MIGRATION, MINORITIES AND CITIZENSHIP

General Editors: Zig Layton-Henry, *Professor of Politics, University of Warwick*; and Danièle Joly, *Director, Centre for Research in Ethnic Relations, University of Warwick*

This series has been developed to promote books on a wide range of topics concerned with migration and settlement, immigration policy, refugees, the integration and engagement of minorities, dimensions of social exclusion, racism and xenophobia, ethnic mobilization, ethnicity and nationalism. The focus of the series is multidisciplinary and international. The series publishes both theoretical and empirical works based on original research.

Titles include:

Muhammad Anwar, Patrick Roach and Ranjit Sondhi (*editors*)
FROM LEGISLATION TO INTEGRATION?
Race Relations in Britain

Naomi Carmon (*editor*)
IMMIGRATION AND INTEGRATION IN POST-INDUSTRIAL SOCIETIES
Theoretical Analysis and Policy-Related Research

Adrian Favell
PHILOSOPHIES OF INTEGRATION
Immigration and the Idea of Citizenship in France and Britain

Simon Holdaway and Anne-Marie Barron
RESIGNERS? THE EXPERIENCE OF BLACK AND ASIAN POLICE OFFICERS

Danièle Joly
HAVEN OR HELL?
Asylum Policies and Refugees in Europe

SCAPEGOATS AND SOCIAL ACTORS
The Exclusion and Integration of Minorities in Western and Eastern Europe

Jørgen S. Nielsen
TOWARDS A EUROPEAN ISLAM

John Rex
ETHNIC MINORITIES IN THE MODERN NATION STATE
Working Papers in the Theory of Multiculturalism and Political
Integration

Carl-Ulrik Schierup (*editor*)
SCRAMBLE FOR THE BALKANS
Nationalism, Globalism and the Political Economy of Reconstruction

Steven Vertovec and Ceri Peach (*editors*)
ISLAM IN EUROPE
The Politics of Religion and Community

Östen Wahlbeck
KURDISH DIASPORAS
A Comparative Study of Kurdish Refugee Communities

Migration, Minorities and Citizenship
Series Standing Order ISBN 0–333–71047–9
(*outside North America only*)

You can receive future titles in this series as they are published by placing a standing order.
Please contact your bookseller or, in case of difficulty, write to us at the address below with
your name and address, the title of the series and the ISBN quoted above.

Customer Services Department, Macmillan Distribution Ltd
Houndmills, Basingstoke, Hampshire RG21 6XS, England

From Legislation to Integration?

Race Relations in Britain

Edited by

Muhammad Anwar
Research Professor
Centre for Research in Ethnic Relations
University of Warwick

Patrick Roach
Principal Officer for Education and Equal Opportunities, NASUWT
and Associate Fellow
Centre for Research in Ethnic Relations
University of Warwick

and

Ranjit Sondhi
Senior Lecturer
Department of Community and Youth Studies
Westhill College, Birmingham

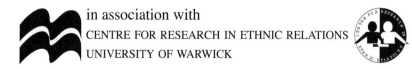

in association with
CENTRE FOR RESEARCH IN ETHNIC RELATIONS
UNIVERSITY OF WARWICK

First published in Great Britain 2000 by
MACMILLAN PRESS LTD
Houndmills, Basingstoke, Hampshire RG21 6XS and London
Companies and representatives throughout the world

A catalogue record for this book is available from the British Library.

ISBN 0–333–73316–9

 First published in the United States of America 2000 by
ST. MARTIN'S PRESS, INC.,
Scholarly and Reference Division,
175 Fifth Avenue, New York, N.Y. 10010

ISBN 0–312–22574–1

Library of Congress Cataloging-in-Publication Data
From legislation to integration? : race relations in Britain / edited
by Muhammad Anwar, Patrick Roach, and Ranjit Sondhi.
p.   cm. — (Migration, minorities, and citizenship)
"In association with Centre for Research in Ethnic Relations,
University of Warwick."
Includes bibliographical references and index.
ISBN 0–312–22574–1 (cloth)
1. Great Britain—Race relations—History—20th century.   2. Great
Britain. Laws, statutes, etc. Race relations act 1976.
3. Immigrants—Great Britain—Social conditions.   4. Minorities–
–Great Britain—Social conditions.   I. Anwar, Muhammad, 1945–   .
II. Roach, Patrick, 1964–   .   III. Sondhi, Ranjit.   IV. Centre for
Research in Ethnic Relations (Economic and Social Research Council)
V. Series.
DA125.A1F7   1999
305.8'00941—DC21   99–26812
                                                          CIP

This book is printed on paper suitable for recycling and made from fully managed and
sustained forest sources.

10   9   8   7   6   5   4   3   2   1
09   08   07   06   05   04   03   02   01   00

Printed and bound in Great Britain by Antony Rowe Ltd, Chippenham, Wiltshire

Contents

v

0006122359001

Preface

The structure of British society has changed considerably since the last major reform was made to British race relations legislation (in 1976). New economic and social relationships have developed as a result of the settlement of a new wave of immigrants to Britain and, more recently, as a consequence of Britain's attempts to negotiate new relationships on the world stage.

Yet any consideration of the contribution of the Race Relations Act of 1976 cannot begin without some explanation as to the purpose of the legislation itself and the factors which brought the legislation into being. The 1976 Act is rooted within a clear historical context. It is no accident that the nature and scope of the legislation passed in Britain took the form it did nor that the public response to the legislation itself has remained deeply ambivalent to this day.

Before the passing of the 1976 Act several attempts, successful and unsuccessful, had been made to introduce controls in response to the arrival of labour from the New Commonwealth. Indeed, throughout the 1960s and 1970s, a small number of dedicated policy-makers struggled to establish a race relations legislative framework against the background of ever-tightening and increasingly oppressive immigration controls which were being introduced at frequent intervals. For some, the struggle for race relations legislation was necessary to establish at least a minimum level of protection for newly arrived minority communities. For others, the framework to address the problem of racial discrimination would always remain fundamentally flawed in so far as it remained tied to the central principles behind immigration control.

In the decade which passed between the Race Relations Act 1965 and the enactment of the Race Relations Act 1976 four major instruments of immigration control were also put into place. Moreover, since the Commonwealth Immigrants Act 1962 several major pieces of immigration legislation and numerous changes to immigration rules have been introduced to date.

Throughout the 1960s, 1970s and 1980s, the fundamental question of the status of Britain's black and ethnic minorities

vii

was being defined and transformed not as a result of new race relations legislation but as a consequence of the passing of complex immigration controls – measures designed to stem mainly the tide of black and Asian immigration to Britain as a prerequisite to the maintenance of social order. Immigration legislation established over three decades continued to define the problem of 'race relations' in terms of the 'black' presence within 'white' society. Black immigration was a problem to be controlled; its effects were regarded as potentially destabilising to notions of Britishness and the effective operation of British society.

Moreover, it is no accident that immigration control was determined to be outside the scope and remit of the Race Relations Act. In this way racially discriminatory immigration controls were allowed to continue to operate and such practice was effectively enshrined by law. However, some degree of fairness of treatment also came to be regarded as a necessary response to those black and ethnic minorities who had already arrived and settled in Britain and who were British citizens. It is within this historical context that the Race Relations Acts of 1965, 1968 and 1976 emerged.

It cannot be assumed, therefore, that the emergent race relations framework was determined solely by the desire to protect the rights of newly arrived immigrant populations. It has been argued that the legislation itself performed three functions: first, to afford protection from racial discrimination; secondly, to provide a further mechanism for social control; and thirdly, to limite political and civic legitimacy to specific social groups. However, its limited scope placed constraints on the processes available to citizens seeking to challenge racially discriminatory practice, and afforded direct protection under the law to certain groups but not to others, i.e. religious minorities.

Assessing the contribution of the 1976 Act poses some challenging questions. What were the objectives of the legislation? Is it possible to determine what British society would have been like without a race relations legislative framework? Is it possible to reach an agreement on all sides that legislation has indeed made a difference? What indicators could be used to assess the relative success or failure of the legislation? Could Britain have achieved more had its legislators adopted a different approach? These and other questions are addressed by the contributors to this book. Some of the papers included in the book were presented at a conference organised by the Centre for Research in Ethnic Relations (CRER), University of Warwick, jointly with the Commission for Racial Equality and the Runnymede Trust, in September 1996. The conference discussed the contribution made by the Race Relations Act 1976 to the development of British race relations over the last two decades. In order to gain a wider range of views on the subject, the editors have deliberately sought contributors from very different backgrounds, all of whom have achieved eminence in their own professional fields. They include a politician, lawyer, political philosopher, journalist, race relations experts, academics, researchers and even a retired Chairman of the Commission for Racial Equality (CRE). Their distinct disciplines, unique sets of experiences, and different styles combine to provide a book that has coherence, depth and character.

In reaching any conclusions as to the contribution made by the existing legislation, it is necessary to remember also that the CRE – as the agency charged with statutory responsibility for reviewing the effectiveness of the 1976 Act – has also repeatedly argued for a substantial reform of the law. During the 1980s the CRE's recommendations were virtually ignored by the Government. Whilst no assurances have so far been given, there are indications that a more sympathetic response may be taken by the present Government.

As we look towards the future of race relations in Britain in the twenty-first century, there are a number of trends which also need to be borne in mind. The spectre of economic recession – and its attendant consequence of rising levels of unemployment and poverty – within the states of Europe and globally, will continue to heighten the appeal of extremist political parties and lead to increased ethnic tensions around the globe. This may require definitive action from governments – singly and in concert – to address the problems of social and economic inequality, poverty and alienation through more effective programmes for the redistribution of social and cultural resources. At the same time, trends towards ethnicism and fundamentalism are increasingly becoming a global feature and signal the need for new policy responses for the creation of inclusive societies which extend beyond the framework for equal opportunities and immigration control, which has been deployed by Britain over the past three decades.

We would like to thank all the contributors for their co-operation in the preparation of this book. We would also like to thank the CRE for a small grant for the administrative help. We are grateful to many colleagues at CRER for their help, in particular Zig Layton-Henry and Beryl Pine-Coffin. Finally, we would like to thank Rose Goodwin and Gurbakhsh Hundal for preparing the manuscript.

MUHAMMAD ANWAR
PATRICK ROACH
RANJIT SONDHI

List of Abbreviations

ADA	Americans with Disability Act
BSA survey	British Social Attitudes
CARD	Campaign Against Racial Discrimination
CRC	Community Relations Commission
CRCs	Community Relations Councils
CRE	Commission for Racial Equality
CRER	Centre for Research in Ethnic Relations
ECOA	Equal Credit Opportunity Act (US)
EEC	European Economic Community
EEOC	Equal Employment Opportunity Commission (US)
EFTA	European Free Trade Association
EOC	Equal Opportunities Commission
GLC	Greater London Council
HUD	The United States Department of Housing and Urban Development
ICERD	International Convention on the Elimination of All Forms of Racial Discrimination
IPPR	Institute for Public Policy Research
JCWI	Joint Council for the Welfare of Immigrants
NACRC	National Association of Community Relations Councils
NASUWT	National Association of Schoolmasters and Union of Women Teachers
NCCI	National Committee for Commonwealth Immigrants
NEMDA	National Ethnic Minority Data Archive
OCR	Office for Civil Rights (US)
OFCC	Office of Federal Contract Compliance (US)
PEP report	Political and Economic Planning
PSI	Policy Studies Institute
RECs	Racial Equality Councils
RRA	Race Relations Act
RRB	Race Relations Board
SCORE	Standing Conference on Race Relations in Europe
UCCA	Universities' Central Council on Admissions

Notes on the Contributors

Yasmin Alibhai-Brown came to this country in 1972 from Uganda. She completed her M.Phil. in literature at Oxford in 1975 and then went into teaching adults, particularly immigrants and refugees. Since 1985 she has been a journalist writing for the *Guardian*, *New Statesman* and other newspapers and is now a regular columnist on *The Independent*. She is also a radio and television broadcaster and author of several books. At present she is Research Fellow at the Institute for Public Policy Research and has recently published *'True Colours': Public Attitudes to Multiculturalism and the Role of Government* (1999). She is a member of the Home Office Race Forum and advises various key institutions on race matters. She is currently working on a book on mixed-race Britons, having been awarded a fellowship by the Rowntree Foundation to work on this project.

Muhammad Anwar is Research Professor in the Centre for Research in Ethnic Relations (CRER), University of Warwick, having formerly been Director of CRER (1989–94) and Head of Research, Commission for Racial Equality (1981–9). He has written extensively on ethnic and race relations. His publications include *Between Two Cultures* (1976), *Who Tunes into What* (1978), *The Myth of Return* (1979), *Votes and Policies* (1980), *Ethnic Minority Broadcasting* (1983), *Ethnic Minorities and the 1983 General Election* (1984), *Race and Politics* (1986), *Race and Elections* (1994), *British Pakistanis* (1996), *Between Cultures* (1998) and *Ethnic Minorities and the British Electoral Process* (1998). He is co-author of *Participation of Ethnic Minorities in the October 1974 General Election* (1975), *Television in a Multi-Racial Society* (1982) and *Overseas Doctors* (1987). He is also the editor of *Muslim Communities in Non-Muslim States* (1980) and co-editor of *Black and Ethnic Leaderships* (1991).

Michael Banton was Professor of Sociology in the University of Bristol from 1965 to 1992. Since 1986 he has been a member of the UN Committee on the Elimination of Racial Discrimination and was its chairman from 1996 to 1998. His most recent books include *International Action against Racial Discrimination* (1996), *Ethnic and Racial Consciousness* (1997) and *Racial Theories* (1998).

Geoffrey Bindman is a solicitor and senior partner of Bindman & Partners which he founded in 1974. He has specialised in civil liberty and human rights issues. From 1966 to 1976 he was Legal Adviser to the Race Relations Board and thereafter, until 1983, to the Commission for Racial Equality. He is a Visiting Professor of Law at University College, London, and an Honorary Fellow in Civil Legal Process at the University of Kent. In 1982 he was Visiting Professor of Law at the University of California at Los Angeles. He has contributed many articles in journals and edited the report of the International Commission of Jurists' 1987 mission to South Africa (published as *South Africa: Human Rights and the Rule of Law in 1988*, revised edition 1989). He is co-author with Lord Lester of Herne Hill, QC, of *Race and Law* (1972). He has contributed chapters to several books, including *Halsbury's Laws of England* (4th edition).

Sir Michael Day, OBE, read English at Cambridge and Social Studies at LSE, and joined the Probation Service in 1960. He was appointed Chief Officer of Surrey in 1968 and moved to manage the West Midlands Service in 1976. He encouraged developments relevant to the needs of an ethnically more diverse population. In cooperation with the CRE he published *Probation and After-Care in a Multi-Racial Society* (1981). Prominent in probation and penal concerns at a national level, he was the first chairman of the Association of Chief Officers of Probation, and served as Chairman of the Commission for Racial Equality from 1988 to 1993. In retirement he has continued to play an active part in the Telford and Shropshire Race Equality Council and other community provisions.

Ann Dummett has worked in the race relations field for over thirty years, as a local Community Relations Officer, researcher and later Director at the Runnymede Trust, research officer and lobbyist for the Joint Council for the Welfare of Immigrants (JCWI), and most recently as a consultant, working chiefly for the CRE, on European law concerning minorities. She is the author of numerous books, pamphlets and articles on racism, immigration and nationality law.

John Goering is currently Acting Deputy Director for Policy and Research for the President's Initiative on Race at the White House, while on secondment from the Office of Research at the US Department of Housing and Urban Development (HUD). He received his PhD in sociology and demography at Brown University and has taught at the University of Leicester in England, Washington University in St Louis, and at the Graduate Center of the City University of New York. He has conducted and managed research for the US Department of Housing and Urban Development where his research has focused on housing discrimination, segregation and civil rights policies. He is currently managing the multi-year implementation and research on HUD's 'Moving to Opportunity' demonstration which makes use of an experimental design to address neighbourhood and household effects changes on low-income public housing families as they move into non-distressed neighbourhoods. His latest book is *Mortgage Lending, Racial Discrimination and Federal Policy* (1996). He is currently completing a collection of essays analysing the thirtieth anniversary of the Fair Housing Act and another book, *Choosing a Better Life: The Impacts of the 'Moving to Opportunity' Demonstration* (forthcoming). He has served on the editorial boards of the journals *Ethnic and Migration Studies*, *Urban Affairs Review* and *Housing Studies*.

Lord Lester of Herne Hill, QC, is a practising member of the English Bar and Liberal Democrat peer. He specialises in constitutional and administrative law and European human rights law. He has argued many leading cases not only before English courts, but also before both European and Commonwealth courts. Lord Lester is President of Interights (the International Centre for the Legal Protection of Human Rights) and Honorary Professor of Public Law at University College London. He is co-editor of the forthcoming book *Human Rights Law and Practice*.

Bhikhu Parekh is Professor of Political Theory at the University of Hull. He has been Visiting Professor at several

North American universities, including McGill, Harvard and the University of Pennsylvania. He was Vice-Chancellor of the University of Baroda in India and Deputy Chair for the Commission of Racial Equality, UK. He is the author of several widely acclaimed books in political philosophy, including *Hannah Arendt and the Search for a New Political Philosophy* (1981), *Marx's Theory of Ideology* (1982), *Contemporary Political Thinkers* (1982), *Gandhi's Political Philosophy* (1989) and *Colonialism, Tradition and Reform* (1989). He is currently completing *Re-thinking Multi-Culturalism* (to be published by Macmillan).

Patrick Roach is Principal Officer for Education and Equal Opportunities at the NASUWT and Associate Fellow at the Centre for Research in Ethnic Relations. He was formerly Research and Development Officer at the University of Warwick and prior to that spent over ten years as a policy and research officer within local government. His main interests concern the development of responses to ethnic diversity and equal opportunities in the provision of education and information services as a prerequisite for active citizenship and democratic participation. He is currently engaged in research into ethnic minority youth transitions, racism and leisure and examining the factors which impact on the educational attainment of ethnic minority children. His recent publications include *Public Libraries and Ethnic Diversity: A Baseline for Good Practice* (with M. Morrison, 1998), *Public Libraries, Ethnic Diversity and Citizenship* (with M. Morrison, 1997), *Education Interventions: Local Measures to Improve the Educational Attainment of Ethnic Minority School Pupils* (with R. Sondhi, 1997), and *Monitoring and Evaluating Organisational Performance: Developing Good Practice in the Voluntary Sector* (1997).

Ranjit Sondhi was born in India and has lived, studied and worked in Birmingham for over thirty years. Since 1969 he has worked on a number of community action projects in inner-city areas. In 1976, he founded the Asian Resource Centre in Handsworth and worked there until 1985. He left to join Westhill College as a Senior Lecturer in the Department of Community and Youth Studies where he is also coordinating a new degree in race and ethnic studies. He has served on a number of public bodies and until recently he was Deputy

Chairman of the Commission for Racial Equality, Chairman of the Refugee Employment, Training and Education Forum, and a member of the Ethnic Minority Advisory Committee of the Judicial Studies Board. He is presently serving on the Lord Chancellor's Advisory Committee on Legal Education and Conduct, on the DfEE's Task Force on Disability Rights, and on the Home Secretary's Race Relations Forum. He has recently been appointed as a Governor of the BBC with special responsibility for the English Regions. He remains involved in various local projects involving the mentoring of pupils at risk of school exclusions, South Asian arts and black oral history.

1 Introduction

Muhammad Anwar, Patrick Roach and Ranjit Sondhi

It is in the last fifty years that Britain has received in significant numbers workers and their dependants from the former colonies whose colour differs from that of the white indigenous population, although the presence of black and ethnic minority people is not new.[1] The main sources of this immigration are the New Commonwealth countries of the Indian subcontinent and the West Indies. The estimated present-day number of people of New Commonwealth origin, now known as ethnic minorities, is 6.3 per cent of the total population and of these over 50 per cent are British born. Thus over half of the ethnic minority population is not 'immigrant' but native-born British. Most of those who arrived as immigrants have now become full British citizens.

The process of migration was helped because Commonwealth citizens had free entry into Britain under the Commonwealth rules. In addition, the colonial links and knowledge of Britain of several thousand soldiers and seamen from India and the West Indies during the Second World War encouraged some of them to stay in Britain and others to come back to work in the expanding industry during the period of postwar boom.[2] They were initially welcomed by the British public as allies, who had defended their nation.[3] Foreign sailors had settled in this country for many years and there were already established communities of non-white people in the ports, notably Bristol, Cardiff and Liverpool. The start of mass migration, however, was the arrival of the *Empire Windrush* ship in June 1948 with 492 migrants from Jamaica. This was followed by SS *Orbita* and SS *Georgia* in the same year. After this the immigration progressed slowly by air and sea and during the 1950s the number of immigrants from the West Indies increased, reaching an annual rate of 30,000 in 1955 and 1956.

Immigration from India and Pakistan started later than that from the West Indies, but also reached a very high level from

1

1960 onwards as people tried to enter the UK while there was still time before the Commonwealth Immigrants Act 1962 came into force, which restricted the free entry of Commonwealth immigrants.[4] In the beginning the migration was unorganised but later on it resolved into a pattern of chain migration where friends and relatives were encouraged and helped by pioneer migrants to follow them to new opportunities in Britain. Mass migration in some cases resulted in the establishment of institutions, agents and organisations to facilitate the migration. This way even after the 1962 Act, the introduction of the voucher system reinforced the sponsorship and patronage of friends and relatives because the migrants in Britain were in a position to obtain vouchers for their kin and friends.[5] Later immigration legislation and debates on immigration forced the migrants to bring their dependants to Britain because of the fear of losing their right of entry. Table 1.1 shows how the New Commonwealth origin population increased between 1951 and 1981.

The 1991 British Census included for the first time an ethnic origin question instead of 'birth place of the head of household' as was used in the 1981 Census. The 1991 Census showed that out of the almost 55 million total population, ethnic minority population had risen to just over 3 million.[6] The Census showed that most of the ethnic minorities were to be found in the South-East (56 per cent) especially in the Greater London area (45 per cent), the Midlands (20 per cent), the North and the North West (9 per cent), Yorkshire and Humberside (7 per

Table 1.1   *New Commonwealth (NC) estimated population in England and Wales, 1951–81 (thousands)*

Year	West Indian	Indian	Pakistani*	Bangladeshi	Other NC	Total
1951	15	31	5	–	23	74
1961	172	81	25	–	58	336
1971	237	322	166	–	591	1316
1981	546	673	295	65	627	2207

*Figures for 1951–71 include Bangladeshis as East Pakistan was then part of Pakistan.

Sources: Rose et al., *Colour and Citizenship* (1969); 1971 and 1981 Census Reports

cent) and the remainder (8 per cent) in East Anglia, the South-West, Wales and Scotland (mainly in Glasgow and Edinburgh). The 1991 Census also showed that out of the 3 million ethnic minority population almost half (49 per cent) were of South Asian origin, about 30 per cent were black and the remaining 21 per cent of ethnic minorities were Chinese or from other parts of the New Commonwealth.

Research has shown that New Commonwealth workers filled a gap for labour in the unskilled sectors and poorly paid jobs which arose as a result of the reconstruction and expansion of the British industry after the war. However, it appears that the reactions of the British public and politicians to immigration from the New Commonwealth were more vigorous than they had been to the previous waves of immigration.[7] It also appears that successive governments were persuaded by arguments for stricter immigration controls as a prerequisite for good community and race relations. But the fact remains that the political response in terms of the immigration legislation and the strict control policies were a response to racist attitudes in society, and in the process some discrimination was also taking place. Increasingly hostile immigration controls began to have a marked effect on race relations within Britain.

The treatment of ethnic minorities began to be characterised by prejudice and discrimination. Therefore, arguments were put forward for the strict immigration legislation to be matched by legislation to tackle racial disadvantage and racial discrimination faced by ethnic minorities.

It is thirty-three years since the first Race Relations Act in Britain was passed in 1965. The Act was the first step towards eliminating racial discrimination. The Race Relations Board (RRB) was set up under the 1965 Act, which coordinated the work of nine regional conciliation committees established to deal with complaints of racial discrimination. The Act dealt only with discrimination in places of public resort, although the majority of the complaints received were about employment, housing and the police. However, these were outside the scope of the Act. It is worth mentioning that Maurice Foley MP was appointed as the Coordinator of Policy on Integration in March 1965. However, this initiative did not make much difference to the worsening situation of racial discrimination.

The Political and Economic Planning (PEP) Report in 1968 showed that there was intolerable racial discrimination and it called for urgent remedial action.[8] This report, together with pressure from the RRB and the National Committee for Commonwealth Immigrants (NCCI), persuaded the then Home Secretary, Roy Jenkins, to extend the scope of the 1965 Act. As a result, the second Race Relations Act of 1968 made racial discrimination unlawful in employment, housing and the provision of goods, facilities and services, including education. The RRB was given powers to investigate complaints, and secure redress for the victims of racial discrimination. The 1968 Act also set up another organisation, the Community Relations Commission (CRC), in parallel with the RRB. The function of the CRC was to promote good community relations and to advise the Home Secretary on such matters. It also took responsibility for dealing with the local Community Relations Councils (CRCs).

In the early 1970s many research projects and several reports by the Select Committee of the House of Commons on Race Relations and Immigration had demonstrated that there was entrenched racial inequality in Britain and that this situation was leading to deteriorating race relations. In 1975 the Government accepted the views of the Select Committee, the CRC and the RRB that there were major structural weaknesses in the Race Relations Acts of 1965 and 1968 and that the legislation was in urgent need of reform. It therefore published a White Paper in September 1975, which outlined the Government's proposals for the Race Relations Act 1976. In Chapter 2 Lord Lester of Herne Hill provides an overview of the purpose and origins of the Race Relations Act. He examines the impact of the arrival of large numbers of Commonwealth citizens on the development of immigration policy and observes that the pattern of Caribbean and South Asian immigration provided a central spur for the development of both immigration controls and race relations policy. Nevertheless, Lester argues that despite the original intention that the 1976 Act would contribute towards addressing the interrelated problems of immigration, cultural diversity, racial discrimination and disadvantage, there remains at the end of the 1990s a need for a more effective framework for enforcement and redress.

It is worth mentioning here that ethnic minorities in the 1970s were facing the cycle of cumulative disadvantage by which low paid and low status jobs for the first generation immigrants went hand in hand with poor and overcrowded housing conditions and poor educational facilities. This affected the next generation who would grow up less well equipped than others. The CRC's Reference Division provided research evidence that proved these points. At the same time, the PEP survey in 1974 showed that an ethnic minority unskilled worker had a one-in-two chance of being discriminated against when applying for a job, an ethnic minority skilled worker a one-in-five chance, and an ethnic minority white-collar worker a one-in-three chance.[9] The housing conditions data showed that the ethnic minorities' situation had not improved since the mid-1960s despite the legislation of 1965 and 1968. They still lived in over-crowded conditions or shared basic amenities, compared with their white neighbours. Ethnic minorities were under-represented in the council housing sector and were over-represented in the private furnished rented sector, which had greatest insecurity and worst housing conditions.[10] The research studies in the field of education also showed that ethnic minority children were relatively under-achieving in education compared with white children and that this was not simply because they were recent arrivals in this country. If we look at the number of West Indian children in schools for the educationally subnormal at that time they were over-represented, the proportion being four times as large. In Greater London, West Indian children comprised a quarter of the ESN children; in one London borough their proportion was as high as 55 per cent, which was not a reflection of their numbers in the population.

On 6 December 1973 Roy Jenkins (who later became Home Secretary) said in the House of Commons that ethnic minorities in Britain 'are here to stay and that on every ground of morality and expediency, they must not be treated as second-class citizens'. Yet in 1974 the unemployment rate among West Indian young people was twice as high as amongst the age group as a whole. We also know that by this time more than a third of ethnic minorities were British born and educated. It was recognised widely by those who worked in the race relations field that the gap between ethnic minorities and white people was significantly due to racial discrimination and that the 1968

Race Relations Act was too weak to deal with the patterns of racial discrimination. The then Chairman of the RRB, Sir Geoffrey Wilson, said in a speech to a Bow Group Conference in 1973 'the Act does not bite on discriminatory patterns of employment and housing which help to determine income levels and concentrations of populations'. Both the CRC and RRB pointed out the weaknesses of the 1968 Act both in the scope of the law, and even more in its enforcement.[11] It was also pointed out that various procedures and practices of employers and others could also discriminate indirectly against ethnic minorities. Thus it was argued by some that the definition of discrimination had to be sufficiently flexible to permit positive action to overcome the effects of wider discrimination and disadvantage.[12]

A PEP survey in 1974 had shown that more than half of the large employers practised some form of racial discrimination and that ethnic minority workers had to make twice as many applications as white workers to find a job. It was also found that ethnic minority workers were heavily concentrated in non-skilled manual jobs and that they were likely to work on permanent night shift.[13] Anwar found a similar pattern among Pakistanis in the early 1970s.[14] The PEP study also found that while 79 per cent of white men with degree level qualifications were in professional/managerial jobs, only 31 per cent of Asian/Afro-Caribbean men with the same level qualifications were in such jobs. Also, 83 per cent of white men with 'A' levels were in non-manual jobs, compared with 55 per cent of Asian/Afro-Caribbean men with the same level qualifications.[15]

By 1975, there was enough research evidence to show that racial discrimination was widespread but had become covert, and that very few people under the 1968 Act in fact complained. Therefore, when the Select Committee decided in January 1975 to examine the 'organisation of the Race Relations Administration' it was welcomed by the CRC and the RRB. It received over a hundred submissions and memoranda on the subject from various organisations, including government departments, organisations working in community relations and associations representing ethnic minority groups. The Committee recommended that the existing legislation should be strengthened, that powers of enforcement for cases of racial discrimination should at least match those being provided against sex discrimination, and that greater resources needed to be provided to deal with racial inequality. The Committee also recommended that there should be a Minister for Equal Rights, that the Home Office and other government departments should strengthen both their staffs and policies for dealing with race relations issues. The Committee further recommended that the civil service and the public sector generally should have effective monitoring procedures which could encourage a positive response in the private sector.[16]

The Committee stressed in its report that there was a growing lack of confidence among the second generation non-immigrant ethnic minorities, and the risk of their becoming permanently alienated. Therefore, it recommended that tackling discrimination needed to be combined with a more comprehensive programme to deal with racial disadvantage – in particular, urban disadvantage more generally. The CRC also published a report entitled 'Urban Deprivation, Racial Inequality and Social Policy' in 1977 which clearly stated that:

> The extent and type of differences between the needs of the urban deprived and the needs of ethnic minorities is the difference between 'urban deprivation' and what has been called 'racial disadvantage', that is, the disadvantages experienced by racial minorities which spring from racial prejudice, intolerance and less equal treatment in society.[17]

At the same time a CRE study in an inner area of London found that black school leavers were three times more likely to be unemployed than their white peers. It also found that those in work had taken longer to find employment, had made more applications and had been to a greater number of interviews compared with white young people.[18] A similar pattern of racial disadvantage was found among young Asians.[19] Asian school leavers were found to be at a definite disadvantage in the search for jobs and training. It was clear from the findings that many of these difficulties were due, directly or indirectly, to discrimination, being affected by the cumulative effects of prejudice against themselves and their families. In Bradford a study showed that young non-whites (mainly Asians) found it three times more difficult to find work than young whites, and that overall inner-city unemployment rates were nearly double for non-whites as for whites.[20] All the evidence pointed, therefore, to the deterioration of the situation of ethnic minorities of the first generation; in addition, the cumulative disadvantage was also affecting the second generation of British-born ethnic minority young people. As a consequence the 1968 Act was losing its credibility and its effectiveness. This was acknowledged by the Home Secretary, Roy Jenkins, in a speech to the national conference of Community Relations Councils in September 1975. He said that he had accepted the argument that these weaknesses had 'impaired our ability to ensure equality of treatment and weakened the credibility of the legislation in the eyes of the minority communities.' He added, 'I have drawn the conclusion that unless we can swiftly devise measures to keep the promise inherent in the Race Relations Act, people will lose confidence in the good faith of Governments. That erosion of confidence is something we cannot permit'.[21] It is worth pointing out that this speech was made in the same month as the publication of the White Paper 'Racial Discrimination' in which the Government had put forward proposals for reform of the legislation.

The White Paper also acknowledged the limitations and weaknesses of the 1968 Act. In its White Paper 'Equality for Women' published a year earlier (September 1974), the Government had indicated that 'in preparing proposals for sex discrimination legislation, it had attempted to avoid a number of weaknesses which were experienced in the enforcement provisions of the race relations legislation'. The Government also indicated that it was its ultimate aim to harmonise the powers and procedures for dealing with sex and race discrimination so as to secure genuine equality in both fields: 'Therefore the new legislation would be designed to fulfil that aim'.[22]

It was proposed that under new legislation the principal functions of the new Commission would be to work towards the elimination of racial discrimination and the promotion of racial equality. It would have a major strategic role in enforcing the law in the public interest. The main task of the new Commission would be wider policy: 'to identify and deal with discriminatory practices by industries, firms or institutions.' It would be empowered to issue non-discrimination notices and to bring legal proceedings against those who persistently violated the law but it would also be able to assist and represent individual cases of racial discrimination. The White Paper also indicated that the new Commission would be able to conduct general enquiries and research, to advise Government, and to take necessary steps to educate and persuade public opinion. Therefore, it was proposed that the functions of the CRC would continue under new legislation. It was also stated in the White Paper that the Commission would have adequate powers to require the production of relevant information. It would be able not only to investigate suspected unlawful conduct but also to keep under review wider policies and practices in the public and private sectors, having particular regard to their implications for and effect upon racial minorities.[23] Therefore, the scope of the new legislation and how it would be enforced was made clear in the White Paper and the Bill which followed.

It is relevant to point out that, politically, it was easier for the Labour government to sell the new proposals on racial discrimination in 1976, since it had received cross-party support for similar legislation in relation to sex discrimination when the Sex Discrimination Act 1975 was passed with few problems. The Race Relations Bill received support from the Opposition's Home Affairs spokesperson, William Whitelaw, who said that because of the Conservative Party's commitment to the principle of non-discrimination and in the interest of racial harmony, he would advise his colleagues not to oppose the Bill. (Despite this advice 43 Conservative MPs voted against the Bill at its third reading.) It is clear from the sequence of events that the then Home Secretary, Roy Jenkins, had prepared the ground and had rehearsed the arguments in 1974 and 1975 with the sex discrimination legislation, and the race relations legislation in 1976 was duly adopted. He had made his intentions clear in his September 1975 speech referred to above. He said that:

> we shall provide a comprehensive code of law against racial and sex discrimination, backed by effective means for the victims of discrimination to obtain redress, and supported by powerful commissions able to tackle the real, extensive and continuing problems of discrimination.[24]

This is what the Home Secretary then delivered in the shape of the Sex Discrimination Act 1975 and the Race Relations Act 1976. Whether the new Act has been successful in terms of meeting its objectives is examined in details in Chapters 3 (Bindman) and 4 (Anwar). Here it is relevant to mention that the scope of the legislation remained similar to the 1968 Act but in addition to direct discrimination the concept of indirect discrimination was introduced for the first time. In this context we look at the definition of discrimination as set out in the Race Relations Act 1976, section 1(I)a:

> (1)   A person discriminates against another in any circumstances relevant for the purposes of any provision of this Act if
>> (a)   on racial grounds he treats that other less favourably than he treats or would treat other persons; or
>> (b)   he applies to that other a requirement or condition which he applies or would apply equally to persons not of the same racial groups as that other but
>>> (i)   which is such that the proportion of persons of the same racial group as the other who can comply with it is considerably smaller than the proportion of persons not of that racial group who can comply with it; and
>>> (ii)   which he can not show to be justifiable irrespective of the colour, race, nationality or ethnic or national origins of the person to whom it is applied; and
>>> (iii) which is to the detriment of that other because he cannot comply with it.
>
> (2)   It is hereby declared that, for the purpose of this Act, segregating a person from other persons on racial grounds is treating him less favourably than they are treated.[25]

Therefore, according to the Act, direct racial discrimination takes place where a person treats another less favourably on racial grounds. Indirect discrimination occurs when all persons are apparently treated equally, but when a requirement or condition is applied with which a considerably smaller proportion of one racial group can comply as compared with another racial group, when a failure to comply is a detriment, and when the requirement or condition cannot be shown to be justifiable as quoted above from the Act.

Under the Act the Commission for Racial Equality (CRE) was brought into being and the RRB and the CRC were amalgamated in this new body. It started its work in June 1977 and David Lane became its first Chairman.

Since we are examining partly the impact of the 1976 Act on British race relations, it is relevant to mention the duties of the CRE under the Act. In section 43(1)(C) the CRE is charged with three duties:

(1) to work towards the elimination of discrimination;
(2) to promote equality of opportunity, and good relations between persons of different racial groups; and
(3) to keep under review the Race Relations Act and to recommend amendments when necessary.

It is relevant to point out that when the CRC and the RRB were merged there were some practical difficulties because the 'culture' of the two organisations was different, and as a consequence some friction and mistrust among staff developed in the first few years of the CRE. The CRE was also criticised by the House of Commons Select Committee on Home Affairs in its report about the CRE in 1981. Some of the criticism was unfair. For example, it overlooked the difficulties which resulted from the nature of the legislation. It was in accordance with its duties under the Act and its experience of using the legislation that the CRE made recommendations for changes to the Act to the Home Secretary in 1985 and 1992. It argued that:

the need for effective legislation to promote racial equality is, if anything, greater now than it was in 1976. The facts relating to racial disadvantage are known. The degree to which, in a variety of ways, the disadvantage is compounded by discrimination on racial grounds is increasingly well established.[26]

The CRE never received a formal reply to its 1985 recommendations.

The CRE published its 'strategy statement' in October 1975. It was a bold strategy and included a lot of work. There were high expectations from the CRE's strategic role, in particular its powers of formal investigation. In the first five years it started, for example, 42 investigations, most of them small. At the same time almost 5000 individual complainants were supported. However, in 1982 and 1984 the CRE ran into difficulties on formal investigations because of the Court of

Appeal decision regarding *CRE* v. *Amari Plastics Ltd* (1982) and
the House of Lords decision concerning *CRE* v. *Prestige Group Plc*
(1984). In the first one, it was held that an appeal against a
non-discrimination notice could challenge the findings of fact
as well as the reasonableness of the requirements imposed by
the CRE's notice. In the second decision, which resulted in the
CRE dropping several other active formal investigations, it was
held that the CRE could not investigate a named person unless
it had evidence of possible discrimination. This decision
appeared to be contrary to the debates at the Committee stage
of the Race Relations Bill, at the time, and therefore was not in
line with Parliament's intentions. So far the implications of
these two decisions for the CRE work have not been removed
sufficiently in order for it to play its strategic role as it was outlined in the Race Relations Act 1976. The Conservative Home
Secretaries between 1979 and 1997 had generally paid lip
service to the questions of racial equality and therefore had not
responded positively to the requests of the CRE for necessary
changes in the legislation. In fact, the Conservative Prime
Minister, Mrs Margaret Thatcher, never made a major speech
on race relations during her 11 years in office. This shows that
there had been a lack of political will during most of the 22
years of the Race Relations Act 1976. The work of the CRE
would be enhanced now if the new Labour Government were to
accept immediately some of the recommendations of CRE for
strengthening the Act submitted in 1992. The need for the law
to be strong in order to eradicate discriminatory practices and
behaviour is undeniable as the experience of the last thirty-
three years in Britain has shown. The legislation is an unequivocal declaration of public policy and provides protection and
redress to those discriminated against.

It is a commonly held view among those concerned with
race relations work that our legislation is partly based on
lessons learnt from the United States with regard to its anti-
discrimination laws. For example, the US Civil Rights Act 1964
and the British Race Relations Acts 1965 and 1968 were fairly
similar. The US Fair Housing Act was passed in 1968 and the
1964 Act was amended in 1972 with extended scope. One of the
main differences between the British and the US legislation is
the US legislation's emphasis on equality of results and not
simply on equality of opportunity, as is the case with the British

legislation. That is why there is more force and sanctions behind ethnic monitoring in the US, while in Britain it is seen as a voluntary activity of employers or service providers. John Goering in Chapter 7 provides an assessment of the impact made by legislation in the United States on the social and economic profile of America's black and minority ethnic communities. He examines the response of local, federal and state civil rights agencies and the emergence of civil rights law. He considers the factors which have influenced the relative successes and failures of American public policy in relation to improving the employment, housing and education of black and minority ethnic communities. Goering also considers the relationship between the American and British approaches to race relations and whether the civil rights framework developed in the United States could provide a model for the future of race equality policy and practice in the UK.

In addition to the law enforcement part of the Race Relations Act in Britain there are at least four other methods for bringing about change, and for helping to tackle discrimination and provide equality of opportunity under the Act. The first is the Code of Practice in Employment under section 47 of the Act which was approved by Parliament in 1984. This Code provides practical guidance for the elimination of discrimination and the promotion of equality of opportunity in employment. The Code's recommendations are also admissible in industrial tribunal cases. The cross-examination of witnesses shows that, although many employers have equal opportunity policies, their managers are not implementing the recommendations in the CRE's Code. A survey of employers to look at the effectiveness of the Code showed that the awareness of the Code was high among employers and two-thirds of them had adopted written equal opportunity policies but only a quarter had a monitoring system.[27] Statutory Housing Codes have also been issued by the CRE in the early 1990s and a non-statutory Code of Practice for the Elimination of Racial Discrimination in Education was published in 1989. The effectiveness of these codes is not yet known.

The second method is ethnic monitoring which is also central to the implementation of CRE's codes. It has been acknowledged widely that without ethnic record-keeping and regular monitoring it would be difficult to eliminate discrimination and

to operate effective equal opportunity policies. The experience
of several employers, local authorities and central government
departments in ethnic record-keeping shows that these
methods are essential to tackle racial discrimination. For
example, for any redressive action one needs to find out first
the statistics to establish whether discrimination is occurring
and if so at what levels in the system.[28] This applies to employment, housing, education and all other fields. What the CRE
said in 1984 about the importance of ethnic record-keeping
with built-in monitoring is equally relevant in 1998:

> the point the Commission has been trying to hammer home
> is that there is no substitute for finding out what is actually
> happening. That means getting at the facts and then doing
> something effective about them. In many hundreds of organ-
> isations equal opportunities policies are now developing.
> They need to be as efficiently audited as any profit or loss
> account. Otherwise, they may be no more than cosmetic.[29]

Because of the importance of ethnic record-keeping and monitoring they need to become mandatory, as in the United States.
One way to make this method work is to look at the obligations
of local authorities both as large employers and also as
providers of services. Under section 71 of the Race Relations
Act there is a general duty on local authorities to make appropriate arrangements with a view to ensuring that their various
functions are carried out with due regard to the need: (a) to
eliminate unlawful racial discrimination; and (b) to promote
equality of opportunity and good relations, between persons of
different racial groups. However, it appears that this statutory
duty imposed on local authorities is not very effective. It needs
strengthening in line with section 43(1) of the Act, and section
71 also needs to be extended to cover other public bodies.
In particular any positive action these bodies have taken
to redress the situation and its effectiveness should be dis-
seminated for the benefit of others. This brings us to the
third method to provide equal opportunity, that is, positive
action.

Positive action is provided for in the Race Relations Act
under sections 35, 37 and 38. It is a series of measures by which
people from particular racial groups are either encouraged to
apply for jobs in which they have been under-represented or

given training to help them develop their potential and so improve their chances in competing for those jobs. It is worth emphasising that the elements of competition and standards remain important in the policies of positive action. The Act does not provide for people to be taken on because they belong to a particular racial group, except in very limited circumstances where racial group is a genuine occupational qualification for the job. What it does is to provide for fair competition. It needs to be pointed out that the concepts of 'reverse' and 'positive' discrimination as used in the United States are illegal according to the Act and these should not be confused, with the term positive action as used in Britain; for example, positive discrimination in selection for employment to achieve racial balance in the work force is not permitted under sections 37 and 38 of the Act. Positive action should, therefore, be seen as a remedy for past racial disadvantage and discrimination in employment, rather than a substitute for a general programme for ending racial discrimination.

There are many industries and organisations in Britain where informal recruitment methods are prevalent. Ethnic minorities are often disadvantaged as they never come to know of vacancies because they have never worked in those industries. They are unable to pass on to their friends and children the information on vacancies. Therefore such establishments will always remain all white. The CRE's formal investigations have shown that informal recruitment, for example, by word of mouth, is unlawful as it discriminates indirectly against particular racial groups. However, even when these methods of recruitment are corrected to remove their unlawful effect, it can take many years before an impact is made on opportunities for ethnic minority people. Therefore, some urgent positive action is needed to correct the effect of past discriminatory policies and practices of employers in this regard.

Another situation could be where ethnic minorities may not apply for jobs in an organisation because they do not see anybody from their racial group working there; or because of past direct or indirect discrimination which occurred in a particular organisation where it is well known that the employer does not employ ethnic minorities at all or does not employ them in particular posts. Here again, just to remove discriminatory practices will not be enough. More needs to be done to win the confidence of ethnic minorities in that employer and to encourage and help them to apply. This help could be the encouragement and training as permitted under the positive action provisions of the Act. Section 35 of the Act allows for meeting the special needs of racial groups. It says:

> Nothing in Parts II to IV shall render unlawful any act done in affording persons of a particular racial group access to facilities or services to meet the special needs of persons of that group in regard to their education, training or welfare, or any ancillary services.

Also under section 5(2) of the Act relevant persons to provide personal services for people from the same racial group could be appointed. However, it appears that some local authorities, in particular, have misinterpreted this section of the Act and the CRE had to intervene after receiving complaints from the public. Some sections of the media have also exploited such situations, which has not helped good race relations.

The fourth method for bringing about change and for helping to tackle racial discrimination is the effective use of research for law enforcement and for policy. Under section 45 of the Act the CRE can carry out research itself or grant funds to other organisations and individuals, which directly assist in its investigative, promotional and advisory work. Therefore, the research activity is integrated with the other aspects of the CRE's work to fulfil its duties as outlined in section 43 of the Act referred to above. In the last two decades several research projects have been completed by the CRE in the field of employment, housing, education, services, the media, etc. Some of these have directly helped the CRE's formal investigations while others have highlighted the racial disadvantage that ethnic minorities face in various walks of life, including the National Health Service, the teaching profession, the criminal justice system and the media. The CRE has also benefited from relevant research taking place in universities, in particular, at the Centre for Research in Ethnic Relations at the University of Warwick and at the Policy Studies Institute (PSI). Although more recently the CRE has reduced its in-house research activity, ethnic relations as a research area at academic institutions is gaining increased prominence.

In addition to anti-discrimination law enforcement in Britain the voluntary sector makes an important contribution in eliminating racial disadvantage and discrimination. The role of more than 100 Racial Equality Councils (RECs), partly funded by the CRE under section 44 of the Race Relations Act, is crucial at local level in the elimination of racial discrimination, and the implementation of redressive action policies. The RECs' funding is now dependent on their producing and implementing satisfactory work programmes, which are closely monitored by the CRE. Therefore, the RECs' work at local level is also contributing to the law enforcement and strategic work of the CRE. In addition, their work includes community service and development, public education, campaigning on relevant issues, and policy development in the field of race relations.

We mentioned above that the 1975 Sex Discrimination Act and the 1976 Race Relations Act were influenced by the anti-discrimination legislation in the United States. For example, the Street Committee Report in 1967 had influenced the scope of the 1968 Act.[30] This Committee had specially studied the American and Canadian situations to learn what lessons there were for Britain in terms of dealing with racial discrimination. Then in 1975 some members of the Select Committee on Race Relations and Immigration visited the United States to find out what lessons Britain could learn from their experience in terms of anti-discrimination legislation. (Roy Jenkins, the Home Secretary, hd also visited the USA the previous year.) They were clearly influenced, bearing in mind that the two judicial systems were different and that the American courts had adopted a broader interpretation of the statutory provision against discrimination. Jenkins' visit proved useful in many ways, however, and two important developments in this context are worth mentioning. First, that he was convinced that dissemination should not only be seen in terms of the attitude and intention of the discriminator but also in terms of its effect. Second, that after studying the benefits of positive discrimination in the United States for women and ethnic minorities, he reluctantly agreed to the provisions of 'positive action', as discussed above.

The idea of contract compliance is also American – it puts emphasis on the role of the state. The Local Government Act 1988 now enables local authorities in Britain to ensure that companies with which they have contracts for goods or services

achieve minimum standards in their equal opportunity policies
and practices. Under the 1988 Act contractors may be required
to give satisfactory answers to six questions, approved by the
Secretary of State, and local authorities may include clauses
requiring contractors to take particular measures to ensure
that they operate equal opportunity policies.[31] This is not a very
strong provision compared with the US Executive Order 11246
of 1965. This order requires that Federal Government contractors take affirmative action to ensure that applicants' employees are treated equally without regard to their race, colour or
national origin and it applies to all their operations and not
simply to a Government contract. The Office of Federal
Contract Compliance (OFCC), as part of the US Department
of Labour, is responsible for ensuring that Government contractors comply with the Executive Order. There is no similar
arrangement in Britain and no organisation has responsibility
for monitoring the operation and effectiveness of the working of
contract compliance, which is fairly weak to start with in terms
of statutory provision compared with the US. However, some
strong measures in this context are already being undertaken
in another part of the United Kingdom, namely Northern
Ireland, where, under the Fair Employment (Northern Ireland)
Act 1989, all public and private sector employers with more
than 25 employees are required to monitor their work force.[32]
The Northern Ireland legislation is even stronger than the
United States Presidential Orders because those orders cover
only Federal contractors while in Northern Ireland all public
and private sector employers are included. (This comparison
has been dealt with in more detail in Chapter 4.) Here we
would like to mention that, if the political will is there, the
central Government can set an example in this context by
monitoring its own contracts as a starting point. It is well
known that the Northern Ireland legislation was passed by
pressure from the Irish lobby in the United States.[33] However,
ethnic minorities in Britain do not have similar support abroad,
but, as citizens of this country, they are entitled to equal
treatment.

Geoffrey Bindman (Chapter 3) begins by examining the contribution made by the previous attempts at developing a legislative framework for race relations and the major differences
between these and the emergence of the 1976 Act. He identifies

the central role played by research as a principal driver in shaping political attitudes to the problems of racial discrimination and disadvantage. Bindman considers the relative strengths and weaknesses of the 1976 Act in terms of its conception, the scope of the definition of racial discrimination and in terms of the Act's implementation. He identifies the critical problem of British legislation in terms of the mechanisms available for enforcement and the limited scope and powers available to the CRE as the main enforcement agency.

In Chapter 4 Muhammad Anwar provides an assessment of the impact of the 1976 Act using quantitative indicators of social and economic changes which have occurred in the last twenty-two years. He identifies the continuing experience of discrimination in access to employment for Britain's ethnic minorities. He confirms that the patterns of inequality of access to jobs, housing, education and health have remained fundamentally unaltered since the passing of the 1976 Act, although there are now significant differences in the social and economic experiences of Britain's ethnic minority groups. Anwar identifies the increase in the levels of racial attacks and harassment as linked, in part, to the limited impact of the Act in shaping public attitudes on 'race' and cultural diversity. Sir Michael Day, in Chapter 5, has reflected on his experience as a Chairman of the CRE, by providing examples of some of the issues he had to deal with. He has also offered a number of solutions for the issues faced by a multiracial Britain in the late 1990s.

In addition to the influence of the American legislation and its operations on British anti-discrimination legislation, Britain is also part of the European Union. There is the European Court of Justice, the European Community's own Court to interpret EEC legislation. The European Community Treaty has nothing strong enough on racial discrimination but it protects against sex discrimination. The European Commission in its White Paper in 1994 recommended the introduction of Community legislation against racial discrimination. As a result, racial or ethnic discrimination, along with discrimination based on sex, religion and belief, disability, age or sexual orientation are part of fundamental rights as principles underlying the European Union. Ann Dummett in Chapter 6 has dealt with the historical developments in this context and the implications for Britain. There is also the European Convention on Human Rights and Fundamental Freedoms and its Article 14 which prohibits racial discrimination, but its scope is limited. The European Court on Human Rights at Strasbourg has limited powers to deal with racial discrimination. The European Parliament has been more active and has produced reports on racism and xenophobia in Europe and as a result 1997 was declared as European Year Against Racism, Xenophobia and Anti-Semitism. Dummett cites the growth of far Right parties across Europe, and the extent of collaboration between far Right parties as a principal concern which requires action from all member states. She identifies the spate of European developments in the past decade aimed at addressing the issues of racism and xenophobia and considers the likely impact of the recently established European Observatory established in Vienna for the monitoring of racism and xenophobia. Dummett considers the potential of the Amsterdam Treaty in extending the provisions available in Britain for the protection of religious as well as ethnic minorities. She concludes that whilst Britain has much to share in the development of race relations policy and practice within the European Community, it has been more obstructive than most in the development of community-wide policies in this area. For Dummett, the need for greater commitment from Government to the eradication of racism is perhaps more important than the need for changes to the existing national and European legislative frameworks.

There is also the International Convention on the Elimination of All Forms of Racial Discrimination, adopted by the UN General Assembly in December 1965, which applies to Britain. Michael Banton in Chapter 8 has dealt with the international context and also commented on the International Bill of Human Rights. He argues that the United Nations 'has been promoting the establishment of independent national institutions for the promotion and protection of human rights, so this is now a matter of more than domestic interest.' Therefore, Banton argues for the British Government to develop a strategic vision for racial equality as a basis for developing effective practice. He maps the key differences in the international, European and British visions of racial equality and human rights as a means of highlighting the differences in practice which have emerged. Banton questions the need for changes to be made to the existing race relations legislation and raises the importance of case law in clarifying and extending the reaches of the 1976 Act. Referring to the case of Britain's Muslims, Banton draws our attention to the importance of, and distinction between, religious difference and ethnic difference and argues for greater recognition to be afforded to faiths outside the established Christian Church as a prerequisite for greater equality.

Some have argued, including the Liberal Democrats and the Institute for Public Policy, for the establishment of a UK Human Rights Commission to cover all forms of discrimination. However, others, including the CRE and the EOC, defend the separate legislations and administrations on the basis that work against racial discrimination and sex discrimination will be marginalised in a single Human Rights Commission. In fact, the new Labour Government has also decided to establish a Commission for Disability.

It is clear from the evidence presented in Chapters 3 and 4 that there are difficulties with the 1976 Act both in terms of legislation and its interpretation by British courts. The system is too cumbersome and complex and results are not very significant in terms of changing the nature and patterns of discrimination. Both Anwar and Bindman have put forward suggestions for improvements. But Anwar has also argued that, to tackle racial disadvantage and discrimination, the Race Relations Act 1976 and the CRE are essential but not sufficient, and a comprehensive programme, led by the Government, is needed to provide equality of opportunity, so that ethnic minorities are able to play their full part as British citizens as we enter the twenty-first century.

Yasmin Alibhai-Brown in Chapter 9 also considers the need for measures beyond the law to tackle the problems of racial discrimination, harassment and inequality. She argues that there is a need to develop an improved understanding of the perceptions of different ethnic communities in relation to issues of racism, exclusion and the measures needed to combat these problems. She considers how and to what extent British attitudes towards 'race' and diversity have changed. She further examines the implications of prevailing racial attitudes in terms of their influence on the implementation and review of the 1976 Act. For Alibhai-Brown, these public attitudes will play a critical role in determining the shape and scope of any future legislative agenda.

Finally, Bhikhu Parekh (Chapter 10) examines the importance of developing a shared national identity for the future of Britain as a multicultural society. He argues that whilst ethnic, cultural and national differences help to define the society in which we live, there is also a need for the nature of what it means to be British to be clearly defined in a way that is both inclusive and plural. Parekh outlines the challenge presented by the need to establish a unified national identity whilst encouraging diversity to flourish. He explores what is meant by national unity, how Britain has sought to establish national unity, and considers the scope which can be afforded to the practice of diversity within a society. Parekh argues for a coherent model of British multiculturalism to be established and outlines the conditions upon which a stable multicultural society would depend.

NOTES

1. P. Fryer, *Staying Power: The History of Black People in Britain* (London: Pluto Press, 1984), and R. Visram, *Ayahs, Lascars and Princes* (London: Pluto Press, 1986).
2. M. Anwar, *The Myth of Return* (London: Heinemann, 1979).
3. Cabinet Papers, 'Coloured People from British Colonial Territories', (50) 113 Public Records Office (1950).
4. E. J. B. Rose *et al.*, *Colour and Citizenship* (London: Oxford University Press, 1969).
5. Anwar, *The Myth of Return*.
6. Office of Population Censuses and Surveys, *1991 Census: Ethnic Group and Country of Birth* (Great Britain) (London: HMSO, 1993).
7. M. Anwar, 'New Commonwealth Migration to the UK', in R. Cohen (ed.), *Cambridge Survey of World Migration* (Cambridge: Cambridge University Press, 1995).
8. W. W. Daniel, *Racial Discrimination in England* (Harmondsworth: Penguin, 1968).
9. D. Smith, *The Facts of Racial Disadvantage* (London: Political and Economic Planning, 1976).
10. Ibid.
11. G. Bindman, 'The Changes in the Law in Racial Discrimination', in *A Guide to the Government's White Paper* (London: Runnymede Trust, 1975).

12. A. Lester, 'Anti-Discrimination Legislation in Great Britain', *New Community*, XIV:1, 21–31.
13. Smith, *The Facts of Racial Disadvantage*.
14. Anwar, *The Myth of Return*.
15. Smith, *The Facts of Racial Disadvantage*.
16. Select Committee on Race Relations and Immigration, *The Organisation of Race Relations Administration*, vol. 1 (London: HMSO, 1975).
17. Community Relations Commission, *Urban Deprivation, Racial Inequality and Social Policy* (London: Community Relations Commission, 1977).
18. Commission for Racial Equality, *Looking for Work – Black and White School Leavers* (London: Commission for Racial Equality, 1978).
19. M. Anwar, *Between Two Cultures* (London: Community Relations Commission, 1976).
20. Bradford Council, *District Trends* (Bradford: City of Bradford Metropolitan Council, 1979).
21. Community Relations Commission, *Press Release* (London: Community Relations Commission, 12 September 1975).
22. Home Office, *Racial Discrimination*, White Paper, Cmnd 6234 (London: HMSO, 1975).
23. Ibid.
24. Community Relations Commission, *Press Release*, op.cit.
25. Her Majesty's Stationery Office, *Race Relations Act 1976* (London: HMSO, 1976).
26. Commission for Racial Equality, *Review of the Race Relations Act: Proposals for Change* (London: Commission for Racial Equality, 1985). Also *Second Review of the Race Relations Act* (London: Commission for Racial Equality, 1992).
27. Commission for Racial Equality, *Are Employers Complying?* (London: Commission for Racial Equality, 1989).
28. M. Anwar, 'Redressive Action Policies in the United Kingdom', paper presented at XI World Congress of Sociology, New Delhi (1986).
29. Commission for Racial Equality, *Annual Report 1983* (London: Commission for Racial Equality, 1984).
30. H. Street, G. Howe and G. Bindman, *Report on Anti-Discrimination Legislation* (London: Political and Economic Planning, 1967).
31. Her Majesty's Stationery Office, *The Local Government Act 1988* (London: HMSO, 1988).
32. Her Majesty's Stationery Office, *The Fair Employment (Northern Ireland) Act 1989* (Belfast: HMSO, 1989).
33. R. Osborne and R. Cormack, 'Fair Employment Towards Reforms in Northern Ireland', *Policy and Politics*, 17 (4) (1989).

2 The Politics of the Race Relations Act 1976

Anthony Lester

My involvement with the vexed problems of racial injustice, bigotry and intolerance began long before 1976. My involvement was shaped by my origins and experience: by the nightmares of a fortunate British Jew who escaped the Nazi Holocaust only by the accident of birth in Britain; by English anti-Semitism; by revulsion at the Sharpeville massacre and indignation at apartheid in South Africa; by two profoundly influential years in the United States at the beginning of the 1960s, witnessing the heroism of the civil rights movement in using non-violent action to overcome racist oppression in the Deep South; by observing the intractable patterns of racial discrimination and disadvantage in the cities of the Northern States; and by exploring the benefits and the limitations of constitutional guarantees of legal equality.

In 1964 I returned from an Amnesty International mission to report on justice in the American South in the wake of the Mississippi burnings. I was more than ever convinced that the affliction of racism in the United States was taking root in Britain in the absence of powerful political leadership and effective action by government and parliament. That bleak prospect was obvious to anyone with a knowledge of the human condition or of the painful history of race relations in Britain and the former empire.

It had been strident anti-Semitic hostility to the arrival of a relatively small number of Jewish immigrants, escaping persecution in Central and Eastern Europe a century ago, which had led to the Aliens Act of 1905. In the 1930s the government of the day decided not to arouse that ancient and persistent light sleeper, anti-Semitism, by allowing asylum to more than a tiny number of Jewish refugees from Nazi Germany.

The much more substantial immigration from the Commonwealth Caribbean and South Asia in the 1950s and early

1960s met at least as strong a tide of racial feeling in Britain, aggravated by colour prejudice, imperial nostalgia and a decline in national self-confidence. In the 1950s, the problems of racial prejudice and xenophobia were ignored or condemned by the political class; then, in the first Commonwealth Immigrants Act of 1962, the problems were dealt with by purely negative, defensive measures restricting the immigration of persons of colour. The Labour Opposition, led by Hugh Gaitskell, had fiercely and courageously resisted that first Commonwealth Immigrants Bill, in 1961. But by 1964, Labour had come reluctantly to accept that racially discriminatory controls were a necessary condition of good race relations and of winning and retaining power.

Meanwhile, during the autumn of 1964, a group of friends and I attempted to persuade the newly elected Labour Government to introduce legislation, modelled on US and Canadian precedents, to tackle racial discrimination in employment, housing, education, and commercial services, using an equality agency to enforce the law with civil proceedings.[1] Labour's meagre electoral commitment had been to use criminal law to forbid discrimination in public houses and other places of public resort and to create the offence of deliberately stirring up racial hatred. We persuaded the Home Secretary, Sir Frank Soskice, that a civil law was more appropriate and effective than criminal sanctions in tackling racial discrimination, and that an equality agency – the Race Relations Board – should be set up; but Soskice refused to widen the scope of his Race Relations Bill, observing to the Commons, in July 1965, that it would be 'an ugly day in this country if we had to come back to Parliament to extend the scope of this legislation'. The small size of the Government's parliamentary majority, the prospect of another General Election in the near future, and the electoral unpopularity feared to have been incurred by passing the Race Relations Act 1965, also led Harold Wilson's first Government to tighten the screw of immigration control, fixing a quota for the number of Commonwealth immigrant workers (but not of aliens) who could settle in Britain each year.

The immigration White Paper of 1965 was to be followed, three years later, by Home Secretary Callaghan's Commonwealth Immigrants Act 1968. This was rushed through Parliament as an emergency measure in three turbulent days and nights to deprive British Asian passport holders (made destitute by the policy of 'Africanisation' in East Africa) of their right of entry to the United Kingdom. The United Kingdom was, in fact, their only country of citizenship – a citizenship which they had retained instead of opting for local African citizenships, relying upon a pledge made to them by a previous Conservative Government. They were British citizens in a legal sense, but citizens now reduced to second-class status because of their colour. It was an unsightly measure which would be plainly unconstitutional in the many Commonwealth countries whose legislatures are bound by enforceable constitutional Bills of Rights guaranteeing the equal protection of the law for all their citizens.

Because the British Executive-controlled Parliament was omnipotent, there was recourse to the European Commission of Human Rights, which decided that Parliament had subjected a group of British citizens to racial discrimination which was inherently degrading and in breach of fundamental human rights.[2] Happily, the Commission's decision was promptly implemented by Home Secretary Roy Jenkins,[3] who changed the immigration rules in 1974. However, the underlying premise on which these statutes and administrative measures were based – that non-white immigration from the New Commonwealth had to be severely restricted – was extended and made permanent by the Conservative Government's Immigration Act 1971 and its requirement of patriality.

If one of the aims of these successive immigration measures was to take race out of politics, then they were a notable failure. They may even have had the opposite effect by conceding to the demands of a blatantly racist campaign, and thereby giving respectability to the proposition that skin colour was of the essence and that ethnic minorities were to be admitted on sufferance.

Of course we need a firm and effective system of immigration control. However, the subsequent law-making on immigration and British citizenship has not built a fair, non-discriminatory and efficient system of immigration control, or created a code of enforceable civil and political rights based upon equal citizenship.

Our law has two faces. One face confronts the stranger at the gate, grudgingly and suspiciously; the other is turned benevolently towards the newcomer and his descendants within the gate, guaranteeing the treatment of members of ethnic minorities as individuals on their merits, rather than discriminatory treatment on the basis of racial stereotypes, prejudices and assumptions. With one face, the law embodies and reinforces racial inequality; with the other, it expresses and urges racial equality. The positive impact of race equality law continues to be diminished by the negative impact of unfair and discriminatory immigration and asylum law.

To revert to the making of the race relations laws, in late 1964 a multiracial Campaign Against Racial Discrimination (CARD) was set up, on the initiative of Dr Martin Luther King, supported by some leading members of the main immigrant groups. It was chaired by Dr David Pitt. I became its legal officer. During the next three years, CARD played an important role in lobbying for comprehensive and effective legislation on behalf of the victims of racial discrimination, until it disintegrated in December 1967, taken over by militant Maoists and other militant tendencies, brought together under the tattered banner of 'Black Power'.

The destruction of CARD was a severe blow to those of us who had worked to build a multiracial movement for racial equality, led by members of the ethnic minorities, and reflecting their needs and aspirations. Tragically, nothing like CARD has since been created, though, in 1968, Jim Rose and I founded the Runnymede Trust, whose brilliant first Director, Dipak Nandy, did so much to counter prejudice with hard objective facts and reasoned argument, and to explain the dilemmas of democratic leadership: the need for 'a political process which would take account of popular grievances without succumbing to popular prejudices, a political process which at one represents and educates.'[4] Similarly, Jim Rose and Nicholas Deakin in their masterly study *Colour and Citizenship*, published in 1969, provided a public philosophy based upon ideals of fair play and equality before the law.[5]

At the end of 1965, Soskice retired and was replaced by Roy Jenkins. The change was to be of decisive importance to the making of the Race Relations Acts. Jenkins was firmly committed to the view that legislation had an important role to play in combating racial discrimination. He possessed the political skill needed to extend the 1965 Act, even though Parliament had legislated only shortly before he became Home Secretary.

The Government had no mandate to legislate for equal treatment in the key areas of employment, housing, education and commercial services. Any extension of the law would be electorally unpopular, and there was precious little support in the Government, the Labour Party or the trade union movement for bold and rapid action. Yet Jenkins decided upon his objectives and his strategy at the outset, and he remained true to both in the face of formidable opposition.

In a book on race and law that I wrote with Geoffrey Bindman and published in 1972, I told the story of what happened during the brief liberal interlude when Jenkins was Home Secretary before becoming Chancellor of the Exchequer, in November 1967.[6] One of Jenkins' first decisions was to appoint Mark Bonham-Carter to the chairmanship of the Race Relations Board. Bonham-Carter, whose recent death has left a large gap on the Liberal Democrat benches in the House of Lords, made it a condition of his appointment that he should be able to put the case after only a year's operation for the extension of the scope of the Act and a revision of his Board's powers.

Jenkins and Bonham-Carter conducted a shrewd campaign to reform the law, much of it masterminded by the Board's Chief Officer, John Lyttle. Jenkins made a series of carefully timed speeches, to which I was proud to contribute, committing himself and, by implication, his Ministerial colleagues further and further in the direction of reform. Jenkins and Bonham-Carter supported independent research into the nature and extent of racial discrimination, and an inquiry by Professor Harry Street, Sir Geoffrey Howe QC and Geoffrey Bindman to examine overseas experience in using law to tackle racial discrimination. Meanwhile, Dipak Nandy organised a grassroots project for CARD using volunteers in Leeds, Manchester and Handsworth to reveal the true extent of racial discrimination.

The campaigners lacked the advantages enjoyed by their US counterparts from whom they drew their inspiration. Britain's ethnic minorities did not have significant voting power; the non-white population consisted mainly of recent immigrants, whose claim to equal treatment was made with less insistence and was understood with less sympathy than if they had been born in Britain. When the campaign began, there was little public awareness of the nature or extent of racial discrimination. There was also no ideal of equality, embodied in a written constitution or elsewhere, to which the campaigners could turn in support of their case for using law to combat racial discrimination. The common law had at best been neutral, at worst giving preference to property and contract rights over the right to equality of treatment, and failing to treat racial discrimination as contrary to public policy. The campaigners' objective was radical and without precedent in this country. The notion of positive civil rights and the use of law to combat discrimination were as novel and unfamiliar to the ethnic minorities as they were to the majority of the community. After the disintegration of the CARD alliance, leaders from the immigrant communities no longer formed the vanguard of the lobby for legislation. During the passage of the 1968 Race Relations Bill, the main work of lobbying for a strong statute was done by 'Equal Rights', an *ad hoc,* hastily-created, temporary body which sought no following among immigrants. And the political climate of the 1960s, characterised by increasingly frequent and effective attacks on coloured immigration and immigrants, grew steadily less favourable to those who were working to reduce racial prejudice and discrimination.

Despite the unpromising political climate, the first annual report by Bonham-Carter's Race Relations Board in 1967, argued strongly and bravely for extending the 1965 Act. The Board summarised the role of legislation in five principles which remain equally valid thirty years later: (1) a law is an unequivocal declaration of public policy; (2) a law gives support to those who do not wish to discriminate, but who feel compelled to do so by social pressure; (3) a law gives protection and redress to minority groups; (4) a law thus provides for the peaceful and orderly adjustment of grievances and the release of tensions; (5) a law reduces prejudice by discouraging the behaviour in which prejudice finds expression.[7]

What thoughts were in our minds when we sought to use the law to promote equality within a plural and liberal democracy? What was our philosophy and our understanding of the notion of 'race'?

We shared a moral ideal of the equality of human beings which affirms that, although we are unequal in our skill, intelligence, strength and virtue, we are morally equal because of our common humanity. We also believed that, because of imperatives of a modern society, equality of opportunity, based on individual merit, has been transformed from a moral ideal into an economic, social and political necessity. We were convinced that the unequal characteristics of human beings are not the result of innate inferiority or superiority but of the unequal environments into which we are born and must live. If the inequalities are removed, people are able to fulfil their real potential. Our belief was reinforced by the evidence of social science about the social conditioning of people by their environment. Human potential may be limited by genetic inheritance, but genetic differences are now seen to be a far less powerful source of inequality than environmental factors. And, so far as *racial* inequality is concerned, biological evidence indicates that the socially significant group differences are culturally not genetically transmitted. The range of difference within individuals in ethnic groups is at least as great as the range of difference between ethnic groups. Although this evidence is relevant and important, we also remembered, in Professor Michael Banton's well-chosen words, that 'The validity of the declaration that all men are created equal in dignity and rights does not depend upon a permit from the biologists that has to be renewed at regular intervals.'[8]

Our philosophy was conveyed in a memorable public statement given thirty years ago, by Roy Jenkins, on his attitude towards racial discrimination and integration.[9] The new Home Secretary began by observing that 'integration' is rather a loose word. He said:

> I do not regard it as meaning the loss, by immigrants, of their own national characteristics and culture. I do not think we need in this country a 'melting-pot', which will turn everybody out in a common mould, as one of a series of carbon copies of someone's misplaced vision of the stereotyped Englishman. ...
>
> It would deprive us of most of the positive advantages of immigration which ... I believe to be very great indeed.
>
> I define integration, therefore, not as a flattening process of assimilation but as equal opportunity, accompanied by cultural diversity, in an atmosphere of mutual tolerance. This is the goal.

Later, in the same speech, Home Secretary Jenkins referred to the great economic, commercial and intellectual benefits of immigration, observing that to live apart, for a person, a city, a country, is to lead a life of declining intellectual stimulation. 'Let there be no suggestion', he said, 'that immigration, in reasonable numbers, is a cross we have to bear, and no pretence that if only those who had come could find jobs back at home, our problems could be at an end. There is ... no overall rational basis for resentment of the coloured immigrant population in our midst. ... But resentment does not always spring from rational causes, particularly when, as is the case with coloured immigrants, their skin and their cultural differences make them natural targets for those who are looking for scapegoats.' No Home Secretary or shadow Home Secretary has spoken like this in the subsequent thirty years. What was unique was Roy Jenkins' perception, as a liberal reforming Home Secretary, that in the moral and political climate of the post-war period, no civilised society could permit the growth of racial injustice, and his unblinking determination to use his public office to promote racial equality. He understood the feebleness of reason before the power of fanatically believed doctrines. He knew the truth of Kant's famous observation that 'Out of the crooked timber of humanity no straight thing can ever be made'. He did not strive officiously to use the law to straighten the crooked timber of humanity, but to encourage the enlightened ideals of a plural democracy and to provide effective redress for the victims of injustice.

In referring to 'equality of opportunity, accompanied by cultural diversity', Roy Jenkins had also referred to 'an atmosphere of mutual tolerance'. *Mutual* tolerance means tolerance of cultural differences by minorities as well as by majorities. It means that not only white racism but also black racism is invidious, as is the prejudice of members of one ethnic minority against members of another. It means that those who worship as believers of one religious faith should respect believers in other faiths, as well as those who have no religious faith – one person's religious faith often being blasphemy to the faith of another person. It means acceptance of universal human rights and fundamental freedoms by which all democratic societies are internationally bound, including the right to free expression.

Roy Jenkins has always valued freedom of speech as much as he has valued racial equality and human dignity, fighting censorship as well as discrimination. I share his commitment to each of these fundamental values. I mention this because of the insistent pressure from some religious and ethnic groups to ban the public utterance of evil racist ideas which insult their faith, their culture or their humanity. I share their revulsion, but I am firmly opposed to using the criminal law to punish political or religious speech or writings which offend, shock or disturb, unless they create a serious risk of imminent violence or stir up racial or religious hatred; such are the demands of that pluralism, tolerance and broadmindedness without which there can be no democratic society. There is a panoply of offences against public order and against the person at the disposal of the police service and the courts to combat racial incitement, racial harassment and racially-motivated violence. What is needed is the vigorous and effective enforcement of these existing laws, rather than new-fangled legislation to extend the outmoded offences of blasphemous and seditious libel.

To return to my potted political history, before Roy Jenkins swapped offices with Jim Callaghan, he had effectively committed his colleagues to amending the Act to cover racial discrimination in employment, housing, education, and the provision of goods, facilities and services to the public. It was Home Secretary Callaghan who executed the plan. His Race Relations Act 1968 extended the law's reach to cover these vast areas, and established a Community Relations Commission to complement the work done by the Race Relations Board. But the 1968 Act was marred by unnecessary exceptions, and above all by serious weaknesses in its provision for enforcement.

In February 1974, Labour was narrowly returned to power and Roy Jenkins became Home Secretary again, with a mandate to introduce legislation dealing with sex as well as race discrimination. I abandoned my practice at the Bar to help him, as Special Adviser, between 1974 and 1976. It was my particular responsibility to develop policy in this area with Ministers and civil servants. It was a challenging and exacting task because there was strong hostility from some of my civil service colleagues to our central aims and to our chosen means of achieving them.[10]

It was a minority Government facing a strong Conservative opposition, and its staying power was at best uncertain. Jenkins decided that the best way of persuading Parliament to enact strong legislation on race equality was by first introducing separate legislation on sex equality for which there would be much greater political support, and then modelling the race equality legislation upon what became the Sex Discrimination Act 1975. I therefore wrote the first drafts of two White Papers,[11] one on 'Equality for Women',[12] and the other on 'Racial Discrimination'.[13]

Our stated aim in tackling racial discrimination was to fashion 'a coherent and long-term strategy' to deal with the interlocking problems of immigration, cultural differences, racial disadvantage and discrimination. This was to be achieved both by strengthening the existing statute law, and by promoting administrative and voluntary measures to give prac-tical effect to the objectives of the law. Legislation was intended to be but one part of what would eventually become a comprehensive strategy for tackling racial disadvantage.[14]

The Race Relations Act 1976 widened the scope of the 1968 Act which it replaced, and removed loopholes and anomalies. The Act forbids colour bars in private social clubs and political parties,[15] and racial discrimination in the selection of Parliamentary candidates.[16] It also permits a limited measure of special provision and of positive action in favour of ethnic minority groups, without allowing racial quotas or reverse discrimination.[17]

The Act also radically extended the key concept of unlawful racial discrimination to include not only direct discrimination on racial grounds but also indirect discrimination. Neutrally-framed and well-intentioned practices and procedures were made unlawful, if they have a disproportionate adverse impact on ethnic minorities and lack any objective justification.[18] This means having to treat individuals, for the purposes of the Act, as belonging to particular 'racial' groups; to that extent, the concept of indirect racial discrimination may be said to lend credence to the idea that there are separate races, or that group reasoning is appropriate.[19] That is the price which has to be paid if the legislation is to tackle the mischief of discrimination effectively.

The excessively technical way in which the Race Relations and Sex Discrimination Acts were drafted has cramped the potential reach of the crucially important concept of indirect discrimination through a strict textual interpretation.[20] The European Court of Justice has liberated the concept of indirect sex discrimination from the crabbed and identical language of the Sex Discrimination Act.[21] However, the concept of indirect racial discrimination has not yet been set free.

It is also very unfortunate that a majority of the House of Lords interpreted the Act as applying to the provision of services and facilities to the public by government bodies only if those bodies are performing similar functions to private bodies in the market place.[22] This interpretation is inconsistent with the international human rights law by which the United Kingdom is bound,[23] and means that the Act does not apply to the exercise of public powers in many significant areas of life.[24]

As regards redress for the victims, the 1976 Act made a major departure from the previous legislation. Instead of channelling all complaints through the new Commission for Racial Equality (CRE) as an exclusive enforcement agency, we decided to give individuals a direct right of access to legal redress, and to combine this with the key strategic function of the CRE in enforcing the law in the public interest with strong new powers.

Mark Bonham-Carter persuaded Roy Jenkins that the Community Relations Commission and the Race Relations Board should be amalgamated into the new CRE. I had argued unsuccessfully that this would inevitably weaken the CRE's ability to carry out its crucial law-enforcement functions. I well understand the political factors which led to that decision, but I believe that the experience of the past two decades has demonstrated the flawed legacy which the CRE inherited at its birth by virtue of this amalgamation. The White Paper explained that, although the CRE would be able to assist individuals in appropriate cases, its main task would be wider policy: 'to identify and deal with discriminatory practices by industries, firms or institutions', using its power to issue non-discrimination notices and to bring legal proceedings against those who persistently violate the law.[25] The leadership of the amalgamated CRE has not always believed that a major part of the CRE's work should be the strategic enforcement of the law.

When the CRE has attempted to use its investigative and enforcement powers, it has not been helped by the complex procedures insisted upon by the courts in their laudable concern to ensure fairness to those alleged to have acted contrary to the law.[26] In the words of Lord Denning MR,[27] the CRE has also 'been caught up in a spider's web spun by Parliament from which there is little hope of their escaping. ... The machinery is so elaborate and cumbersome it is grinding to a halt.'[28] This is a serious defect in the statutory scheme, crying out for reform.

A key part of the strategy behind the 1976 Act was that an undertaking to comply with the provisions of the Act would be a standard condition of all Government contracts. As we recognised in the White paper: 'the policies and attitudes of central and local government are of critical importance in themselves and in their potential influence on the country as a whole'. A Government Department was therefore to monitor compliance with these clauses by requiring contractors to provide reasonable information about their employment practices and policies.

Yet in sharp contrast to the position taken in Northern Ireland,[29] successive governments have failed to introduce this type of positive monitoring.[30] Indeed current legislation actually hobbles local authorities in performing their duty, under section 71 of the Act, to have regard to the need to eliminate unlawful racial discrimination and to promote equal opportunity.[31] The time is over-ripe to remove this fetter and to fulfil the promise of the 1975 White Paper. It is time to heed the recommendations made by the CRE in their two reviews to remove the weaknesses in the Act revealed by twenty years' experience and case law. It is time to restore the CRE's budget, cut by £1 million in 1995, and expected to be cut further in its twentieth birthday year.[32] It is time for the political parties to ensure that ethnic minority Parliamentary candidates are selected so that Parliament and its handiwork better reflect the multiracial nature of the nation.

Under the incoherent constitutional arrangements of this country it is unlawful to discriminate on religious grounds in Northern Ireland, but not in Great Britain:[33] it is unlawful to discriminate on racial grounds in Great Britain, but not yet in Northern Ireland; and it is unlawful to discriminate on grounds of sex throughout the United Kingdom. The Fair Employment Commission has monitoring powers in tackling religious discrimination in Northern Ireland, which have been denied to the CRE and the EOCs (Equal Opportunities Commissions). The legislation forbids the various equality Commissions from sharing information provided to them in the course of their investigations. The EOC for Great Britain cannot even share this information with the EOC for Northern Ireland. As for discrimination against the disabled, the new legislation is as full of holes as a colander, and the pathetic National Disability Council has neither teeth nor even the power to give legal advice and assistance to aggrieved victims. This is a profoundly unsatisfactory state of affairs, which again cries out for reform.

We need comprehensive equality legislation, constructed on the basis of coherent and consistent principles. We need a speedy and efficient system of enforcement and redress applied to all forms of unlawful discrimination in all parts of the country. We need to bring our law into line with the International Convention on the Elimination of All Forms of Racial Discrimination, as repeatedly recommended by its Committee.[34] We need to make the guarantees of non-discrimination by which we are internationally bound part of our national law. We need to allow people in this country as elsewhere to take cases to the Human Rights Committee, under the Optional Protocol to the International Covenant on Civil and Political Rights, enabling them advantage of the Covenant's powerful guarantees of equality.[35] We need to persuade the governments of the Member States of the European Union to create an enforceable right for all their inhabitants to equal treatment without racial or religious discrimination.[36]

Somehow we need to rediscover the political will and skill that put the Race Relations Act into law twenty years ago, the same year in which the United Kingdom also ratified the International Covenants on Civil and Political and on Economic, Social and Cultural Rights. To quote Dipak Nandy again, 'It is the duty of politicians to heed popular opinion. It is equally the duty of politicians to educate public opinion. But nothing in the theory of democratic politics requires politicians to give way to popular prejudices, especially where the rights of minorities are at stake.'[37] That was well said in December 1968. It needs to be said again and again to politicians of all parties as we approach another contest for the popular vote. We will never attain all that we seek, but it is our duty to redouble our efforts now, in preparation not only for the next election but for the next century.

NOTES

1. Nicholas Deakin, Bernard Donoughue, Jeffrey Jowell, Ian MacDonald, Jim Rose, Roger Warren Evans and Michael Zander. Julie McNeal who was General Secretary of the Campaign Against Racial Discrimination (CARD) also played a key role.
2. *East African Asians* v. *United Kingdom,* 3 EHRR 76 (1973).
3. Instead of challenging the decision before the European Court of Human Rights.
4. Dipak Nandy, 'Race as Politics', in *Towards an Open Society: Ends and Means in British Politics,* proceedings of a seminar organised by the British Humanist Association, December 1968 (London: Pemberton Books, 1971) p. 70.
5. E. J. B. Rose *et al., Colour and Citizenship: A Report on British Race Relations* (London: Oxford University Press, 1969).
6. A. Lester and G. Bindman, *Race and Law* (London: Longman and Penguin Books, 1972) pp. 122–30.
7. Annual Report of the Race Relations Board, April 1967, paragraph 65.
8. Michael Banton, *Race Relations* (London: Tavistock, 1967) p. 4.
9. 'Racial Equality in Britain', speech made on 23 May 1966 to a meeting of voluntary liaison committees of the National Committee for Commonwealth Immigrants, in Roy Jenkins, *Essays and Speeches,* ed. Anthony Lester (London: Collins, 1967).
10. See A. Lester, 'Discrimination: What Can Lawyers Learn from History?', *Public Law,* 224 (Summer, 1994) p. 225. The hostility remained until the Government won another General Election in October 1974, and a new team was put in place at the Home Office.
11. With considerable assistance from my own Special Adviser, Angela Byre, and from Dipak Nandy, who acted as a consultant.
12. Cmnd. 5724, September 1974.
13. Cmnd. 6234, September 1975.
14. Ibid., at paragraphs 22 to 26.
15. RRA 1976, section 25.
16. RRA 1976, section 12.
17. RRA 1976, sections 35, 37 and 38.
18. RRA 1976, section I (I)(b).
19. See, e.g., Kenan Malik, *The Meaning of Race* (Basingstoke: Macmillan, 1996), p. 25.

20.   See, e.g., *Perera* v. *Civil Service Commission* (1983) IRLR 166 (CA); and *Meer* v. *Tower Hamlets LBC* (1988) IRLR 399 (CA).
21.   Case C-127/92, *Enderby* v. *Frenchay Health Authority* (1993) IRLR 591, in relation to the EC principle of equal pay, but rejecting restrictive arguments derived from the language of section 1(1)(b) of the Sex Discrimination Act 1975.
22.   *R* v. *Entry Clearance Officer, ex parte Amin* (1983) 2 AC 818 (HL), In Re Amin (an appeal from *R* v. *Entry Clearance Officer, Bombay, ex parte Amin* (1983) 2 AC 818).
23.   Namely, Articles 2 and 26 of the International Covenant on Civil and Political Rights, and Articles 1, 13 and 14 of the European Convention on Human Rights read with its substantive provisions, including Protocol No. I to the Convention.
24.   However, since the common law now recognises a principle of equality without unfair discrimination, the problem can to some extent be dealt with by the judicial review of administrative action: see De Smith, Woolf and Jowell (1995), *Judicial Review of Administrative Action*, 5th edn (London: Sweet and Maxwell) paragraphs 13–036 to–045.
25.   See note 13 above (esp. paragraph).
26.   See *CRE* v. *Prestige Group Plc* (1984) I WLR 335 (HL); *R* v. *CRE, ex parte London Borough of Hillingdon* (1982) AC 779 (HL).
27.   CRE v. Amari Plastics Ltd (1982) IRLR 252 (CA).
28.   Lord Denning was not entirely sympathetic to the investigative powers of the CRE and EOCs: see *Science Research Council* v. *Nassé* (1979) I QB 144 (CA), at p. 172G, where, after referring to their powers, he said 'You might think we were back in the days of the Inquisition.'
29.   Where sections 38 to 43 of the 1989 Fair Employment Act place employers under an obligation to provide religious monitoring data, which has been tied to their eligibility for public contracts. They are also bound to carry out periodic reviews aimed at fair participation and to draw up affirmative action plans. The preface to the Government's White Paper, *Fair Employment in Northern Ireland* (Cm 380, 1988), explains that the measures there contained 'use the Government's economic strength to support good practice'.
30.   Despite the recommendations of the CRE: Second Annual Review of the Race Relations Act (1992), p. 41, *Guidance for Officials on Policy Appraisal for Equal Treatment* (June 1996), is welcome and useful in enabling the impact of policies and programmes on ethnic groups, among others, to be appraised. However, it is no substitute for an effective Government contract compliance programme and the monitoring of employment practices and procedures.
31.   Local Government Act 1988, section 18.
32.   *New Law Journal*, 21 June 1996, p. 907.
33.   Although Gypsies (*Commission for Racial Equality* v. *Dutton* (1989) 1 All ER 306 (CA)), Sikhs (*Mandla* v. *Dowell Lee* (1983) 2 AC 548 (HL)), and Jews (*Seide* v. *Gillette Industries Ltd* (1980) IRLR 427 (EAT) at 430) have been classified by English courts as 'racial groups'.
34.   See, for example, the comments by the Committee on the Elimination of Racial Discrimination of 15 March 1996 on the UK's Thirteenth Report.

35. See, for example, the Human Rights Committee's comments on the UK's Fourth Periodic Report, CCPR/C/79/Add. 55, 27 July 1996.
36. The Government's White Paper on the IGC strongly opposes this. It states that 'As for questions of discrimination, the Government is proud of its national record, and convinced of the adequacy of the legal framework already in place. It believes that the problems of discrimination (particularly on such sensitive questions as race and religion) are best dealt with in this way, through national legislation.'
37. See note 5 above, p. 70.

3 Law Enforcement or Lack of It
Geoffrey Bindman

Law can have a useful declaratory effect. In its often repeated list of the uses of the law published in 1967, the Race Relations Board placed first its role as an unequivocal declaration of public policy.[1] But without effective enforcement by the courts its value is severely limited. It achieves no practical redress for those who suffer hurt and loss as the victims of discrimination. Effective enforcement needs:

- statutory powers which enable courts and tribunals to make necessary orders and awards;
- judges able and willing to implement the law creatively and positively in order to carry out its purposes;
- an institutional framework and environment which ensures that victims and those representing them have access to courts and tribunals.

WEAKNESSES IN THE LAW BEFORE 1976

The Race Relations Acts which preceded the 1976 Act were conspicuously deficient in enforcement powers. The 1965 Act did not touch at all on the areas in which discrimination was most prevalent: employment and housing. After 1965 discrimination in those areas continued unabated. Although discrimination was prohibited in access to certain public facilities, such as pubs, restaurants, museums and public transport, individuals had no right to take a case themselves to a court or tribunal. The only sanction against those who broke the law was tortuous and remote. The Race Relations Board, whose voluntary conciliation committees had primary responsibility for investigating complaints of discrimination, could as a last resort, and only if satisfied that discrimination was likely to be repeated, refer a complaint to the Attorney-General. He alone had power to ini-

40

tiate legal proceedings in a county court. Only four cases during the lifetime of this statute – from 1966 to 1968 – were referred and the Attorney-General found reasons for not proceeding in all of them.[2] In the absence of any realistic sanction, no effective redress was provided to any victim while the 1965 Act was in force.

The 1968 Act was only marginally more effective although on paper it contained much stronger enforcement powers. The Board itself could now take cases to the county court and damages could be claimed. Discrimination in employment and housing became unlawful. Yet sanctions against those who broke the law remained extremely weak. Individual complainants continued to be denied the right given to victims of other civil wrongs to take legal proceedings on their own initiative. Only the Race Relations Board could do this, and then only after going through a laborious process of attempted conciliation. In employment cases, an additional hurdle was erected: complaints made to the Board had to be referred to so-called 'industrial machinery' – bodies set up jointly by employers' organisations and trade unions for the purpose of investigating and attempting to resolve complaints. Only in the event of failure could a case be taken to court by the Board. Unhappily, the employment cases referred to industry machinery were so delayed or ineptly conducted that they ended without result in almost every case. Only a handful of employment cases were taken to court by the Board during the lifetime of the 1968 Act.

The number of cases outside the employment field which provided any effective redress for the victim was extremely small. In those which were successful the damages awarded were often of a token amount. The typical sum awarded to a complainant refused service in a pub operating a colour bar was £5.[3]

FRAMING THE 1976 ACT

Parliament had an opportunity to provide effective enforcement mechanisms and a wider range of sanctions in the 1976 Act. It made several promising improvements. It removed the cumbersome requirement of a formal conciliation process prior to the initiation of legal proceedings. The power to bring proceedings

on behalf of individuals was not given to the Commission for
Racial Equality, which replaced the Race Relations Board, but
was granted to the individuals themselves, with assistance, if
they needed it, from the Commission. Employment cases were
to be brought in the industrial tribunal, instead of the county
court, which was to continue to hear cases relating to matters
other than employment. Courts and tribunals were explicitly
empowered to award compensation for injury to feelings, as
well as for specific losses. There is little doubt that they already
had this power but it was considered important to spell it out in
order to encourage higher awards.

A Dual Framework

Before the 1976 Act the law failed to give adequate recognition
to the dual nature of discrimination. It not only unjustly harms
individuals who need to be able to seek redress for the wrong
done to them, but because it arises from attitudes and practices
which are directed at groups or supposed groups, it is also
susceptible to collective forms of enforcement. The latter were
virtually ignored in the earlier legislation. Although the 1968
Act gave the Race Relations Board power to conduct investigations in the absence of an individual complaint, the provision
conferring this power was limited and rarely used.

The draftsmen of the 1976 Act made a serious effort to con-
struct a framework for tackling collective or institutional discrimination. Relieved of the responsibility for investigating and
pursuing cases on behalf of individuals, the new Commission
was intended to focus its efforts on a strategic and wide-ranging
assault on what in the United States came to be described as
'patterns and practices' of discrimination.

Indirect Discrimination

An important change was to expand the definition of discrimination to include indirect as well as direct discrimination.
Indirect discrimination refers to those situations, ignored by
the earlier legislation, in which an ostensibly neutral requirement – such as education in the United Kingdom, or mother-
tongue English – has a discriminatory impact because of the
inability of many members of a particular group to comply with

it. It is especially characteristic of institutional situations affecting a large number of people because it arises from the imposition of a standard of general application. An individual from a relevant group unable to meet this standard could bring an indirect discrimination claim, but a collective claim, attacking the standard itself and seeking a remedy for all those disadvantaged by it, would necessarily have a much wider effect and be a more economical way to proceed. The CRE was intended to pursue such collective cases.

A New Mechanism

The mechanism chosen was the 'formal investigation'. The statute apparently gave the CRE extensive powers to conduct such investigations. Section 48 says: ' ... the Commission may if they think fit, and shall if required by the Secretary of State, conduct a formal investigation for any purpose connected with the carrying out of those duties.' So far so good. But how could the CRE make its investigation productive and effective? Obviously it needed information which would determine whether discrimination had occurred. That meant giving it access to subpoena powers. Then it needed to have power to take action in the light of its findings. Where it uncovered discrimination, which might affect a large number of individuals, there needed to be a mechanism for ensuring that all the victims secured suitable redress. So, it was reasoned by those who devised the scheme of the Act, the CRE must be empowered to make orders requiring the discriminator to take suitable remedial action.

A Legal Transplant

The scheme was seriously flawed. One error was to give enforcement powers to the CRE instead of giving them to an independent court or tribunal. This was partly the result of falling into the trap of the 'legal transplant'.[4] What was acceptable in other jurisdictions did not necessarily fit into the English legal tradition.

The CRE was modelled on the American administrative enforcement agency. Starting in New York and Massachusetts soon after the Second World War, human rights commissions were set up in many states to administer anti-discrimination laws. Their function was to investigate complaints of discrimination and, when necessary, convene a public hearing at which the validity of the complaint would be determined. If it was upheld, the discriminator was ordered to remedy the wrong. The commissioners who heard the complaint were not involved in the investigating process and were obviously required to exercise independent judgement in adjudicating on the complaint, but they were part and parcel of the agency. This was not thought to constitute a conflict of interest because the parties, if aggrieved by a decision, had the right to challenge it in court.[5]

In the English legal culture, an administrative body given such powers is required to observe strict standards of impartiality, and its decisions are open to legal challenge if it fails to apply the principles of natural justice. These principles consist of three main requirements: that one accused of wrongdoing should be given particulars of what is alleged, that he or she should be given an opportunity of answering those allegations, and that the adjudicating body should be free of bias or the appearance of bias. In Parliament there was much disquiet about the intrusive powers proposed for the CRE. From both Government and Opposition there was ambivalence about using the law coercively. In the interests of getting an already weak Bill passed, further compromises were made. The result was a series of limitations on the CRE's investigative powers far greater than those which natural justice would in any event have demanded. The powers themselves were drastically curtailed. The greatest failure was to omit the two most effective and far-reaching features of the American system: the power to order specific remedial action through changes in management systems and policies; and the power to secure redress for members of a class subjected to discrimination. The absence of the latter – the 'class action' – is a general weakness in the English legal system, but in the United States it has been of particular importance in discrimination cases and the 1976 Act was an ideal opportunity to introduce it into our system.[6]

Confusion of Aims

The drafting of the Act suffered not only from political fear of intrusive powers but from a confusion of aims. It was not uni-

versally agreed that the law had a role to play in effecting institutional changes other than by providing individual redress.
The duties given to the CRE do not specifically include enforcement of the law. Its main functions are to work towards the
elimination of discrimination and promoting equality of opportunity and good relations between persons of different racial
groups generally.[7] The encouragement of equal opportunity
policies, unaccompanied by any threat of legal action, has been
seen from the outset by the CRE as a major function. In
November 1982 an internal working party played down the
investigative role, saying: 'It is important to place on record the
fact that the law does not support the concept of primacy of
investigative work ... promotional work is of equal importance
to investigative work as an alternative route to the common
objectives set for the Commission.'[8] This may be literally true
but it also reflects an undercurrent of scepticism in the CRE
about the use of what were perceived as coercive powers. But
the power to conduct investigations need not be only a tool for
law enforcement. Nor indeed is there anything to prevent the
CRE from conducting enquiries outside the context of a formal
investigation, provided they are within the scope of its general
duties. Only if it seeks to use the subpoena and other powers
accompanying a formal investigation need it use that mechanism. Even if it does choose to embark on a formal investigation,
the only necessary consequences of doing so are that terms of
reference must be drawn up and general notice must be given
of the holding of the investigation. It is not surprising that the
CRE, under a severe battering from the courts, lost the will to
make the most of its investigative role.

Named-Person Investigations

Major legal and practical problems have arisen particularly in
relation to those investigations in which the CRE has wanted to
investigate possible unlawful discrimination by 'named persons'
– usually companies or institutions but sometimes individuals.

Before embarking on such an investigation, the person must
be informed of that intention and given an opportunity to
make oral or written representations.[9] Oral representations
may be made by a solicitor or counsel. Not surprisingly, large
and wealthy companies or institutions, anxious to head off a

time-consuming and potentially damaging investigation, were prepared to invest considerable resources in exploiting their right to make representations. On several occasions, Queen's Counsel were employed to make representations over several days. In order to meet the requirements of natural justice these representations had to be heard by Commissioners in a quasi-judicial setting. The CRE had to prepare its ground carefully to avoid further legal pitfalls. A range of technical issues had to be resolved. How far must the CRE disclose the evidence which led to its wish to investigate? Should witnesses be allowed to give evidence when representations were made? Should cross-examination be allowed? Should the Commission issue a formal response to the representations? Generally the CRE erred on the side of caution to avoid as far as possible further legal challenges. What cynical Parliamentarians perceived as safeguards against abuses of power by the CRE led to absurd complexity. Lord Denning – no friend of the CRE – summed it up: 'The machinery is so elaborate and cumbersome that it is in danger of grinding to a halt. I am very sorry for the Commission, but they have been caught in a spider's web spun by Parliament, from which there is little hope of their escaping.'[10] It was as if the police were required to justify in court every decision to prosecute before arresting a suspect. The representation process often took months and, even after deciding to proceed, the CRE could face court proceedings challenging its decision.

Appeals to the House of Lords

A series of challenges ended in the House of Lords, which effectively sabotaged the strategy envisaged by the framers of the Act. The CRE decided to embark on an investigation into the housing policy of the London Borough of Hillingdon after a highly publicised incident when the leader of the Council, Terry Dicks (subsequently MP), sent an immigrant family, who had sought Council housing as homeless persons after arriving at Heathrow, to 10 Downing Street in a taxi. Mr Dicks' complaint was that the Government should be responsible for housing immigrants, not Hillingdon, merely because Heathrow happened to be within its area. There was evidence that a white family arriving from Rhodesia had been housed without fuss and the CRE decided to investigate the Council's policy towards homeless families on the footing that it might be unlawfully discriminatory. After a three-day hearing of representations by Hillingdon, with solicitors and counsel, the CRE amended its terms of reference in some respects but decided to proceed. The Council challenged the decision by judicial review. Mr Justice Woolf (now Lord Woolf, Master of the Rolls) said the terms of reference were too wide and not justified by the evidence relied on by the CRE. He pointed out that the CRE was free to start afresh with narrower terms of reference but meanwhile its decision was quashed. The ruling was upheld by the Court of Appeal and the House of Lords.[11]

The Dicks incident which prompted the CRE's action was on 5 November 1978. The House of Lords gave its judgment on 17 June 1982. Not surprisingly, after spending many thousands of pounds on this abortive exercise and after so much time had gone by, the CRE lost its appetite for investigating Hillingdon's housing policies and proceeded no further.

THE IMPACT OF THE NEW LAW

The effect of the Hillingdon decision, reinforced by the House of Lords decision in the Prestige case two years later,[12] was to prevent the CRE from starting a formal investigation of a 'named person' without evidence to justify a strong suspicion that he, she or it had discriminated unlawfully. While this might not on the face of it seem a serious obstacle, since one would expect investigations to be targeted on such cases, it proved a devastating blow to the CRE's strategy. The Courts had signalled that they were ready to monitor the CRE's detailed compliance with the law. Those threatened with investigation were encouraged to resist and the CRE was conversely discouraged, knowing that resistance could be enormously costly and time-consuming for its staff.

More Hurdles

It must also be remembered that the Hillingdon and Prestige investigations never got past the first hurdle. The CRE was not allowed even to 'embark' on the investigations. After an investigation has got off the ground, the Act places several further pitfalls in the CRE's path. If the investigators identify illegality and the CRE is minded to find unlawful discrimination, it must warn the putative discriminator who then has a chance to make representations once again, this time against the prospective finding. If the CRE sticks to its guns after that and makes the finding of discrimination it can face an appeal to a court or industrial tribunal.

In July 1978 the CRE decided to embark on an investigation of Amari Plastics Limited, on the basis of evidence that the company was refusing to recruit black employees. The company fought tooth and nail at every stage. It made unsuccessful representations before the investigation started and before the finding was made. After the finding, the CRE issued a non-discrimination notice, whereupon the company exercised its right to appeal to the industrial tribunal against the requirement in the notice that it cease to discriminate unlawfully. The tribunal is empowered to quash a requirement on appeal where it considers it 'to be unreasonable because it is based on an incorrect finding of fact or for any other reason'.[13] The tribunal took this to mean that the factual basis of the CRE's finding could be challenged. In other words the whole of the evidence could be examined all over again in a formal judicial setting. The High Court and Court of Appeal upheld this interpretation. Lord Denning made the famous comment quoted earlier but still felt he had to rule in the company's favour.[14] The Court of Appeal decision was in February 1982. After that the case had to go back to the industrial tribunal in September 1983, more than five years after the CRE first decided to investigate.

In effect, after going through the laborious double representation process, the person investigated could tell the CRE: 'having failed to persuade you to drop this investigation, we now want you to prove the case against us in a tribunal'. An ostensibly unrestricted power to investigate and make findings was thus transformed by the courts into a power only to make findings which the CRE could prove in court. If that had been Parliament's intention, why not simply give the CRE power to take a case to court at the outset, saving a huge amount of time and expense?

In the Prestige investigation the House of Lords ruled that the CRE had no power to undertake a named person investigation at all without a belief (supported by evidence) that there might have been unlawful discrimination. It had previously been supposed that a general investigation, not alleging discrimination, could be mounted into a named person without offering representations. This decision, coming after Hillingdon, had a devastating effect on the CRE's formal investigation strategy. As a direct result of the Prestige decision, no less than eight investigations already in progress were abandoned.[15] In the following years the number of investigations has rarely exceeded one or two a year, including both general and named person investigations.

Who is Responsible?

Who is to blame for this débâcle? How damaging has it been to the effectiveness of the Act? Was Parliament responsible or was it the judges' fault?

Undoubtedly the judges, with a few exceptions, have viewed the cases coming before them narrowly, legalistically and without sympathy or understanding of the purposes which the law was designed to achieve. Lord Denning, for example, in the Nassé and Vyas cases completely misunderstood the extremely limited extent of the CRE's powers and the feebleness of the threat which they posed to those whom the CRE chose to investigate. He spoke of the 'inquisitional' powers of the Commission, 'of a kind never known to the law', which enabled the CRE to 'interrogate employers and educational authorities up to the hilt and compel disclosure of documents on a massive scale. You might think that we were back in the days of the Inquisition. You might think we were back in the days of the General Warrants.'[16] Lord Wilberforce, in the House of Lords in the same case, was more objective: 'The powers have been conferred upon statutory bodies as part of the machinery for eliminating discrimination in situations where the parties are of unequal strength: no instance was given to us of the oppressive use of them and we should presume that they will reasonably be used for the purpose for which they are given.'[17]

A MORE SYMPATHETIC APPROACH

Judicial hostility was directed at the investigative powers, and this was Parliament's fault. However, the Nassé and Vyas decisions illustrate a much more sympathetic approach to the problems faced by individual victims in proving discrimination. On the whole the courts have tried to assist complainants to overcome these problems. Where, for example, discrimination in recruitment was claimed, the employer would have details of the qualifications of all the applicants. Without access to this knowledge it would be impossible for the complainant to establish whether a rejection was grounded in race or merely that the better qualified candidate was chosen. The House of Lords agreed that the alleged discriminator must disclose the information which the complainant needs to pursue his case.

In other ways the courts over the years since 1976 have made it easier for discrimination to be proved. An early question was whether discrimination only became unlawful if it was intentional. Lord Denning in a sex discrimination case caused confusion by deciding that even deliberate discrimination could be lawful if benevolently motivated.[18] The employer who allowed female employees to leave five minutes early to avoid the rush to leave the building was held by Lord Denning to have acted lawfully because his motivation was chivalrous. The Appeals Committee of the House of Lords refused leave to challenge this decision. Viscount Dilhorne asked (and he was not joking) whether the captain of a sinking ship would break the law by shouting 'women and children first'.[19]

The courts eventually settled for a simple test which ruled out considerations of motive and intention.[20] Would the discriminatory treatment have occurred but for the race (or supposed race) of the victim? The 'but for' test is not a comprehensive solution – it does not deal with the case where a racial ground for the treatment is chosen even though there might have been a non-racial justification for it – but it is wider and simpler than any test depending on proof of motive or intention.

The courts also made it easier for complainants to prove discrimination by encouraging the drawing of inferences in suitable cases. To prove discrimination two hurdles must be surmounted. The first is to establish that the complainant has been 'less favourably' treated. The second is to prove that the ground for that treatment is race. While the courts have consistently held that the burden of proving unlawful discrimination rests with the complainant on the balance of probabilities, it is now established that once discrimination has been demonstrated, the tribunal or court should be prepared to infer that the ground of discrimination was racial if the respondent cannot demonstrate a plausible alternative explanation.[21] The CRE has argued that this is not enough: the respondent should shoulder the burden of demonstrating that the plausible alternative explanation was indeed the true one. The judges could reasonably maintain that so radical a change in the ordinary burden of proof goes beyond interpretation and requires legislative amendment. Indeed the CRE has recommended that there should be a legislative change.[22]

The courts have also gone some way to encourage more generous assessment of compensation than was practised in the early days of the Act. Some judges have made it clear that the hurt caused by discrimination must be treated as serious and that compensation for injury to feelings must be expressed in substantial awards. Since the Race Relations (Remedies) Act 1994 the employment tribunals are no longer limited in the amount of compensation they may award. A study in early 1996 showed that following abolition of the limit the average award was £4596, an increase of 63 per cent over the average for the year before abolition.[23] In 1997 the average rose by a further 62 per cent, to £7405 (excluding the two exceptional cases of Chan and D'Souza (under appeal) in which awards were made of £170,043 and £358,288.[24] The latter record was exceeded in September 1998 when Sam Yeboah settled his claim against Hackney Borough Council for £380,000. These figures combine awards for injury to feelings and for actual financial loss. Awards for injury to feelings have steadily increased but the Employment Appeal tribunal has reduced some awards recently for injury to feelings, in one case from £13,500 to £7500 and in another from £8000 to £4500.[25] While in a blatant case aggravated damages can be awarded, the courts have ruled against awards of exemplary or punitive damages.[26] Compared with awards in defamation cases, for example, average awards are still modest, and are unlikely to have a serious deterrent impact on corporate discriminators. Nor are they a powerful incentive to victims to go through the trauma of litigation, especially considering that discrimination is proved in only a small percentage of cases.[27]

The courts have been less progressive in their interpretation of indirect discrimination. The use in the statute of the phrase 'condition or requirement' has been interpreted narrowly so as to reject claims of those who were not able to demonstrate that a criterion applied by a respondent was any more than a preference.[28] Mr Perera complained that when he was rejected for a legal appointment in the Civil Service, his considerable practical experience as an advocate in Sri Lanka was not taken into account. The Civil Service Commission acknowledged that UK experience was given greater weight and there were more than enough candidates with that experience. The Court of Appeal held that UK experience was not a 'requirement or condition' but merely a preference, and therefore outside the definition. From Mr Perera's point of view the distinction was arbitrary and irrelevant. The effect on him was manifestly discriminatory and unfair. The court could have given a broader interpretation to the statutory language having regard to the purpose of the law. The CRE in 1992 and again in 1998 recommended that the statutory language be changed to remove this anomaly but nothing has been done to implement this (and virtually every other) CRE recommendation.

On the other hand, the courts made it harder to escape liability for indirect discrimination by showing it to be justifiable. Those seeking to establish indirect discrimination have always argued that the test adopted in the United States, from which the concept of indirect discrimination was borrowed, should be used in the Race Relations Act, namely, that only where the discriminatory requirement or condition was 'necessary' for the effective conduct of the respondent's business should it be allowed to outweigh its discriminatory impact. English judges preferred the weaker test of 'reasonableness', until decisions of the European Court in equal pay cases adopted a stricter approach which UK courts have now tended to follow.[29]

A Mixture of Success and Failure

What could and should have been done (and should still be done) to remedy the weaknesses of the law as they have become apparent since 1976? The response of Government to the recommendations for reform made by the CRE and by others has been lamentable.

The CRE has a statutory responsibility 'to keep under review the working of this Act and, when they are so required by the Secretary of State or otherwise think it necessary, draw up and submit to the Secretary of State proposals for amending it'. On three occasions the CRE has initiated a review, without any prompting by the Home Secretary of the day, and in 1985, 1992 and 1998, after putting out draft proposals for public consultation submitted them for Government action. Little or no action has followed.[30]

In its Second Review of the Act in 1992, the CRE was able to print a long list of recommendations made in its first review which had not been implemented. Among the weaknesses and anomalies which it had urged the Government to put right seven years before were several of those which have already been described. They included those attributable to judicial timidity or muddled drafting: the Perera and the Prestige decisions among them; and others which had more to do with the failure of the Government in 1976 to provide a proper framework of powers and remedies which would give decent redress to individuals and enforceable powers to the CRE to tackle institutional discrimination. Among the structural reforms which the CRE has fruitlessly advocated were: establishing a separate specialised discrimination division of the industrial tribunals; extending legal aid to discrimination cases in the industrial tribunals; extending the powers of the CRE to take legal proceedings; extending the remedies available to industrial tribunals.

The Second Review (1992) and the Proposals for Change published in April 1998 repeated most of these recommendations. They identified three main areas which needed attention: the coverage of the anti-discrimination provisions of the Act; the framework for achieving equality; and the hearing of racial discrimination complaints. The need to solve the problems arising from the Perera and Amin cases is reiterated.[31]

In relation to the powers of the Commission and their erosion by the Hillingdon and Prestige decisions, interpreting the grossly cumbersome and wasteful restrictions on the investigative process, the CRE's recommendations were to extend the coercive powers of the CRE by giving it power to issue directions for specific action by those whom it found to have discriminated unlawfully.

The response of the courts to the interpretation of the Race Relations Act at first sight seems inconsistent. On the one hand they have adopted a very restrictive attitude to the exercise by the CRE of its investigative powers, virtually rendering the formal investigation valueless as a means of uncovering unlawful discrimination. On the other hand they have been largely sympathetic to the difficulties of individuals seeking to prove discrimination and over the years have made their task easier.

The paradox arises from the nature of the powers given to the CRE in the 1976 Act. The courts are extremely sensitive to the exercise of coercive powers by statutory bodies. In order to make its investigations effective it was assumed that the CRE would need power to compel the disclosure of information from those who did not wish to supply it. It was therefore given power by notice to require any person to provide written information or to attend to provide it orally.[32] The power is limited to 'named person' investigations except where the Secretary of State authorises its use. If the CRE's notice is not complied with, it can apply to the county court requiring compliance. Furthermore, it is a criminal offence wilfully to alter, suppress, conceal or destroy a document of which production has been required by notice from the CRE.[33]

Secondly, the CRE was of course given the power to issue a 'non-discrimination notice'.[34] Although there are precedents for the issue of enforcement notices by statutory bodies in other contexts (for example by planning authorities) the non-discrimination notice exists only in the Sex Discrimination and Race Relations Acts. It is a very weak sanction. The preliminary hurdles before a notice can be issued have already been discussed. But suppose a notice is issued? What effect can it have? Its coercive effect is minimal. It can demand that no further acts of discrimination like those found by the CRE to have occurred shall be done and it can demand that, where changes of practice are needed in order to avoid further acts of discrimination (of which apparently the respondent himself is the judge), the respondent must tell the CRE and anyone else concerned what those changes are. It can also demand information at specified times in order to verify that the notice has been complied with. No sanction is provided by the Act against failure to make changes or to provide the required notification.

All the CRE can do is start a fresh investigation to ascertain whether there has been compliance,[35] or, if it has evidence of the likelihood of further discriminatory acts, it may apply to the court for an injunction.[36] Not surprisingly, this tortuous process has rarely been used.

The truth which needs to be faced is that the English judicial tradition makes it undesirable to vest quasi-judicial powers in a body like the CRE. The investigative strategy envisaged by those who framed the Act has failed because it has fallen between two stools. On the one hand, the quasi-judicial enforcement powers are so weak that even when fully exploited they can make little impact. On the other hand the existence of such powers prompts the judges to make it virtually impossible to use them. It is hardly surprising that in 1997 no new investigations were started.

The CRE's proposals for strengthening these enforcement powers are sadly counter-productive. If enacted they would only produce even more judicial resistance. A far better way of dealing with the matter would be to take away the CRE's subpoena powers and power to issue notices. It could investigate freely within the powers available to any individual. Rather than having the power to make enforceable orders itself, it should be required to seek them from a court or tribunal. Those investigated would then have no complaint against the CRE. They could only be made to cooperate in an investigation if ordered by a body with recognised judicial authority.

The story of the Race Relations Act is a mixture of success and failure. Its symbolic impact as a declaration of policy has had some value. Even as a vehicle for achieving compliance with the law this symbolic value is not insignificant. Many institutions and individuals are inclined to obey the law because it is there. They may be encouraged to do so because in their particular circumstances they are not faced with strong enough prejudices to persuade them to defy the law. Others will comply because it is the softer option to facing an investigation or because they fear the publicity associated with a finding of discrimination, however remote a possibility that might be and however trivial the sanctions resulting from it.

But it remains a daunting uphill struggle for any individual to pursue redress for discrimination, in spite of some judicial effort to lighten the burden of proving it. The small number of successful cases and the often pitiful awards of compensation are little to set in the balance against the massive extent of discrimination revealed in a series of surveys.[37] The weakness of the individual victim is greatly enhanced by the absence of legal aid in the industrial tribunals and by the lack of resources available to the CRE to fund individual cases. Furthermore, there is no effective machinery for enabling the CRE or anyone else to secure redress for individuals affected by institutional discrimination. The 'class action' is not properly developed in the United Kingdom and even in those few formal investigations in which unlawful discrimination has been identified it would be difficult to find a single individual for whom the CRE had secured financial redress as a result. This again is due partly to a failure in the drafting of the Act which imposes short time limits on individual claims and does not explicitly allow for delays in the investigation process, even though they could hardly be blamed on individual victims.

What is important now is to learn the lessons of the last twenty years. Discrimination remains a blot on our society and as we extend our concern beyond race and gender discrimination to disability, age, sexual orientation and other areas, it becomes increasingly important to establish an efficient and effective framework for both individual and collective enforcement of the law.

NOTES

1. Report of the Race Relations Board for 1966–77, para. 65.
2. Report of the Race Relations Board for 1967–68, pp. 7 and 35.
3. For example, see Report of the Race Relations Board for 1973, p. 42.
4. See Otto Kahn-Freund, 'On Uses and Misuses of Comparative Law', in *Selected Writings*, ed. Lord Wedderburn of Charlton (London: Stevens, 1978) pp. 294–319.
5. H. Street, G. Howe and G. Bindman, *Report on Anti-Discrimination Legislation* (London: Political and Economic Planning, 1967).
6. In June 1997 the Lord Chancellor announced that he was considering introducing a better framework for representative and class actions but no firm proposals have yet appeared.
7. RRA 1976, section 43(1).
8. Quoted in 'Racial Justice at Work' by Christopher McCoudden, David J. Smith and Colin Brown (London: Policy Studies Institute, 1991) p. 66.

9.   RRA 1976, section 49.
10. *CRE* v. *Amari Plastics* [1982] QB 1194 at p. 1203.
11. [1982] AC 779.
12. *CRE* v. *Prestige Group Plc* [1984] ICR 473 HL.
13. RRA 1976, section 59(2).
14. See note 10 above.
15. 'Racial Justice at Work', p. 77.
16. In *Science Research Council* v. *Nassé and Leyland Cars* v. *Vyas* [1979] QB 144.
17. [1980] AC 1028.
18. *Peake* v. *Automotive Products* [1978] QB 233.
19. The writer was present.
20. *James* v. *Eastleigh Borough Council* [1990]2 AC 751.
21. *King* v. *The Great Britain–China Centre* [1991] IRLR 513 CA, approved by the House of Lords in *Zafar* v. *Glasgow City Council* [1998] IRLR 36.
22. *Second Review of the Race Relations Act 1976* (London: Commission for Review Equality, 1992) p. 53. In its more recent proposals published in April 1998, however, it appears to argue only for codification of the present law.
23. *Equal Opportunities Review*, May/June 1996, p. 13.
24. *Annual Report* of the CRE for 1997, p. 6.
25. *EOR Discrimination Case Law Digest*, no. 30 (Winter 1996), p. 9.
26. *Deane* v. *London Borough of Ealing* [1993] IRLR 209 EAT.
27. In 1995, the CRE settled 113 cases; 42 were successful after a hearing, and 38 were dismissed after a hearing. In the previous year there were 1937 applications for CRE assistance to pursue claims (*Annual Report* of the CRE for 1995).
28. *Perera* v. *Civil Service Commission* [1983] IRLR 166 CA.
29. *Bilka-Kaufhaus GmbH* v. *Weber von Harz* [1986] IRLR 317 ECJ.
30. However, following the publication in February 1999 of the Macpherson Report on the Stephen Lawrence case the Government has announced that it will amend the Act. The scope of the amendments is not yet known.
31. In *R* v. *Entry Clearance Officer, Bombay ex parte Amin* [1983] 2 AC 818, the House of Lords held that the phrase 'goods, facilities, and services' in s. 20 of the Act must be interpreted narrowly so that it only covered acts similar to those that could be done by a private person. It did not cover, therefore, the services of immigration officers. An amendment (s. 19A) has extended the law to the services of planning officers but otherwise this restrictive interpretation survives.
32. RRA 1976, section 50.
33. RRA 1976, section 50(6).
34. RRA 1976, section 58.
35. RRA 1976, section 60.
36. RRA 1976, section 62.
37. The studies published by Political and Economic Planning in 1967, the Policy Studies Institute in 1973, 1985 and 1991, and a number of other studies show that only a minute fraction of cases ever result in any redress for the victims.

4 The Impact of Legislation on British Race Relations
Muhammad Anwar

INTRODUCTION

There are different ways of analysing the impact of the race relations legislation on British race relations. This chapter examines that impact by using three broad indicators, namely, the facts of racial disadvantage and discrimination; the number of racial harassment and racial attack cases; and attitudes of both whites and ethnic minorities towards race relations and their views on race relations legislation. The weaknesses of the Race Relations Act 1976 are also discussed and suggestions are made for improving it. Finally, proposals are made for what else needs to be done to improve race relations.

It is worth pointing out at the outset that as a result of race relations legislation much has been achieved in terms of equal opportunity policies and practices in employment and in services. Statutory codes of practice in employment and housing and non-statutory codes in education and health have been published by the CRE. In addition to practical guides for various purposes the CRE has recently published three racial equality standards for employers, for local government and for services working for young people. A number of individuals have been successful in industrial tribunals and county courts. However, in the last twenty-two years their number remains insignificant, that is under 2000, (on average less than 100 a year). The CRE's formal investigations and individual complaints have also helped to uncover many practices which were unlawful indirect discrimination. Examples include: the practice of recruitment by word of mouth, or through internal applications only, long residency requirements for access to public housing, and offers of insurance only to those born in the UK. Many employers and service providers have used the positive action provisions of the Act to provide equality of opportunity. Some local authorities have also made good progress following their obligations under section 71 of the Act. And we should not forget the important work of the local Racial Equality Councils in terms of community service, public education, campaigning on relevant issues, community development and policy development in the field of race relations. But I am afraid, as we will see from the research and other evidence, that despite some progress a lot more needs to be done to achieve racial equality and to provide services which meet the needs of multicultural Britain in the late 1990s.

FACTS OF RACIAL DISADVANTAGE AND DISCRIMINATION

Leon Brittan, as Home Secretary, in 1983 said 'racial discrimination and racial disadvantage are a daily reality for far too many black and brown people in this country'.[1] This is true even in 1998. A few latest research and other findings will help to gauge the extent of racial disadvantage and discrimination in Britain and show how the situation has changed in the last fourteen years, in particular.

A national survey of racial minorities published by the Policy Studies Institute (PSI) in 1984 showed that serious inequalities, to which racial discrimination contributed, persisted in employment, housing, education and other services.[2] Several other surveys, including some by the CRE along with its formal investigations have confirmed that racial disadvantage and racial discrimination are widespread. The pattern of racial and ethnic disadvantage has also been demonstrated, in a comprehensive way, by the 1991 Census, not only nationally but also for local areas. The 1991 Census was the first British census that included an ethnic question.

A survey conducted by the PSI in collaboration with the CRE, over the period of February 1984 to March 1985, revealed that over a third of employers discriminated, against ethnic minority job applicants. This survey showed the extent of direct discrimination only. In addition, there is indirect discrimination, as the CRE's several investigations and individual complaints in employment have revealed. The PSI survey put the nation-wide figure, even on a conservative estimate, at tens of thousands of acts of racial discrimination in job recruitment, every year. The results were based on the first stage of recruitment alone, and if the candidate had progressed to subsequent stages such as interview, other forms of racial discrimination could have occurred, as shown in some formal investigations conducted by the CRE. The 1994 PSI survey also discovered that over 40 per cent of ethnic minorities in the sample felt that most or about half of the employers would refuse someone a job for racial/religious reasons. Also 27 per cent of white respondents felt the same way. In fact, 19 per cent of ethnic minority respondents said that they were refused a job because of their race or religion.[3]

A CRE formal investigation into the accountancy profession discovered that the success rate of white applicants for accountancy posts was nearly three times as high as that of ethnic minority applicants. In addition, for those reaching the interview stage, the white candidates' success rate was nearly twice that of ethnic minority applicants.

A study of ethnic minority graduates in the late 1980s discovered that a greater proportion of them were unemployed, they had to make more job applications than their white peers, they received fewer interviews, job offers and early promotions.[4] This pattern is confirmed by another study of graduates published in 1996.[5] It concluded that compared with whites, graduates from ethnic minorities were unemployed more often, had to apply for a greater number of jobs initially, and took longer to get their first job, and were more likely to feel slightly underemployed. Similar trends were found in a study of overseas doctors published in 1987 and a study of ethnic minority teachers published in 1988.[6] The CRE also found through a formal investigation that St George's Medical School had racially discriminated against certain applicants who were identified as 'non-Caucasian' through the use of a computer programme which gave negative mathematical weighting to such applicants.[7] Therefore, racial discrimination does not only start when one becomes a doctor but well before one qualifies. In fact, racial or ethnic origin may prevent entrance at the gate to the medical profession. Therefore, we can conclude that tens of thousands of acts of racial discrimination in employment take place in Britain, every year and most of the victims have no way of knowing. One result of this is a very high level of unemployment among ethnic minorities, even for those with a degree who are British-born. Therefore, higher qualifications do not necessarily help to remove the racial differences. Let us now examine how the unemployment situation of ethnic minorities has changed in the last sixteen years. In 1982 a survey showed that almost 60 per cent of Afro-Caribbean young people were unemployed compared with 42 per cent of whites from the same areas. The PSI survey in 1982 also showed that unemployment was a major new factor of racial inequality for both young and old. The 1991 Census revealed that the unemployment rate for ethnic minority males (20.3 per cent) was nearly twice the rate of white males (10.7 per cent) and almost 2.5 times higher for ethnic minority females (15.5 per cent) compared with white females (6.7 per cent). However, there were significant variations between different ethnic groups. For example, Bangladeshi males (30.9 per cent) and Pakistani males (28.5 per cent) had significantly higher unemployment rates compared with Indian males (14.4 per cent). Afro-Caribbean males (25.2 per cent) also had a very much higher unemployment rate. The pattern of unemployment is almost similar for females of various ethnic groups. Ethnic minority youth unemployment is also very high and those 16–24 years old, according to the 1991 Census, had an unemployment rate of 30.9 per cent for males and 24.9 per cent for females compared with 17.4 per cent and 11.4 per cent for white males and females respectively. The 1994 PSI survey showed that unemployment rates for some ethnic groups were even worse. For example, the unemployment rate for Bangladeshi and Pakistani men was 42 and 38 per cent respectively compared with 31 per cent for Caribbean men and 19 per cent for Indian men. However, only about 15 per cent of white men were unemployed.[8]

More recent evidence from the Labour Force Surveys confirms earlier trends. For example, the unemployment rate for all ethnic minority groups was more than double in autumn 1995 compared with whites. However, for Pakistani and Bangladeshi males the unemployment rate in autumn 1995 was 28.7 per cent compared with 8 per cent for white males, more than three times higher. For Pakistani and Bangladeshi females for the same period the pattern is similar except that it is four times higher (29.2 per cent) than white females' unemployment rate (6.5 per cent).[9] Recent research shows that one of the significant contributory factors to this situation of ethnic minorities is racial discrimination. Therefore, the comparative unemployment rates of whites and ethnic minorities clearly are the most dramatic illustration of continuing inequality in Britain. It is also worth pointing out that discrimination and inequality in employment has a magnifying effect on other key areas like education, housing and health. Therefore, it would be useful to review, very briefly, inequality in other areas. The CRE's formal investigation into council housing in the London Borough of Hackney, and its research and a formal investigation into council housing allocations in Liverpool in the 1980s showed widespread discrimination against ethnic minority applicants and tenants. Another report by the CRE based on testing in 13 areas in 1990 showed that a fifth of all accommodation agencies consistently treated the ethnic minority testers less favourably than the white testers.[10]

Research and the 1991 Census have shown that ethnic minorities live in poorer quality accommodation than whites. For example, about one-third of Pakistani and almost half of Bangladeshi households are overcrowded compared with under 2 per cent white households in this situation. A similar pattern of overcrowding was discovered by the PSI survey in 1994. It showed that 43 per cent of Bangladeshi and 33 per cent of Pakistani households were overcrowded compared with 2 per cent whites. Like the 1991 Census this survey also showed that 13 per cent of Indian households were also overcrowded.[11] Also ethnic minorities are more likely to be homeless, particularly in London, where ethnic minority families were four times as likely as white families to be homeless. It is estimated that over 30 per cent of people living in temporary accommodation are from ethnic minorities.[12] Tower Hamlets was also investigated by the CRE on its homeless policies regarding ethnic minorities and was found guilty of racial discrimination.[13] Oldham Council was also found to be contravening the Race Relations Act 1976 by its discriminatory housing allocation policies which affected the Bangladeshi community disproportionately. It is worth pointing out that the Government's new policy of investigating a homeless person's immigration status by the housing officials could also affect race relations.

In education, it has been accepted that racial inequality exists,[14] particularly institutional racism contributes to discriminating practices in educational institutions. The CRE found that in Birmingham black pupils were four times more likely to be suspended than white pupils.[15] The Swann Committee in 1985 had revealed that there was discriminatory behaviour in the class room. A recent formal investigation by the CRE into English as a Second Language Units in Calderdale found that the arrangements were indirectly discriminatory and contrary to the Race Relations Act, and as a result the Language Centres were replaced by a Language Support Service, a programme which was incorporated into mainstream schools. It is worth mentioning that analysis of the University admission data has shown that some ethnic minority students face disadvantage in terms of getting admission to universities compared with white applicants of similar qualifications.[16] Also over one-third of young Asians in a survey by the author felt that there was evidence of racial discrimination in schools they had attended. This was also confirmed by 27 per cent white young people in the same survey.[17]

It has been shown by research and the CRE's formal investigations that racial discrimination in the provision of public and private services is still widespread, although this happens discreetly and often the victim is not aware of it. In immigration, for example, the CRE found that the procedures operated by the Immigration Service were to the disadvantage of people from the New Commonwealth countries who were entering the UK and it made several recommendations to improve them. Discrimination in health and the caring services is usually indirect or sometimes unintended. For example, recent research has suggested that despite the greater use of primary health care made by most ethnic minorities compared with whites, the quality of the care offered to ethnic minorities was poorer, in particular, in terms of meeting language needs and preference for the gender and ethnicity of doctors consulted.[18]

If we look at the number of complaints relating to racial discrimination which reach industrial tribunals or county courts, it is not very significant. However, it is well known that this number is, no doubt, the tip of the iceberg, because an overwhelming majority of the victims either never come to know that they have been discriminated against or do not have the courage or motivation to complain.

However, I must point out that despite the widespread racial discrimination, there are many individuals from ethnic minority communities who have been successful in various professions – businesses, sports, in the media, music and public life – and are making important contributions in this country. However, my analysis has looked at patterns of racial disadvantage and discrimination for groups and not individuals, although individuals act as role models. Generally, ethnic minorities are under-represented in public appointments, such as membership of health authorities and trusts, in the judiciary, at senior levels in the civil service, the armed forces and the police. They are also seriously under-represented in the House of Commons, with only nine MPs out of 651. To reflect the multiracial nature of our society there need to be 40. There is a slow progress at local government level and now more than 400 out of 23,000 councillors in England and Wales have ethnic minority backgrounds.

RACIAL HARASSMENT AND RACIAL ATTACKS

I believe strongly that the incidence of an increasing number of racial harassment and racial attacks cases is having an adverse effect on race relations. One Home Office study in 1981 showed that the rate of racial attacks against Asians was 50 times that for white people and the rate for Afro-Caribbeans was 36 times that for white people.[19] The Home Affairs Committee in its report in the mid-1980s on Racial Attacks and Racial Harassment said the most shameful and dispiriting aspect of race relations in Britain is the incidence of racial attacks and harassment.[20] In 1989 the Home Affairs Committee looked at these issues again and concluded that there was a significant level of under-reporting of racial incidents.[21] In 1994 it was reported that there were about 130,000 incidents of crime and threats against Asian and Afro-Caribbean people.[22] Therefore, the police figures of only a few thousand racially motivated crimes per year nationally are nowhere close to the reality, because many people do not report such incidents and because they know that the police have a very poor detection rate for such incidents. For example, in London in 1989 the clear-up rate for racial incidents was just over 30 per cent. However, as a result of more publicity of such incidents, more ethnic minority people are coming forward to report racial incidents. Two further points are worth making: (1) that racial attacks on individuals affect not just one person but their families and friends as well and (2) that it is estimated that between 1970 and 1989, 74 people died as a result of racially motivated attacks.[23]

In 1990 the then Metropolitan Police Commissioner, Sir Peter Imbert, wrote 'racial attacks are not only against the law, they are also socially divisive and morally repugnant'. The Home Affairs Committee added to this

> we would go further. We believe that if racism is allowed to grow unchecked it will begin to corrode the fabric of our open and tolerant society. For this reason crimes and anti-social behaviour become more serious when they are racially motivated than when they are not. This belief lies at the core of our review of this subject and our recommendations.[24]

The fact that the Home Affairs Committee published three reports within eight years on racial attacks and harassment (1986, 1989, 1994) shows the serious nature of the subject and its likely impact on race relations.

The British Crime Survey in 1991 showed that 56 per cent of racially motivated incidents involving Asians were assaults and 66 per cent were seen as threats.[25] However, racial violence in any form creates a climate of fear, intimidation and insecurity. One recent development is that there is now a greater recognition of this problem at government levels. For example, the Home Secretary, speaking at the Conservative Party Conference in October 1993 said, 'racial attacks will not be tolerated, and those who perpetuate them must be caught, convicted and punished.' It is clear, however, from officially recorded figures that the number of reported racial incidents is increasing every year. For example, in 1989, the cases reported to the police in Britain were 5420 and this number increased to over ten thousand in 1994. This means that the reported racial incidents almost doubled within the five-year period. However, we know that this number only represents the tip of the iceberg.[26] Also 'low level' racially motivated incidents are neither recorded by the police nor by the British Crime Survey, which estimated racially motivated crimes to be 130,000 every year. Recently a Minister at the Home Office estimated them to be 140,000 a year. However, the Labour Party estimated such incidents to be between 175,000 and 200,000 a year.[27] The results from the PSI Survey in 1994 suggested that in a 12-month period there were about 20,000 people who were racially attacked, 40,000 who were subjected to racially motivated damage to property and 230,000 people who were racially abused or insulted. These estimates are higher than other recent estimates. In the sample survey 26 per cent of whites said that they were prejudiced against Asians as well as 20 per cent of whites who were prejudiced against Caribbeans.[28]

Several studies have shown that racial attacks affect Asians more than some other ethnic groups.[29] The CRE revealed in 1993 that 49 per cent of victims of racial attacks were Asian, 23 per cent Afro-Caribbean, 22 per cent white and 7 per cent Jewish.[30] Asian shopkeepers and Asian women seem to be special targets of racial attacks. For example, one study in London in 1993 showed that 32 per cent of Asian shopkeepers were racially abused within one twelve-month period and this figure rose to 37 per cent in the Midlands.[31] This seems to be the pattern in other areas of Asian settlement. Asian women have recently become targets where their jewellery and purses are snatched. It appears that such incidents are likely to rise in the future and the police and other authorities, such as housing and education authorities, need to take appropriate action to reduce the level of intimidation and the feelings of insecurity as they exist currently throughout Britain. On the whole, a significant proportion of ethnic minorities worry about being racially harassed. A lot of them avoid certain situations which affect the quality of their life. This brings me to move on to my third indicator, that is attitudes towards race relations.

ATTITUDES TOWARDS RACE RELATIONS

In the light of the above evidence of racial disadvantage, racial discrimination and racial harassment and attacks, how far have attitudes of ordinary people towards race relations – both whites and ethnic minorities – changed in the last twenty years? Lord Scarman stressed in 1981, when he was carrying out his inquiry into the Brixton disorders, that 'The point has often been put to this Inquiry, and I think everybody accepts it, that we are as much concerned with attitudes and beliefs as we are with facts.[32] Many surveys during the twenty-two year period have used questions on 'race relations' but I have selected only a few to show the trends over time.

In 1975 a survey commissioned by the Community Relations Commission (CRC), in which respondents were asked whether race relations in the country as a whole were getting better, remaining the same, or getting worse, found that 44 per cent of ethnic minority respondents felt race relations were getting better, as did 32 per cent of whites. On the other hand, only 13 per cent of ethnic minority and 20 per cent of white respondents thought that race relations were getting worse in the country as a whole.[33] However, in a similar survey in 1981 commissioned by the CRE, the situation was dramatically different from that revealed in the 1975 survey. In the 1981 survey nearly half of the ethnic minority respondents and one-third of the whites thought race relations were getting worse and only 18 per cent of ethnic minorities and 25 per cent of whites thought they were getting better.[34] Most noticeable was the change in the opinion of ethnic minority people in those six years: fewer ethnic minorities than whites thought race relations had improved. It was interesting to note from the 1981 survey that among the ethnic minorities, those born in Britain and those more fluent in English were more likely to think race relations had deteriorated.

In the 1981 survey respondents were also asked 'whether they thought the feelings between whites and ethnic minorities would get better, worse, or stay the same over the next five years.' Respondents generally did not show much optimism. Over half (53 per cent) of the ethnic minorities thought race relations would get worse, as did 43 per cent of the whites. Again, among the ethnic minority respondents, it was the young people, those born in Britain, educated, fluent in English, who were more pessimistic about race relations in the future.

Two other findings from the 1981 survey are relevant to the topic under discussion: white people's views of ethnic minorities and the overall status of ethnic minorities in British society compared with whites. As far as the views of white respondents were concerned, over three-quarters said that they did not mind them being in this country. The younger the person, the more likely they were to say 'I have never minded them being here.'

As far as the overall status of ethnic minorities in British society was concerned, almost 70 per cent of ethnic minorities felt that their status was worse. However, it is significant that 58 per cent of white respondents also agreed that the position of ethnic minorities was worse. It is clear that the ethnic minorities felt they were disadvantaged in comparison with the white population and this has clear implications for race relations. The third PSI survey in 1982 also included a few questions on views on race relations.[35] When asked whether life in Britain for people of Asian and West Indian origin has improved over the last five years, half of Asian and West Indian informants said that life had become worse for their ethnic group and only 15 per cent of Asians and 20 per cent of West Indians said that it had become better. The same question was asked in the 1974 PEP survey and the responses were totally different. At that time over half (54 per cent) of West Indians and over a third of the Asians (35 per cent) said that things had got better and fewer than 20 per cent of informants said things were worse.

When asked about the trend in racial discrimination, over 40 per cent of Asians and West Indians said that this was worse compared with five years earlier. Also a quarter of Asians and West Indian respondents said that the level of discrimination had remained the same. It would be useful to mention the views of white respondents on discrimination, from this survey. Almost 40 per cent of whites said that there was more discrimination now than there was five years ago but a third (33 per cent) said that there was less discrimination. What was more interesting was that 73 per cent of white respondents acknowledged that there were employers in Britain who would refuse a job to a person because of their race or colour. One other finding from the PSI survey is directly relevant and that is that 50 per cent of white respondents agreed that the present laws against racial discrimination should be enforced more effectively. The comparative figures for West Indian and Asians were 80 per cent and 86 per cent respectively. However, when asked whether there should be new and stricter laws against racial discrimination, 75 per cent of West Indians and Asians but also 43 per cent of white respondents agreed with the statement. Therefore, it appears that even in 1982 when the 1976 Act was only six years old, there was enough feeling about its ineffectiveness for a higher proportion of ethnic minorities – but also a significant number of white people – to want stricter laws to deal with racial discrimination.

The British Social Attitudes Survey in 1984 showed that 90 per cent of the respondents felt that British society was racially prejudiced against its black and Asian members.[36] Forty-two per cent of the respondents thought racial prejudice would be worse in five years' time and in fact one-third of them classified themselves as racially prejudiced.

Similar trends were found in 1991 in another survey of attitudes commissioned by the Runnymede Trust.[37] It showed that 67 per cent of white people thought Britain a very or fairly racist society compared with 79 per cent of Afro-Caribbeans and 56 per cent of Asians. Almost 40 per cent (39 per cent) of whites, 42 per cent of Asians but a high 67 per cent of Afro-Caribbeans believed that employers discriminated against non-white workers. A similar pattern of attitudes emerged regarding the police (worse: 48 per cent white; 75 per cent Afro-Caribbean; and 45 per cent Asian). This survey also showed that over 60 per cent of Afro-Caribbeans, 45 per cent of Asians and 31 per cent of whites thought that British laws against racial discrimination were not tough enough, with the implication that some action is needed in this context.

The 1992 British Social Attitudes (BSA) survey also confirmed that the public still perceived Britain as a racially prejudiced society.[38] In 1993 a Gallup survey for the American Jewish Committee revealed that 25 per cent of white British would object to living next to non-white people, 10 per cent wanted anti-discrimination laws to be abolished and 45 per cent of the total sample thought that anti-Semitism was not a problem. The survey also showed that the 'most racist respondents' tended to be working class, elderly and those least educated. It is also interesting to point out that over three-quarters of respondents felt that race relations in Britain were 'only fair' or 'poor', and over 40 per cent thought that anti-racist laws should be strengthened. Once again there is support for more action. The more recent evidence is worrying. An ICM survey in July 1995 in 52 randomly-selected constituencies revealed that two-thirds of the respondents admitted to being racist, and only one in ten said that people they knew were not racist. Also over

half of the respondents believed that there was racial discrimination in the labour market.[39]

It is worth pointing out that racial disadvantage and discrimination is also being transmitted to the British-born and
second- and third-generation ethnic minorities. As a consequence the gap between ethnic minority and white young
people is widening. Furthermore, there is now enough research
evidence which shows that ethnic minority young people are not
prepared to tolerate any longer their disadvantaged position in
society. Their immigrant parents might have accepted racial
discrimination as the price to pay for economic opportunities in
Britain but they will not.

CONCLUSIONS AND THE WAY FORWARD

There is no doubt that due to the Race Relations Act some
progress has been made in terms of discovering patterns of discrimination and in promoting racial equality. However, the evidence in this chapter shows that racial inequality persists in
Britain in the 1990s, that racial harassment is seen as a serious
problem and that white peoples' attitudes towards ethnic
minorities are still a cause for concern, bearing in mind that
more than half of the ethnic minority population is now British
born and most of the others have British citizenship.

It appears clearly from the evidence that the prevalence of
racial prejudice and discrimination is acknowledged, by both
white and ethnic minority people, and that there is enough
support for anti-discrimination legislation; and also that
the majority would like to see the race relations legislation
strengthened. Therefore, let us examine some of the weaknesses of the Race Relations Act 1976 which are making it
ineffective and assess how it should be strengthened.

A new definition of indirect discrimination is needed which
should cover any policy, practice and situation which is introduced, allowed or continued and which has a significant adverse
impact on a particular ethnic or racial group and which cannot
be demonstrated to be necessary. It is still difficult to prove
cases of discrimination and the remedies are so feeble.
Therefore, many people do not feel that it is worth while to go
through all the publicity, stress, time and costs. The number of

individual complainants remains low although, as pointed out above, research shows that tens of thousands of acts of discrimination take place every year. To use the law as a deterrent, effective sanctions are needed as now exist in Northern Ireland under the Fair Employment (Northern Ireland) Act 1989.[40] Furthermore, it is important that in addition to employers and service providers, individuals who discriminate against ethnic minorities should also be punished. Racial discrimination is always difficult to prove by the individual complainant. Most cases are of direct discrimination, and very few cases of indirect discrimination or alleged victimisation come forward. The formal investigation was seen as the main tool for the CRE's strategic role in tackling discrimination, as it can look into the policies and practices of employers and other organisations to find out whether they have discriminated on racial grounds. These formal investigations, sometimes supported by research, give the CRE powers to look into what the individual complainant and victims cannot see. The CRE's formal investigations can be divided into three categories: general investigations into a particular activity; investigations into a named person where an unlawful act was suspected; and investigations into a named person where no unlawful act was suspected. In the first ten years of the Act's operation the CRE had started 52 investigations. These included: 28 in employment, 12 in housing, eight in the provision of goods, facilities and services, three in education and one into the immigration service. It is worth pointing out that the majority of the early completed investigations (42) did not involve large organisations. Therefore, their deterrent effect is difficult to judge. However, the effect of subsequent large investigations, such as housing in Hackney, has been considerable. In most of the early investigations, however, the CRE found discrimination. In the last ten years the CRE has not been able to start and complete many investigations.

In fact in 1995 it started only one investigation and proposals were prepared for another two. However, out of nine investigations, at different stages during the year, five were completed and only one non-discrimination notice was issued. This means that the CRE is not using its powers to investigate sufficiently, in a strategic way, as was intended by Parliament.

One reason for this trend is, however, that the CRE is having difficulties in mounting investigations into named persons because of the House of Lords interpretation of s. 49(4) in an appeal by the CRE in a case against the Prestige Group Plc.[41] This judgment, in 1984, restricted the CRE's investigation powers and as a result seven other investigations of similar type became invalid. I believe that due to the Prestige decision the CRE's effectiveness as a law enforcement body has significantly diminished. To restore its power, the CRE has recommended that subsection 49(4) of the Act should be repealed. This would mean that the effect of the Prestige decision would be reversed and the CRE's powers to conduct a formal investigation for any purpose connected with the carrying out of its duties (s. 48) would thereby be clearly established. The strategic powers and role of the CRE was highlighted in the Government's White Paper, *Racial Discrimination* (1975) and the discussions which followed in the Committee stages of the Race Relations Bill. The Sub-Committee on Race Relations and Immigration of the Home Affairs Committee in its 1981–2 report on the CRE confirmed the importance of the CRE's strategic powers. It said, 'The persuasive power of promotional work is increased hundred-fold where it is supported by experience gained from thorough and detailed examination.'[42] However, I feel that in the meantime, and also to some extent to neutralise the effect of the Prestige decision, the CRE could follow up some of the decisions of industrial tribunals and county courts as evidence of discrimination, start formal investigations in those organisations and issue non-discrimination notices, and, therefore, ask for further corrective action which should be binding.

One area of legislation which has not been tested sufficiently is what happens to those employers or providers of services who are persistently discriminating even after being found guilty. We know that some small and medium-size employers take out insurance cover against legal costs on racial discrimination. In this way, except for the awards which are generally so low, there would not be any additional costs for the guilty employer or provider of a service and, therefore, no deterrent effect. Furthermore, unlike large employers and service providers who may be concerned about 'bad publicity' the small- and medium-sized employers and organisations do not worry too much about a finding of racial discrimination. Moreover, an individual complainant finds it difficult to give evidence or proof of racial discrimination as he or she has not direct access to the employer's or service provider's records, especially if they do not keep ethnic records. Also the resources of individual complainants are always limited compared with respondents. Therefore, the burden of proof should be shifted from individual complainants to respondents.

It is worth pointing out that the CRE's remedial powers are limited. They do not compensate for past discrimination but are more directed to attempting to change future behaviour. Where a respondent decides not to comply with the requirement in a non-discrimination notice, the CRE may apply to a County Court for an order requiring him to comply with it. This is not an injunction and non-compliance with it carries a small fine as the only sanction. Therefore, it appears from the CRE's experience in dealing with investigations that there are considerable limitations in using the law and that the Act needs to be amended to include affirmative action programmes binding all respondents found guilty of racial discrimination, and monetary and non-monetary compensation for individuals who are victims of racial discrimination.

It has been acknowledged widely that without ethnic record-keeping and regular monitoring it would be difficult to eliminate discrimination and to operate effective equal opportunity policies. The usefulness of ethnic record-keeping and monitoring has been mentioned in the CRE's statutory codes of practice in employment and housing and in its non-statutory codes in education and health. For example, for any redressive action one needs to find out first the statistics to establish whether discrimination is occurring and if so at what levels of the system. There is no substitute for finding out what is actually happening. Although many organisations now keep ethnic records, this is only voluntary. In my view ethnic record-keeping and monitoring need to be mandatory, as in Northern Ireland under the Fair Employment Act, where all public and private sector employers with more than 25 employees are required to monitor their work force. This is similar to the United States, with one exception – that the Presidential Executive Orders cover only Federal Contractors. The Office of Federal Contract Compliance Programmes monitors this and American contractors who do not comply are penalised. In Northern Ireland the sanctions for non-compliance include straightforward financial penalties for both government contractors and other employers as well as non-renewal of the contracts. It appears that there is 100 per cent registration of companies with the Fair Employment Commission and almost 100 per cent response to an employers' monitoring exercise, which clearly shows that sanctions do work. Such sanctions do not exist under the Race Relations Act.

It is also important that both the central government and local authorities implement 'contract compliance' and the CRE should be given responsibility of monitoring this. Central government, local authorities and other public authorities should also monitor their contracts in order to establish how many of these go to ethnic minority contractors and suppliers, because it is equally important to provide equal opportunity for ethnic minority businesses.

In fact, a close examination of the Fair Employment (NI) Act shows that there is nothing in that legislation which could not be implemented for racial minorities if the Race Relations Act is strengthened accordingly. It appears quite clearly that the Government is following double standards within the same country. In one part, that is, Northern Ireland, religious groups are covered exclusively by the Fair Employment Act and racial minorities are excluded, while in the rest of the UK racial groups are covered by the RRA but religious groups are excluded. It is now well known that the legislation in Northern Ireland was passed by pressures from the Irish lobby in the US.[43] Ethnic minorities in Britain do not have similar political support. But as citizens of this country they are entitled to equal treatment.

In this context religious groups in Britain are not covered by the RRA. However, there is increasing evidence that discrimination is taking place against members of some religious groups. For example, as a result of the Rushdie affair, the Gulf War and some other recent events, hostility and sometimes discrimination against Muslims has increased and in some situations Muslims feel that they have no protection under the law against discrimination on religious grounds. This feeling is certainly not helping race relations. The race relations legislation has been extended to Northern Ireland to cover racial minorities (The Race Relations (NI) Order 1996). Therefore, it is crucial that religious groups in Britain also have protection regarding discrimination under the law. In 21 international human rights treaties, religious and racial discrimination are treated equally. What else needs to be done to improve race relations? A strong Race Relations Act and the CRE with adequate financial resources are necessary but not sufficient. They need to be accompanied by central government to set a good example, by local government to fulfil their obligations, by employers, trades unions and others including the mass media, to help achieve racial equality and thus good race relations in Britain. There needs to be 'political will' to place racial and religious equality of opportunity at the centre of governmental policy-making, supported by all political parties.

Finally, ethnic minorities need to participate in the structures of society to bring about change. They must become members of advisory committees, industrial tribunals, judges, members of school governing bodies, hospital trusts, members of local councils and Parliament, officers of trades unions and political parties to influence the decision making progress. No doubt some progress has been made in this context but a lot more needs to be done in the future to increase the participation of ethnic minorities in all aspects of British public life, so that they play their full part as equal citizens in its economic, social and political institutions and developments, as we enter the twenty-first century. But I am afraid that as a country we have a long way to go to achieve this goal.

NOTES

1. Speech made in Bradford on 22 July 1983.
2. Colin Brown, *Black and White Britain* (London: Policy Studies Institute, 1984); and Colin Brown and Pat Gay, *Racial Dissemination: 17 Years After the Act* (London: Policy Studies Institute, 1985).
3. T. Modood and R. Berthoud et al., *Ethnic Minorities in Britain: Diversity and Disadvantage* (London: Policy Studies Institute, 1997).
4. John Brennan and Phillip McGeevor, *Employment of Graduates from Ethnic Minorities* (London: Commission for Racial Equality, 1987); and *Ethnic Minorities and the Graduate Labour Market* (London: Commission for Racial Equality, 1990).

5. H. Connor, I. L. A. Valle, N. Tackey and S. Perryman, *Ethnic Minority Graduates: Differences by Degrees* (Brighton: Institute for Employment Studies, Report 309, 1996).
6. M. Anwar and A. Ali, *Overseas Doctors: Experience and Expectations* (London: Commission for Racial Equality, 1987); C. Ranger, *Survey of Teachers* (London: Commission for Racial Equality, 1988)
7. Commission for Racial Equality, *St George's Hospital Medical School* (London: CRE, 1988).
8. Modood and Berthoud *et al.*, *Ethnic Minorities in Britain: Diversity and Disadvantage*.
9. David Owen, *Trends in Unemployment Rates by Ethnic Group from 1992 to 1995* (Coventry: National Ethnic Minority Data Archive (NEMDA) Information Paper 96/1, 1996).
10. Commission for Racial Equality, *Race and Council Housing in Hackney* (London: CRE, 1984); *Race and Housing in Liverpool* (London: CRE, 1989); *Racial Discrimination in Liverpool City Council* (London: CRE, 1989); and *Sorry, Its Gone* (London: CRE, 1990).
11. Modood and Berthoud *et al.*, *Ethnic Minorities in Britain: Diversity and Disadvantage*
12. R. Skellington, 'Homelessness', in R. Dallos and E. McLaughlin (eds), *Social Problems and the Family* (London: Sage, 1993).
13. Commission for Racial Equality, *Homelessness and Discrimination* (London: CRE, 1988).
14. Bhikhu Parekh, 'Educational Opportunity in Multi-Ethnic Britain', in Nathan Glazer and Ken Young (eds), *Ethnic Pluralism and Public Policy* (London: Heinemann, 1983); and Swann Committee, *Education for All* (London: HMSO, 1985).
15. Commission for Racial Equality, *Birmingham Local Education Authority Referral and Suspensions of Pupils* (London: CRE, 1985).
16. Tariq Modood and M. Shiner, *Ethnic Minorities and Higher Education: Why are there Differential Rates of Entry?* (London: Policy Studies Institute, 1994).
17. M. Anwar, *Between Cultures* (London: Routledge, 1998).
18. K. Rudat, *Health and Lifestyles: Black and Ethnic Minority Groups in England* (London: Health Education Authority, 1994); and J. Nazroo, *The Health of Britain's Ethnic Minorities: Findings from a National Survey* (London: Policy Studies Institute, 1997).
19. Home Office, *Racial Attacks: Report of a Home Office Study* (London: HMSO, 1981).
20. Home Affairs Committee, *Racial Attacks and Harassment* (London: HMSO, 1986).
21. Home Affairs Committee, *Racial Attacks and Harassment* (London: HMSO, 1989).
22. *Guardian*, 11 February 1994, based on the British Crime Survey.
23. Paul Gordon, *Racial Violence and Harassment* (London: Runnymede Trust, 1990).
24. Home Affairs Committee, *Racial Attacks and Harassment* (London: HMSO, 1994).
25. Home Office, *British Crime Survey* (London: HMSO, 1992).

26. S. Virdee, *Racial Violence and Harassment* (London: Policy Studies Institute, 1995).
27. J. Ruddock, *Racial Attacks: The Rising Tide* (London: Labour Party, 1994).
28. Modood and Berthoud *et al.*, *Ethnic Minorities in Britain: Diversity and Disadvantage*.
29. P. Mayhew, D. Elliot and L. Dowds, *The British Crime Survey* (London: Home Office/HMSO, 1989).
30. CRE's Evidence to the Select Committee Enquiry into Racial Attacks and Harassment (1993).
31. M. Hibberd and J. Shapland, *Violent Crime in Small Shops* (London: The Police Foundation, 1993).
32. Quoted in M. Anwar, *Race and Politics* (London: Tavistock, 1986).
33. Community Relations Commission, *Some of My Best Friends* (London: CRC, 1976).
34. M. Anwar, *Race Relations in 1981* (London: Commission for Racial Equality, 1981).
35. Brown, *Black and White Britain*.
36. R. Jowell, S. Witherspoon and L. Brook, *British Social Attitudes* (Aldershot: Gower/SCPR, 1984).
37. K. Amin and R. Richardson, *Politics for All* (London: Runnymede Trust, 1992).
38. R. Jowell, S. Witherspoon and L. Brook, *British Social Attitudes* (Dartmouth Publishing, 1992).
39. American Jewish Committee, *British Survey* (London: AJC, 1993), and *Daily Express*, 8 August 1995.
40. Her Majesty's Stationery Office, *The Fair Employment (Northern Ireland) Act 1989* (Belfast: HMSO, 1989).
41. *The Prestige Group Plc* (1984) IRLR335 – the House of Lords decision.
42. Home Affairs Committee (1981–2) H C 46 1 Para 14.
43. R. Osborne and R. Cormack, 'Fair Employment Towards Reforms in Northern Ireland', *Policy and Politics*, 17 (1989) (4).

5 Reflections from the Chair
Michael Day

'Only a failed politician or a desperate seeker after a knighthood would take the job.' I seem to remember it was Bill Morris, himself a former Commissioner, who cheered me with this dismissive comment just as the invitation came my way to chair the CRE. 'Bed of nails' was the usual cliché.

It seemed an unappealing assignment – what authority could I, a middle class, conventional white male, twenty years a Chief Probation Officer, bring to the position? Surely it now needed the experience of someone who had been at the receiving end of racism or a political heavyweight who would have influence over the not obviously sympathetic administration of the time. Yet it is not easy to turn down such a flattering invitation and mighty challenge – though there was enough evidence of the post's likely demands and personal inconvenience to balance the account. I sensed that a third successive chairman from an Oxbridge 'government service' background would be a mistake, it conveyed a lingering colonialism. There must be better-equipped candidates amongst current commissioners, several of them from minority ethnic communities; and how did this 'tap on the shoulder' approach square with equal opportunities? In the end I said yes, though according to *The Times* Douglas Hurd, then Home Secretary, lost house points for standing by his choice. Margaret Thatcher – 'Is he one of us'? – was said to favour Sir Alfred Sherman but he caused timely embarrassment by inviting Fascist Le Pen to address a fringe meeting at the Conservative Party Conference. I suppose the persuasive point was made by a black colleague who argued that as racism was essentially a problem of the white population it was up to someone like me, who had stumbled a few steps down the road of comprehending the injustice of discrimination, to draw others along. If that argument still had force in 1987, it turned more on the Establishment's disinclination to share its power

78

with a black person than on any lack of suitable candidates. Thankfully, the climate had changed enough by the time my period of office was completed to ensure a black successor.

There is no doubt that some of the internal stresses of the Commission arose from a justifiable reservation about white leadership, though it would be naïve to disregard the likely rivalries caused by a perceived favouring of any one minority constituency. The cynical reaction of one black friend – 'Smart move appointing a white Probation Officer to keep us blacks in order' – touched a nerve. This was just two years after terrifying race riots in some inner cities and there was widespread fear of recurring violence. The threat lay in the alienation of young blacks and it was presented as a law and order issue. If that generation were to achieve independence it had to assert itself apart from its parents and separate from the white man's world. It proclaimed itself through Rastafarianism, reggae and ganja. It posed a threat to a system which had no idea how to respond to the kind of defiance never hinted at by their parents' generation. The police and the criminal justice system were expected to deal with this challenge to the wider community and they floundered. The saturation policing and anti-drugs drive which preceded the 1981 and 1985 disturbances simply served to provoke the violent response of the black community.

I had headed a probation service covering an extensive ethnically diverse area, part of which, Handsworth, had witnessed some of the worst 1985 conflict, so I was aware of how disconnected systems were becoming from the community they claimed to serve, and had some notion of the ways in which agencies had to be reframed if they were to remain relevant in a changing environment. The gulf was exposed most sharply in the discrepancy of composition between staff and clientele. The Probation Service drew under 2 per cent, the police 1 per cent, from minority ethnic communities, the judiciary much less. The West Midlands population overall contained about 14 per cent ethnic minorities and comprised 20 per cent of those passing through the Courts. At that time there was no systematic recording of ethnic origin so these are approximate percentages, but it needed only a glance at the inmate population of Brockhill Remand Centre or Winson Green Prison to confirm what was happening. The education, social work and employment services, as well as the rehabilitative parts of the penal

system, had largely given up on young blacks. Many programmes were little more than token gestures and we failed
woefully to address the ingrained racism which made them
victims.

The Probation Service could claim to have made a modest
start in relating to the needs of ethnic minority communities,
though the gulf between the alienated and the Establishment
was then so wide that I suspect we were viewed as just a rather
more devious arm of the system. Attempts by the service to
explain alienation as a cause of antisocial behaviour were
treated with scepticism, and the magistracy in particular found
it hard to acknowledge the injustice of its own stereotyping.
Young Rastas in the dock at Birmingham Court remains a vivid
image of that mutual incomprehension – dreadlocked, defiant,
relating only to their friends in the public gallery.

So I came to the Commission with a rather apocalyptic view
of race relations. I had seen the worst scenario played out here,
and in visiting North American inner cities learned something
of the interplay between discrimination and disadvantage. The
flashpoint came between Afro-Caribbean youth and the white
system over against them. The challenge was to bridge that
widening divide and alert people to the urgent action required
to tackle the root causes of that mistrust. It felt as if all the
effort was being wasted on small-change racism. We were dis-
tracted by the vocabulary and theory of anti-discrimination and
made little investment in ambitious programmes which might
channel the energies of a forceful, talented community. The
troubles of 1981 and 1985 served notice that radical change was
called for if black people were to feel they had a real stake in
the future of this country. They were demanding more than a
liberal tolerance. Britain had no claim to be an equal, inclusive
society while it continued to protect the interests of the 95 per
cent white population, and made no adequate and relevant
provision for the rest.

I held to a rather romantic faith in the integrity of that anti-
discrimination movement so was not totally prepared for the
factionalism, intrigue and range of personal agendas played out
within the body of the Commission and associated organisations. A predecessor, Sir David Lane, wrote feelingly of 'a noble
cause not always matched by magnanimity in personal relationships'. He delicately understated the case. I soon learned to

accept that a body charged with the responsibility of tackling profound prejudices and antagonisms would inevitably draw much of that anger and frustration into itself. As a white chairman and, as it happened, with a white chief executive of similar background, challenges to organisational failure were tediously countered by allegations of racism and there was inter-ethnic rivalry over representation at all levels of the organisation. But it was entirely right that we should have to struggle internally with the same charged issues that we were asking others to confront. We were not preaching harmony but urging individuals and organisations to face some disagreeable features of their behaviour. We were not to be spared some painful learning. We should never delude ourselves that a just, multiracial society is achievable without considerable sacrifice and pain, and perhaps the most difficult part is to accept our own responsibility for colluding with racism. As a body comprising members from different ethnic communities, the Commission had the opportunity to provide a pattern for purposeful collaboration. There were times when we seemed to be setting a pretty poor example but the final story is a good one.

At that time, staff influential within the Commission, and many of those active in Community Relations Councils, were veterans of the early stages in anti-racism campaigning. There were some passionate and volatile activists around who had injected energy into the movement and carried the hurt of victims. They sensed their hour was passing as a more professionally rigorous approach was adopted. There developed something of a power struggle between these old-style campaigners drawing inspiration from civil rights and anti-apartheid movements and carrying through the role of the earlier Community Relations Commission; and those in line from the Race Relations Board putting emphasis on effective law enforcement. Some commentators, most influentially Anthony (now Lord) Lester and a main architect of the 1976 Act, expressed serious misgivings about combining in one body the functions of the predecessor organisations and believed there was an inherent incompatibility which weakened the influence of the Commission on either score.

However, it was not possible without amending legislation to shed any part of the responsibilities enshrined in the 1976 Act 'to work towards the elimination of discrimination and promote equal opportunity and good relations between people of different racial groups.' So the Commission had to ensure that they complemented each other and were not seen as discrete activities. That resolution was not helped by the Labour Government's original agreement to a single body on the understanding that the two functions would be kept well apart. The Commission was required to allocate some part of its resources to education and support of organisations which helped the victims of discrimination but it was vital to direct its specific powers to eradicating discrimination. Promotion would have most influence when built on the authority of successful legal action or compelling evidence of discriminatory practice exposed by well managed investigations. A wearisome sneer was that the Commission lacked teeth. But there was no point in talking tough unless it could deliver. Critics of the Commission failed to appreciate the painstaking effort involved in gathering evidence that would make the case. No person or organisation was eager to concede that they were acting unfairly; quite often they were unaware of the effect of their policies.

An early issue was the future of the Community Relations Councils. A PSI Report was published in 1988 following an examination of their role and functions. They formed a network of race relations activity covering most of the country. Long established and strong in areas with a substantial minority ethnic community, they were notably absent in sparsely populated rural areas – particularly Scotland and the West Country. Partly funded by the Home Office through the CRE budget, they were loosely coordinated by the National Association of Community Relations Councils with its own secretariat and executive but subject to little effective control by the CRE. Some did impressive work in the form of constructive partnerships with local authorities and major agencies; others had become self-indulgent parliaments of local race politics and in their preoccupation with peripheral, trivial examples of petty racism were deflected from the main targets, and brought what was contemptuously referred to as the 'Race Relations Industry' into disrepute.

There was a case for closing that chapter and centralising work in the CRE but that held no guarantee that the Home Office would allow the budget to be redirected and it would sacrifice the matched funding of local authorities, some of whom would be happy to abandon their commitment or allocate the money to an in-house equal opportunities unit which would spare them the discomfort of independent challenge. So it was decided to retain this local outreach – an advantage denied the Equal Opportunities Commission – but bring CRC work into line with the priorities of the Commission and their activities more subject to its control. The partnership was strengthened by the appointment of two deputy chairmen who had been prominent and respected leaders in the CRC movement. The renamed Racial Equality Councils were to be held to the priority of tackling discrimination and draw back from the kind of cultural promotions and internal debates which failed to touch the substance of racism. Predictably, bodies which had locally – and nationally through NACRC and annual conferences – developed their own constituency, resented what they saw as interference from the Commission and what they regarded as an expensive bureaucracy with well-paid officials taking over their cause. New Councils were set up to fill geographical gaps and others controversially closed on their failure to comply with the Commission's requirements. Organisational discipline did not sit easily with the campaigning tradition. Yet it was vital to retain the support of those dedicated campaigners and guard against the Commission becoming remote from community concerns. Their anger and hurt might sometimes surface in undiplomatic expression but they gave heart to the cause. Unlike the United States, we had no civil rights movement to help drive through change and none of the main political parties could be relied on to keep equal opportunities high on their agenda.

Preparation and implementation of the 1976 Act had straddled Labour and Conservative administrations and so it enjoyed broad political support. Roy Jenkins as Home Secretary introduced it but his Conservative successors never failed to back the Commission's work and on occasions defended its case staunchly against the scepticism of ministerial colleagues but there was an obvious reluctance to press their case too hard. The inner city disturbances had scared politicians into recognising that action was called for but it was easier to advocate tougher penalties for rioters and heavier policing than face the resource and policy implications of tackling root causes.

Politicians were not inclined to risk the charge of justifying mayhem. Those, like Bernie Grant, who did, were quickly demonised. Aspects of the Commission's work were at odds with the brand of Tory philosophy dominant through the Thatcher years. Quangos were regarded as profligate bodies beyond Government control and the performance of the Commission was always under close scrutiny. Any perceived slip brought cries for abolition. During her long period of office Margaret Thatcher made no statement nor referred in any speech to race relations, apart from raising the notorious 'swamping' alarm. There was strong resistance to any legislation which might seem to impede the free market or 'management's right to manage'. Looking back, it is astonishing that the CRE's Code of Practice in Employment was approved by Norman (now Lord) Tebbit. Ironically, early resistance to that Code came from TUC representatives on the Commission itself. The overall, rather patronising message from the Government was that the Commission was doing a valuable job acting as a container of racial tensions and that we were armed with the most progressive legislation in the Western world. We should go easy. It would be unwise to push too hard or overstate the case. Avoid the kind of controversy that would provide ammunition to those who would close you down tomorrow. When the occasion seemed justified there were scathing attacks on the Commission from the Conservative back benches and their supporting press gleefully pounced on any apparent excesses on the part of the Commission or associated bodies. It was regularly described as the 'Campaign for Racial Equality' and its statutory role ignored. Quotas and reverse discrimination were caricatured as Commission policy. They indulged their populist mocking of 'race spies' and the *Daily Telegraph* was always eager through commissioned articles and its leaders to promote the views of Ray Honeyford the Bradford headteacher sacked for his allegedly racist views and an implacable opponent of multiculturalism. The editor declined to publish the Commission's letters challenging Honeyford's position. 'You have no claim on our columns' was the haughty response from Max Hastings.

Departmental ministers were generally supportive of policy development within their areas of responsibility and provided introductions and platform encouragement at launches of codes of practice in health, housing and education fields. As Secretary of State for Employment, Michael Howard pledged himself to a ten-point programme to combat racial discrimination in employment and specifically commended targets as a way of improving performance.[1] But Conservative MPs were generally wary of showing enthusiasm for a cause which would bring few votes, though that changed perceptibly as the Asian constituency became more prominent. I recall one comment from a member who subsequently became a high profile minister, in reluctantly forwarding a constituent's complaint of discrimination, that the sooner the Commission was shut down the better. Later he carried responsibilities in the Ministry of Defence whose policies on equal opportunities are now accepted to have been seriously flawed. From the late 1980s there was a noticeable cooling in the Labour Party's own support for anti-racist campaigns. 'Political correctness' became a pejorative term as overzealous practices in some left-wing controlled local authorities seemed to bring the whole policy of equal opportunities into disrepute. Undoubtedly there were individuals and groups who exploited racial discontent in their own power bids and some stretched the law to the point of reverse discrimination. But, as Sir David Lane's enquiry into Brent Education Authority confirmed, the situation was by no means corrupt, as some sections of the media claimed, and those authorities which came under close scrutiny were the ones pioneering imaginative programmes to meet the challenge of ethnic diversity, of which their lampooning critics had no conception and which most authorities did not have to grapple with. It is a fair judgement that at the higher levels there was a lack of political will to tackle discrimination with the urgency and vigour it demanded. We knew enough about methods which would help to achieve greater equality but they required generous resources and above all a readiness to challenge vested interests of power and short-term commercial advantage. Systems needed to be dismantled and replaced. As the influence of local authorities was reduced, particularly with the abolition of the GLC and Metropolitan Counties, their bold, if at times incautious, lead was lost.

The Notting Hill Carnival gave focus to this disquiet. The North Kensington district, particularly that around the

Mangrove Restaurant, was believed by the police to harbour the most subversive and criminal elements of the Afro-Caribbean community. It acquired the reputation of a battle zone and a centre of drug trafficking. Those living there were subject to continuous police surveillance and sporadic raids on their premises. Some of the leading figures in that community were closely identified with Carnival and that in itself was enough to convince local opponents that it must be banned. Those living nearby feared for their properties and exaggerated reports of crime and the problem of crowd control fed national alarm. The Carnival route crossed the local authority boundaries of Kensington and Chelsea, and Westminster and required permission from both. Tory-controlled Westminster, one of the flagships of Thatcherism, wanted no part of it and urged its relocation on open land at Wormwood Scrubs. The black community was represented as an alien force claiming occupation of London streets. There was little sympathy for the argument that this was a substantial part of the local population asserting their right to celebrate in their cultural tradition and at the same time provide wonderful entertainment for the wider community. It was seen as a threat and fear took hold. Stewarding became the great controversy. Some thousands of pounds of Home Office money was authorised for payment through the CRE budget but opponents of Carnival questioned where that was ending up and the police expressed grave doubts about the stewards' ability to control crowds. In that fraught climate of the late 1980s, the Commission played a crucial role in mediating between the opposed interests, winning the necessary assurances and securing the future of what is now widely applauded as the largest and most successful street festival in Europe and is proudly featured on postage stamps. It is difficult now to recapture the frenzy which Carnival caused in those years. No doubt there were villains in the area ready to exploit the situation to their advantage but some of these then cast as troublemakers – Darcus Howe, Alex Pascall, the Critchlows, Lee Jasper – worked to hold the community together and restrain extremists. They have emerged as people of stature who eased us through a tense period of transition to a more relaxed, multiracial Britain, and took responsibility for preserving one of its most conspicuous symbols. It is a nice irony that the current Conservative leader should seek to enhance his political credibility by walking the streets of Carnival in a baseball cap. Not a likely spectacle in 1988. During their years in opposition, race issues slipped down the Labour Party agenda. Probably the cause was too compromisingly associated with the activities of left-wing councils with their threateningly powerful race and equal opportunity units. As Labour struggled to claim the middle ground those units were scaled down, sometimes closed, perhaps from embarrassment at their excesses, perhaps in the mistaken belief that their job was done. Nationally Labour was cautious about supporting strong legislation and the leadership opposed the establishment of a Black section within the party. As in other organisations where activists advocated similar grouping to provide a more effective channel for their concerns, it was viewed as a threat to unity and images of apartheid were conjured up. There was also an element in socialist ideology which regarded racial inequality as but one consequence of a wider social inequality and disadvantage: deal with those structural barriers of class and wealth, and racial discrimination would evaporate. That belief seemed to define the policies of councils like Liverpool, which was served with a non-discrimination notice by the Commission because of its house allocation practices. Hackney and Southwark were similarly criticised following formal investigations. A broad political commitment to equality guaranteed no protection from discrimination.

All political parties seemed wary of putting too much emphasis on legal constraints. It was felt that courts and tribunals should be a last resort; it was better generally to rely on education, exhortation and the gradual process of assimilation. Yet at a time when more severe penalties were advocated to combat criminal behaviour, it seemed inconsistent to resist tougher sanctions in response to widespread breaches of the Race Relations Act. There were several reasons for demanding that the Act be reviewed; it was, after all, a statutory responsibility of the Commission under the Act to do just that. Firstly, decisions of the Courts had frustrated the original intentions of the legislation notably by preventing the Commission from mounting formal investigations unless there was clear evidence of discrimination. Such investigations were conceived as a vital weapon in enabling the Commission to achieve its objectives. It now had to establish that there was discrimination suffered before conducting an enquiry into a particular sector of employment or service delivery. It was becoming increasingly obvious that it was institutional racism embedded in the culture of an organisation which explained under-representation and that required close inspection of its internal world. It was not a matter of exposing a series of easily identifiable discriminatory acts; rather the consequence of many unexamined assumptions. In its early days the Commission could reasonably be criticised for embarking on more investigations than its resources could manage and they may not have been targeted to best advantage. But the complexity of the Act prompted Lord Denning, then Master of the Rolls, to complain in 1982, 'The Commission has been caught up in a spider's web spun by Parliament from which there is little hope of their escaping. The machinery is so elaborate and cumbersome it is grinding to a halt.[2] There has been no significant change in the years since he spoke.

The Commission had no power to require ethnic monitoring, which was the only sure way of confirming over time whether there were even-handed outcomes in personnel practice or service provision. Such record-keeping could be insisted on after discrimination had been proved, as was the case with St George's Medical School where, following insider 'whistle blowing', the Commission's enquiry revealed that candidates with foreign-sounding names, and women, were systematically discriminated against in a computerised initial selection procedure. In 1988 that made the case more widely for ethnic monitoring in the UCCA process and in other areas of personnel selection. It further demolished any fond notion that discrimination happened only in less educated and enlightened areas of society. Those findings also helped to tip the balance in favour of an ethnic question in the 1991 Census. There was considerable debate about what, if any, categorisation should be used and that nearly drove the issue into the sand, which is probably where many politicians would have preferred it to be. At the last minute the Home Secretary was persuaded to use the formula recommended by the Commission, which lacked the refinement some pressed for (no Irish category for instance) but at least it established the principle and a base on which to build in future years.

The first review of the Act presented to the Home Secretary in 1986 did not enjoy even the courtesy of a formal response.

Quite likely there was justifiable anxiety in the Home Office
that parliamentary debate in those years might actually result
in a weakening of the legislation and curtailment of the
Commission's power. But the Commission continued to believe
that experience of operating the Act for over twelve years had
exposed its limitations. The claim made by the Home Office
minister of the time that the Act was working well was not convincing. In industrial tribunals there was little awareness of the
subtle and complex ways in which discrimination occurred and
complainants, perhaps with only the limited legal support of
the Commission, found it hard to prove their case. There were
also key areas of services provided by the 'Crown' most
significantly in the criminal justice system, which were outside
the scope of the Act. It became increasingly apparent that
endemic discrimination in those services undermined the very
principles on which they operated. There was little more than a
token presence of ethnic minorities in any of the main services,
police, prison and probation. There were few magistrates and
only one or two junior judges and recorders from minority
communities. At the same time black people were manifestly
over-represented in the prison population and less likely to
be treated leniently by the courts. Eventually that concern
prompted the scholarly research of Roger Hood into sentencing in some Midlands Crown Courts.[3]

The findings of that research were resented by some of the
judiciary who felt that their professional integrity was
impugned. Those operating in the area of justice could give the
impression that they were safe from any risk of partiality on
racial grounds. The study did not in fact reveal widespread
injustice but did establish that in some courts, and in a limited
number of cases, assessment of offenders was influenced by
racist assumptions and contributed to a bias in sentencing. Five
years later the whole legal/penal system is notably less defensive and prepared through training programmes and monitoring
to examine aspects of their operation which may weigh against
ethnic minorities.

The armed forces was another important sector where there
was an indignant denial of any cultural racism. The Army in
particular, with all its patronising traditions of Empire, seemed
to suggest that years of commanding and serving alongside
foreign troops, its knowledge of Africa and India, ensured a

respect for other cultures and made it immune from racism. The bonding of an élite regiment like the Brigade of Guards relied on recruitment from particular areas and on family allegiance. Interfere with that and pride in a specialist fighting force would be lost. It was no more racist, it was argued, to recruit only tall whites to the Guards than Nepalese to the Gurkhas. The Army was a stark example of policies applying in many other areas where word-of-mouth recruitment and family traditions maintained an image which effectively excluded non-whites. It was a small scale expression of the fear that diversity would destroy national identity.

Reports of racist behaviour in the armed forces were nothing new but its closed system made it hard to assemble evidence for a victim to obtain redress. There was no access to industrial tribunals and a civil organisation like the CRE was judged to have no standing. But over time a few cases came to light where racial harassment had driven the victim to desert. A brave stand by individuals and family concern alerted the CRE and in time the courts. A landmark judgment in the High Court by Lord Justice Taylor upheld Private Anderson's complaint. The Army Board were directed to review their procedures.[4]

At that time the expressed concern of the Prince of Wales at the lack of black forces at ceremonial events like the Trooping of the Colour aroused media interest. The Ministry of Defence was facing a recruitment problem and that also gave incentive to investigate the lack of candidates from the Afro-Caribbean and Asian communities. It was not until 1991, however, that the Ministry accepted there was a serious issue and rather reluctantly agreed to introduce ethnic monitoring, yet then only on a general basis which would fail to reveal particular areas for concern. The complacency was eventually shattered some years later when the CRE threatened to impose a non-discrimination notice on the Ministry itself following revelations of persistent racism.

That experience pointed up the intransigence of major institutions and confirmed that it took some combination of public shaming and self-interest to prompt change. With large-scale immigration in the post-war period to fill low grade vacancies in public services there was a shared assumption that if they stayed that is where they would remain. Discrimination served to ensure that assumption to be correct. A generation on it became obvious that some of the most refreshing talent and creative energy was emerging from those communities and by their inaccessibility organisations were depriving themselves. We were moving beyond the confines of sport and entertainment where black people had long since made their mark. Academic achievement persuaded employers to review recruitment policies, and in their discussions with institutions and employers the CRE was able to put aside any notion of doing favours for disadvantaged minorities and stress the self-interest and commercial good sense of attracting the best available talent. That harder-nosed approach made more impact than the hand-wringing of the past.

Racism is an ugly word and is usually reserved for acts of violence and harassment or the activities of extreme political groups. People recoiled from any suggestion that the way in which most of our systems were framed in order to serve the interests of a white, traditionally Christian, English-speaking community fell into the same category. The expectation had been that as immigrants arrived they would make the necessary adjustments – in a word, assimilate. It did not seem reasonable that systems should be reconstructed to accommodate difference. There was the notion of host and guest and in someone else's house a guest should make the concessions. But the leaders in race relations were beginning to question the assimilationist approach and, although at that time rather simplistic in our use of terms, to stress 'integration'.[5]

For integration to be distinguishable from assimilation, it had to involve a power-sharing in policy and the abandonment of structures which did not comfortably accommodate minority interests. To some that seemed excessively doctrinaire, tedious and expensive but it paralleled the kind of adjustments necessary to give open access to women and the disabled. As ever, the media seized on any examples which made a generally sensible and fair policy appear ludicrous.

But, given that we should value growing diversity and encourage minorities to maintain their cultural traditions, where should be the limits of tolerance? In 1984 a Birmingham school was judged to have acted illegally in requiring a Sikh pupil to wear a cap. Sikh motorcyclists were excused crash helmets. There was further controversy over hard hats on building sites. Should Muslim schoolgirls be allowed to cover their heads and wear the traditional *shalwar?* Most prominently, in Dewsbury, where parents objected to their white children singing 'Paki' songs and so set up their own school in a public house, there was concern that the primacy of English culture was being sacrificed. The complexity of this issue was highlighted when a local authority in Wales defied the Act by requiring fluency in Welsh as a qualification when it was not necessary for the job itself. Some church leaders added to the chorus as Christian-based assemblies gave space to other faiths and joined in celebrating Muslim and Hindu festivals. Were employers expected to interrupt production for Muslim prayer breaks and observe their religious calendar? Hospitals and prisons were required to respond to diverse dietary requirements and cultural habits. Integration, then, was not simply a question of tolerating difference on the margins of an essentially fixed cultural system but giving minorities a say in how that system should be shaped.

Often the concessions made were marginal and rightly dismissed as tokenism. The younger generation of British-born Afro-Caribbean and Asian people were becoming conscious of their own power and impatient for change. They did not inherit their parents' gratitude at being given sanctuary and employment in this country.

Integration at an institutional level, rather than simply accepting a varied population, involved more fundamental adjustments than seemed compatible with the concept of nationhood. The publication of Salman Rushdie's *Satanic Verses* in 1989 literally inflamed the debate with a group of Muslims captured on newsreel setting fire to a copy of the book in Bradford. Probably for the first time people were made aware of a substantial Muslim presence in this country and some were fearful of the threat it appeared to pose. Disconcertingly, even Roy Jenkins who coined the memorable aspiration of 'rich diversity rather than a flattening process of assimilation' expressed the view that with hindsight we might have been 'more cautious about allowing such a substantial Muslim presence into this country'.[6]

Journalists like Fay Weldon chimed in and the tabloid press stoked the fire with lurid images encouraging the belief that the Muslim faith was a destabilising force and amongst much else denied the inalienable right of free speech. It was an extremely tense period and the Commission was concerned at the racist taunts and harassment suffered not only by Muslims but the knock-on hostility towards the wider Asian population. It even had the effect of making Afro-Caribbeans seem less culturally separate and threatening.

The Commission considered how best to respond; some advocated standing well back from the controversy, others suggested that our concern for civil liberties should place us alongside those upholding the writer's freedom of expression and we should not seem to condone the intolerance of book burning. Yet undeniably this episode had profound implications for race relations, even though it was religious sensibilities that were offended rather than any clear case of incitement to racial hatred.

The Commission concluded that it did have a role to play as an intermediary between the various groups involved but it was in new territory. It was hard to hold a neutral line with feelings so polarised. Failure to align the Commission unreservedly with the Muslim cause was resented. A press statement was experienced as racist and patronising because it condemned the death threat of the Ayatollah before expressing sympathy for the hurt inflicted on Muslims by Salman Rushdie.

The network of RECs provided a valuable link with the Muslim community and Commissioners held meetings with police, church leaders and politicians in critical areas. There were discussions with the support group of fellow writers who defended Rushdie's position. A series of seminars was arranged exploring the issues involved – blasphemy, free speech and the plural society – and the papers and discussion subsequently published.[7]

Race relations were under similar strain at the time of the Gulf War in 1990 – Saddam Hussein joined the Ayatollah as a demonic figure threatening Western civilisation. Islam replaced communism as the ideology intent on global domination and followers in this country were viewed as potential subversives. British Muslims felt insecure as hostility towards Iraq spread to all members of their faith. Most were bewildered by events and felt no instinctive loyalty to Saddam but there were extreme populists, notoriously Kalim Siddiqui (a former journalist who had grabbed attention over the Rushdie affair), who continued to act as a self-proclaimed spokesman for this cause. He relished the media attention and his ranting effectively silenced the voices of more thoughtful and moderate Muslim leaders. He projected the spectre of fanaticism and in his advocacy of a Muslim parliament opened up the prospect of up to a million people in this country owing prime allegiance to an alternative authority. Looking back, it is easy to dismiss the now dead Saddiqui as a mischievous charlatan of no account, but he was giving voice to aspirations which were widely shared, especially amongst the younger generation uncertain of their future in this country.

Undeniably, those events exposed deeper dimensions of multiculturalism than were contemplated in the 'sarong and samosas' era. It lifted race relations to a potentially more dangerous and political level with international implications, and if the Commission were to be relevant to the central issues of a dynamic multiracial Britain with its inevitable political strains it could not stand aside and concentrate on the safer territory of individual complaints and interpersonal discrimination. It would be foolish to make any extravagant claims for the Commission's influence in those times but I believe it did develop its role to good effect and mediated across boundaries of misunderstanding and mistrust.

There was thrust on to our agenda the interrelationship between discrimination on the grounds of race and discrimination on the grounds of religion and it made people more aware of the tensions and concessions of a pluralist society. Muslims reasonably argued that they were not afforded the same protection as Jews under the Race Relations Act and that the law of blasphemy was discriminatory by applying only to the established church. Eight years later the death threat stands and Muslims continue to complain of discrimination and vilification because of their religious beliefs and customs. But those who listened beyond the extremist rhetoric learned something of the profound spirituality of the Muslim faith, and the dignity with which the majority of Muslims continued to conduct themselves in the face of extreme provocation helped secure them a respected and permanent place in a multifaith, multiracial Britain.

In a way, the Rushdie episode may be said to have been as significant a watershed for the Muslim/Asian community as inner city disturbances were for the Afro-Caribbean /Black. It represented a catharsis which gave vent to extreme, pent-up emotions. Again the anger found expression mainly through the younger second-generation immigrants claiming their rightful place in the future of this country. It was triggered by crass insensitivity towards a whole sector of our community. Younger people felt more emboldened to assert themselves but they were speaking and acting on behalf of their parents as well. Authorities and politicians have not yet absorbed all the lessons but responded sensibly enough to these eruptions to make us rather more optimistic about the future character of our society and its capacity to manage difference.

The international implications of that episode gave added momentum to the Commission's efforts within the European community. France in particular had a substantial Muslim population who were demanding more political influence and found themselves generally crammed into poor city ghettos and low-level employment, excluded from state services. They met similar objections to their assertion of cultural identity with cases of school exclusion over dress and feared threat to national unity. The CRE gave increasing priority to attendance at conferences and meetings arranged by the Council of Europe and the European Commission debating issues of joint concern. Enthusiasm for the European dimension was not shared by the Home Office who were inclined to the complacent boast that with the strongest legislation and most effective enforcement machinery we had nothing to learn. There was anxiety lest any European-wide legislation might threaten sovereignty and there was interminable argument over subsidiarity, with a determination to retain control over immigration and passport checks. Race policy was regarded as a domestic responsibility and it was contended that freer movement would undermine the 'firm but fair' approach of successive governments.

The CRE, on the other hand, believed there were lessons to be learned from other countries' experience and that the critical influences on race relations worked across national boundaries. Such good practice as we might pride ourselves on ought to be shared. The CRE involved obligations beyond the nation state. There were associated issues of xenophobia, refugees and the status of third-country nationals which all European partners were struggling with. Our own history brought particular problems but too often the political assumptions were of an island apart from Europe with little appreciation of the common difficulties in reconciling a sense of nationhood with wider freedoms and rights. We therefore contended that the Government should take greater heed of the European Court of Human Rights and incorporate its requirements into domestic legislation.

A prime concern was that protection afforded by the Race Relations Act should extend to members of ethnic minorities travelling, working and studying in mainland Europe. That was vital with the advent of the single market in goods and services and in the face of frequent complaints of 'visibly different' travellers being challenged at points of entry and having no protection in law when discriminated against in hotels or when working for a multinational company. Without legislation ethnic minority citizens could not share the benefits of a more open community. The CRE drafted proposals for European legislation, 'The starting line', and the chairman requested the Prime Minister to use his authority in presiding over the European summit at Edinburgh in 1992 to recommend this as the basis for a Directive.

The CRE was required to act in the national interest. Its job was to promote race relations in this country but the CRE saw that as part of the original European Community vision, with its main emphasis on creating a social climate which would lessen the risk of conflict between member states. Although the Treaty made no specific reference to race, as it did to gender, there was strong argument for maintaining that the European Parliament was authorised to legislate in that field. However, to remove any doubts, the CRE advocated an amendment to the Treaty to give explicit authority and that won influential support in other countries. The British government, however, was not persuaded and in its refusal to sign up to the Social Chapter at Maastricht in 1991 made it clear that the Community was seen primarily as an economic collaboration. So the CRE, which had given a lead to European partners and established a high reputation for international cooperation, found itself uniquely without Government endorsement in that very area. But those efforts continued and the network of contacts, the promotion of the Standing Conference on Race Relations in Europe (SCORE) and the Migrants Forum gave a framework for long-term collaboration which should be facilitated by the eventual signing up to the Social Chapter in 1997.

The Commission courted controversy whenever it directed attention beyond specific incidents of discrimination to broader considerations of the policy from which they arose. That ventured into political territory. The Government liked the idea of a body reflecting its determination to tackle racism and promote equality of opportunity. It became uneasy when the Commission questioned policies within its own departments or internationally. For instance, the Commission was repeatedly reminded that it should not meddle with immigration issues.

There was no real political challenge to the virtual ending of immigration from the old Commonwealth in the 1960s and that, together with the stringent 'primary purpose rule', gave a clear message to black people that more of their kind were not welcome. It was not unusual to hear that view supported by those who had successfully settled here earlier. There was no similar concern expressed over the considerable movement of white people to Britain from the European countries and North America. It was clearly a question of colour. As a service of the Crown, any discriminatory action by the Immigration Service was outside the Commission's remit but despite determined opposition by the Government in the High Court the Commission had won the right to examine their work in so far as it touched on its responsibility for good race relations. British citizens who had emigrated from Mirpur in Pakistan or Sylhet in Bangladesh were prevented from bringing elderly parents to live with them or arrange marriages for children from their original home area. The likely number was not great but recurring stories of illegal immigrants, bogus asylum seekers, preferential treatment in housing services in areas such as Tower Hamlets fed the fear of overwhelming immigration. Sections of the media never failed to exploit the mood of xenophobia in relation to mainland Europe and there was disturbing evidence of extreme organisations like the British National Party developing a network with like-minded groups throughout the continent. The terrifying harassment suffered by some ethnic minority families, generally unreported, was of a part with vicious attacks on migrant workers elsewhere in Europe. It contributed to a profound insecurity and holocaust memories were revived whenever Jews and Gypsies were targeted in a period of economic recession. Elsewhere, in Eastern Europe the chilling policy of ethnic cleansing was being applied.

98   *From Legislation to Integration?*

Those wider developments created a climate which affected race relations in Britain. With increasing mobility minorities looked for security in a wider world. The Commission had to make those connections and contribute as best it could to supra-national policies but, like Oxfam, it was reminded that its proper business was attending to casualties not dabbling in politics.

Tackling discrimination is at the core of a wider struggle to create a fair and just society so cannot be a neatly boundaried area of activity. It must reach into the structures which sustain inequality and protect vested interests of the majority. Over the years investigations conducted by the CRE have exposed examples of the institutional racism which exclude minorities. Increasingly aware that self-interest as well as justice required hiring the best available talent irrespective of race, the private sector cautiously followed the early lead set by public authorities. Greater affluence in some parts of the minority communities also had its effect. Victims of discrimination undoubtedly gradually became more confident in complaining even in those organisations which had previously been deaf to their concerns. There will be varying judgements on how much of this change was simply an inevitable adjustment over time and how much was attributable to legislation and the Commission's intervention. No doubt some would maintain that bringing the law into this area has itself created conflict, prompted vexatious litigation and inhibited the development of normal relationships with emerging minorities. Without the 'race relations industry' looking for work and stirring up discontent, any transitional tensions would have resolved themselves naturally, would be the claim. But it is difficult, given the deep-rooted nature of racism, to believe that a process of gradual enlightenment would overcome an instinct to dominate, scapegoat and protect group interests which finds expression along the scale of racist behaviour. It implies also that denying people access to the freedoms and opportunities because of their skin colour is more benign than any actions we label criminal, and requires an entirely different approach.

Two decades of the CRE's life have witnessed the uncomfortable and at times violently disturbing adjustment to the reality of a multiracial society in Britain. No longer does it make sense to talk in terms of a host community and in some areas there has been a remarkable transformation in attitudes. Legislation and enforcement have contributed to that process. It is a continuing one. Power may shift between groups but there will always be the need to protect the interests of minorities from exploitation and the need for a body with the competence to expose the subtle ways in which discrimination operates. As social and economic circumstances change discrimination will find new forms of expression. The blatant aggressive racism which denied black people basic rights in this country and resulted in appalling treatment of Afro-Caribbeans, especially by the police and other authorities, went on without any effective challenge and is a cause for shame. Yet it is of a piece with the exclusion of Paul Robeson and Learie Constantine from London hotels in the 1930s which at the time few people regarded as offensive. That so many stoically endured bitter experiences, and have gained respected positions in our society, is bringing greater benefit than we deserve. There are countless unsung 'Mandelas' in this country. Newsreels from the early 1980s of inner city battles, of the New Cross massacre, are startling reminders of how far we have moved but also of how close the patronising insensitivity of the authorities and a general failure to recognise the hurt inflicted on a whole generation of young people brought us to catastrophe. It would be dangerously complacent to assume that circumstances might not recur when a similarly disaffected group become convinced that their only hope lies in militant action. Elsewhere in Europe we have witnessed immigrants and minorities savagely attacked and blamed for economic and social ills. What will be the longer-term reaction to the humiliation they endure? In such circumstances masks drop and naked racism is exposed, yet even where ethnic minorities appear to have achieved equality the adjustment may be very superficial. Repeatedly in surveys and in investigations the CRE has shown how much additional talent, qualification and persistence is required of ethnic minority candidates. Groups, whether they be tennis clubs or professions, instinctively select candidates who easily fit into their current culture. We talk grandly of celebrating diversity but with varying degrees of conviction. The older generation particularly still have a problem in accepting the organisational or professional authority of those they see as belonging to a different culture, be they well qualified doctors or lawyers, and that unease is frequently voiced in private exchanges. People are offended if their comments are met with a charge of racism. They comfort themselves with the belief that racism is an altogether more obnoxious expression of hostility of which they would have no part.

Sensitive, enlightened programmes in schools where children are learning to enjoy the richness of different cultures in a multiracial setting is bringing enormous benefit. Although some of the most vicious racism (like the most extreme sectarianism in Northern Ireland) is acted out between working-class young men, hope lies in the transformation of youth culture. A coming together is made more possible through enlightened housing and schooling policies, for the mutual suspicion and hostility – whether it be in our inner cities, Northern Ireland or the States – is entrenched by separately housed communities. Aspiring parents, black and Asian as well as white, seek to move away from the areas of likely tension and, if they can afford it, into private schooling where the issues do not have to be worked at in the same way. The poorer, less advantaged groups are then left to struggle with the problems and the message is conveyed that hope lies in escape to the suburbs. The more successful pride themselves on their self-help and ambition and with affluence may become infected by the complacency and denial which typify middle class views on race. They may even succeed in joining the majority in this country whose daily life is free of any exposure to racial tension. The concentration continues of ethnic minorities in poor parts of our towns and cities denied the better housing, health and welfare provision. A combination of exceptional talent and parental encouragement or commercial initiative enables some to escape but, in an increasingly competitive world of specialist skills and a widening gap between the prosperous and those barely coping, the pattern of ethnic minorities' over-representation amongst the dispossessed becomes more fixed.

That social exclusion in the United States so vividly described by J. K. Galbraith in *The Culture of Contentment* will be mirrored here unless there is public investment in those communities on a scale which has never been seriously contemplated.[8] Unless that happens, with all the political unpopularity it would involve, we shall go on deluding ourselves that the marginal adjustments we have made so far represent the equal opportunities of a fair society. To date we may have achieved little more than those authorities and organisations who banner their claim as an Equal Opportunities Employer. They have taken only the first faltering step. Legislation, when it was framed, had the limited objective of eradicating racially motivated obstacles to equality of opportunity. That might lead to only minimal concessions. Beyond that there must be some vision of a society where profound and genuine respect for different cultural traditions erases the mistrust and contempt which has shaped past attitudes. It is a high ideal and requires expression through mainstream political strategies, not regarded as a task devolved to a specific agency. The fine rhetoric of racial harmony is seductive. The challenge comes in the relentless effort to translate that into well-constructed programmes which make a real difference to people's lives. A criticism levelled at legal enforcement was that it failed to tackle underlying attitudes and dealt only with discriminatory behaviour, the symptoms, and that any heavy-handed approach was counter-productive. It aroused defensiveness in those who would respond to more gentle persuasion. The Commission's response was that we need to protect right now the victims of discrimination, that a legal code gave force to the demands for justice and that laws had to be introduced for the very reason that education and persuasion had proved ineffective in bringing about change. Those enduring the misery of racism were not prepared to wait for the process of gradual enlightenment. The Commission had to win support for its cause and was always conscious that lack of rigour in its methods would arm its critics. 'Entrapment' was a frequent charge. Any perceived unfairness in exposing injustice attracted the greater condemnation. Ethnic minority staff, for instance, posed as applicants in an investigation on letting agencies. Evidence of discrimination was incontrovertible. The BBC used hidden cameras to expose racism in hotels, boarding houses and a golf club but somehow that was regarded as cheating.

So the Commission disappointed some by being toothless, lacking urgency, being a government device to give the semblance of action; it upset others by appearing intrusive, threatening a wider freedom and the civil rights of the majority by upholding the grievances of a less eligible 'minority'. There was displaced on to the Commission some of the hostility which it was less acceptable to direct at those with whom it was identified. Its campaigning had to be consistent with the primary role as a law enforcement body and not presume to speak on behalf of ethnic minorities. They must be enabled to present their own case. What the Commission was equipped to do was identify where discrimination was happening and show how it could be stopped. Sometimes that could be achieved by supporting individuals in industrial tribunals where unfair treatment might lay bare a flawed system. The Commission worked methodically with authorities and business leaders to change policies which had discriminatory outcomes. Denial was sometimes because of genuine unawareness of what was happening but more often because removing the unfairness would involve radical revision of organisational behaviour and abolish privileges. That defensiveness was evident in large bodies like the Civil Service, trade unions, the church, just as in private clubs. Working through it involved patient negotiations with policy makers on the inside track but that would not satisfy the demands of those who look for high profile campaigning.

That has to be a continuing process. The deep-seated racist assumptions which buttress power and privilege adapt to change of circumstances and laws and policies have to be reframed in response. Fluctuating economic conditions and attendant social unease can quickly provoke extremism and repression of minorities. We have dealt so far only with the initial tensions involved in managing a multiethnic society within a Europe and a world moving beyond the concept of the nation state. We have to redefine what it means to be British and the determination of some to cling to outdated symbols and myths means it will be an uncomfortable process. Tradition, patriotism and xenophobia are interrelated. In time we shall see the emergence of a more broadly based human rights commission incorporating the responsibilities of the CRE, EOC and other bodies and carrying greater weight in Europe and beyond. The case against such a body has rested on a fear that race might lose its edge alongside less politically contentious issues and that economies of scale might justify fewer resources. To be effective over a wide range would call for considerable authority and skilled professional staff to deal with the complex range of issues that have to be achieved without sacrificing the passionate commitment which had given the drive to anti-discrimination movements.

The raw edge of racism shows on the black/white divide. That is where we have seen its crudest expression. Future tensions will arise from a much more complicated society comprising ethnic and religious groupings which demand accommodation and protection. It will not be easy to retain a sharp national identity from such diversity. Even now it owes more to nostalgia and dated rituals than to any crucial features necessary to sustain a thriving community.

Arguably, once you reach the stage of consciously seeking to preserve characteristics of a system they have lost much of their validity. They cease to make a statement relevant to this time. They reflect a preoccupation with past glories rather than giving expression to current qualities. Many of the examples of discrimination are evidence of a clinging to power and privilege, a preoccupation with preserving systems which are failing to adapt to changing circumstances. Part of us may regret their passing just as John Major looked back wistfully to the time of warm beer and old ladies cycling to evensong, but they have little to do with British life today. A less innocent example is the absurd yet alarming re-enacting of past history in Northern Ireland with bowler-hatted Orangemen proclaiming their shallow power.

Notting Hill Carnival is a truer symbol of current British life than morris dancers. Although they needed much persuasion ten years ago, organisations advertising their products or their staff now rarely fail to display their multiculturalism. Curry has replaced fish and chips as the most popular British dish and there is a substantial Afro-Caribbean influence on popular music and the performing arts. Racism and discriminatory systems are futile attempts to hold back that creative energy and enrichment. True national identity will reflect a fusion of cultures, not the preservation of an historical past. It would be replacing the nostalgic with the romantic to suggest that removing obstacles to opportunity would open up a brave new world with no problems of race and class. All ethnic groups are capable of denying others access to the privileges they enjoy and asserting the primacy of their cultural traditions. Those who have fought hard to secure their space show little enthusiasm for sharing it with others. We are right to be alarmed by the militancy of black power and extremists of Islam. Discrimination is exercised from a position of power so only rarely has the Commission intervened to protect white people from disadvantage. But any future machinery will have to ensure a more extensive and complex-even handedness and determine in what way minority groups are entitled to preserve privileges for their members and assert their valid distinctiveness.

It will be the generosity and open-mindedness of that evolution that will shape the character of our nation and ensure that it plays an effective part in a European and world community. Britain perhaps more than any other country, given its imperial past, is still going through this painful and humbling process of adjustment. Much of our racism reflects an assumption of cultural and political superiority which is not easily discarded. We have had to put aside any prejudices in revaluing the claims of other cultures and needs. Immigration has given us the opportunity to work at that in a way which never happened when the white man was the dominant force. Without immigration Britain would have been denied enormous creative energy and be less well placed to relate to the kaleidoscope of the world beyond.

Twenty years on from the latest Race Relations Act there are grounds for both despair and hope. Many institutions and individuals have, from a combination of motives, learned to value the increasing diversity of our community, with most young people growing up free of the prejudices of earlier generations. But there are still shameful expressions of racism in vicious harassment of minorities: Asians, Afro-Caribbean and, let us not forget, Gypsies. Anti-Semitism is still around. Authorities did just enough after 1985 to avoid immediate repetition but, as the Stephen Lawrence enquiry has startlingly revealed, laudable aspirations at the top can be frustrated by inaction, obstructiveness and organisational defensiveness. Let us hope that that shameful episode has at last forced some understanding of what represents institutional racism. The otherwise admirable Scarman Report served to encourage a complacent belief that the police problem lay with a few bad apples rather than with the nature of the barrel. Perhaps Stephen Lawrence's murder will prove to have made other systems in our society as well as the police face the uncomfortable implications for the cultures they perpetuate. Our experience in the late 1980s and early 1990s was of denial.

In 1986 I presented a post-disturbances report: 'Not back to Normal'.⁹ That title was an explicit contradiction of the authorities' boast that they would soon get things back to where they were. Normal for the white privileged meant misery and denial of opportunity for the black minority. Small-scale, cosmetic projects were not enough. Black people were claiming a real stake in the society of which they were a part. There have been impressive achievements by members of the Asian and Afro-Caribbean community since that time and they are moving to levels where they can influence political and commercial decisions. Certainly the academic distinction of young Asians in particular is providing incentive for others and, as in many areas of life, stripping away complacency about inherent white superiority.

It will be a measure of a greater security when we respect and feel comfortable in that more diverse society but we cannot control its future shape. That will be influenced by the contribution of those who emerge to share in power. Opportunity for all means conceding privilege. The nastiest racism reflects a determination to defend territory and position and as the stakes become higher the tensions may increase.

The very real progress made since 1985 gives confidence that we can manage the transition without any repetition of the eruptions we witnessed in the early eighties. But preventing the explosive pain means bearing the discomfort of radical adjustments and investing in nourishing the very talent which may seem to pose a threat to our own position. Ours is but part of a global challenge. A developing legal framework and an effective enforcement agency will have a continuing part to play in easing us through that process.

NOTES

1. Employment Department, *Equal Opportunities: Ten-Point Plan for Employers* (London: Department of Employment, 1992).
2. *CRE* v. *Amari Plastics* (1982).
3. Roger Hood, *Race and Sentencing: A Study in the Crown Court: A Report for the Commission for Racial Equality* (in collaboration with Grace Cordovil), Centre for Criminological Research, University of Oxford (Oxford: Clarendon Press, 1992).

4.   *R. v. Army Board of the Defence Council ex parte Anderson*, 1990.
5.   See Bhikhu Parekh, 'Integrating Minorities', in Tessa Blackstone *et al.*
     (eds), *Race Relations in Britain: A Developing Agenda* (London: Routledge,
     1998).
6.   Interview in *The Independent*, March 1989.
7.   Commission for Racial Equality, *Free Speech* (London: Commission for
     Racial Equality, 1990), a report of a seminar organised by the CRE and
     the Policy Studies Institute (September 1989).
8.   J. K. Galbraith, *The Culture of Contentment* (London: Sinclair-Stevenson,
     1992).
9.   'Not Back to Normal', a report to the West Midlands Probation Service
     following the Handsworth disturbances of September 1985.

6 Tackling Racism: Britain in Europe
Ann Dummett

Why should it matter to us in Britain, what is happening in the rest of Europe? The term itself, 'the rest of Europe' points towards an answer. You will usually hear people nowadays talking about 'Britain *and* Europe' or 'going *to* Europe' from this country, as though we were a separate entity. On the contrary, we have always been geographically, culturally and politically part of Europe: nowadays we are in some respects legally bound to other parts of the continent. Race relations are not left out of this embrace. The illusion that we are separate has been fostered by a xenophobic tendency in British journalism and politics over at least the last twenty-five years, but it is a myth.

One of the nastiest ways in which race relations here are connected with happenings in other countries is that groups on the extreme Right have long cooperated across borders. This is paradoxical, because most of them have fiercely nationalistic ideologies, but they have proved very efficient at an international style of work. Racist rock bands move from country to country. Racist propaganda is sent through the mail across borders, thus avoiding the legal prohibitions some nations have of posting racist material within the country concerned. Racist games have appeared on the internet. Paramilitary groups from various countries join each other in one place or another for training and exercises.[1] The extreme Right network may be small, but it is mobile and exceedingly dangerous. Tackling it requires measures at European level as well as national level.

The anti-immigrant character of the extreme Right in Britain has been obvious ever since the 1950s. Sir Oswald Mosley returned to the political scene remarkably quickly after the end of the Second World War, with a message hostile not only to Jews and Communists (as it had been already in the 1930s) but to 'coloured' immigration. Other far-Right leaders took the same line, and indeed there was an overlap between their organisations, for example, the Anti-Immigration Society, the Racial Preservation Society and long-standing Fascists like former blackshirts.[2]

In continental countries, however, while Fascist and Nazi organisations also continued their activities soon after the war, the emphasis was at first different. Anti-immigrant propaganda came later. Individual Nazis and Fascists succeeded in obtaining useful positions in Germany, Austria and Italy, and also in Spain which remained Fascist throughout General Franco's lifetime. Escapes for war criminals were organised. Nazi propagandists spread the message that there had been no extermination of the Jews: this was the Allies' great lie. In France, by the early 1950s new extreme-Right groups like 'Action Europe' and 'Nouvel ordre Europeen' had been formed. In Italy, despite legal bans on Fascism, former Mussolini supporters re-formed under a new name, the 'Movimento Sociale Italiano'. Giorgio Almirante, its leader for many years, sat in the Italian and later the European Parliament, but in the 1980s lost his parliamentary immunity and faced charges of helping Fascist terrorists escape from justice.[3] Thus in some places on the continent, the far Right was throughout the post-war period a part – although a very small part – of the ordinary political scene. Its concern was with a return to power of strong leadership – its own: less publicly, many of its exponents were involved in violence and terrorism. There was, as in Britain, an overlap between overtly political groups and secret terror.

In Britain, the arrival of immigrants from the Commonwealth, from the late 1940s onwards, was perceived as entry for settlement by black people, coming to the mother country whose subjects they were. From the beginning, opposition to their coming was set in terms of colour. On the continent, immigration by foreign workers from outside Europe happened some years later, and was regarded as the temporary importation of units for the labour market. Attitudes to them were at first an extension of attitudes to a proletariat, a poor, unimportant and disposable group of use to society at large. They were also, whatever their skin-shade, foreigners and non-citizens, and therefore not part of society proper. Nor, it seemed, would they ever become part of society, because they had been admitted only temporarily on work permits.

These differences of perception have had lasting effects on the politics of immigration in Britain and on the continent. Yet in fact the phenomenon of migration was everywhere much the same: people coming from poor countries outside Europe were arriving in industrial nations with which the sending countries had some historical relationship. Most of them stayed. Economic growth was very rapid on the continent in the 1960s. It drew in migrant labour on a large scale, especially in France and Germany. Then the oil crisis of 1973 and the Iranian revolution of 1979 sent shock waves through Europe's economies. The anti-immigrant rhetoric which had been familiar in Britain since the late 1950s was taken up by those politicians on the continent who scented advantage in it. Some of these (as in Britain) were members of mainstream political parties, but those who used it most crudely were the extreme-Right leaders. As in Britain, the result of anti-immigration propaganda was to stigmatise the immigrants already present as unwanted and undeserving.

The targets of this anti-immigrant propaganda were Turks (the largest migrant group in Germany, and significantly represented elsewhere), north Africans (in France and also in Belgium and the Netherlands) and other foreigners, including some of European origin, such as Italians and Greeks in Germany, Poles in France and so on. But again, as in Britain, people with full citizenship but of foreign or non-European descent suffered from the hostility as well.

'It wasn't any accident,' comments Ray Hill,[4] 'that in the mid to late 70s, the MSI, the German NPD and others all seized upon anti-immigrant agitation and made it the centre of their activities.' For in 1976 the National Front in Britain had achieved startling successes in the local elections, following a sustained campaign that included a television broadcast (ostensibly not made by the NF at all). Events had played into the extremists' hands: newspapers had created an anti-immigrant furore over the arrival of half a dozen families from Malawi,[5] and scare stories about illegal immigrants had abounded. These electoral successes in Britain stimulated the Front National in France, among others, to play the immigration card and to the horror of 'mainstream' party politicians, the far Right began to look like an electoral threat in several countries, most importantly in Germany and France, where they gained significant numbers of votes.

The year 1976, as it happened, was also the year of Britain's major Race Relations Act. At that time, British knowledge of and interest in race relations and immigration on the continent of Europe were minuscule. Stephen Castles and Godula Kosack had produced a study of immigrants and the class structure in western Europe,[6] but there was little other information available in English, and no great interest for such information to feed.

By this time, the United Kingdom had been for three years a member of the European Economic Community, or common market, but there was no strong sense of Europeanness in the country as a result. Paradoxically, around the time of British entry, British popular culture appeared to be turning inward and backward in a wave of nostalgia for the glorious national past. Television series featured the old north-west frontier of India, the nationalism of Henry VIII and Queen Elizabeth I, and were still re-playing stories of British victories over Nazi Germany thirty years earlier. The 'I'm Backing Britain' campaign that originated in 1969 scattered Union Jacks over every kind of manufactured object, from cigarette lighters to underpants. Foreign policy was still dominated, as it had been since the war, by the special relationship with the United States, while anti-racists were mostly resentful of the new European connection for displacing British ties to the Commonwealth.

The new European connection was of far greater legal significance than Commonwealth ties had been. Accepted doctrines and unwritten conventions had characterised the Commonwealth: by joining the Community, however, the United Kingdom committed herself to being bound by the Community Treaty, Community legislation and judgments of the European Court of Justice at Luxembourg. These obligations were written and precise. At the same time, the United Kingdom became a part of the Community's law-making machinery and administration – not outside 'Europe' but of it.

The significance of the change was never conveyed to the British public by politicians or the Press – indeed, many politicians and commentators seemed unaware of its importance themselves. It was not until the late 1980s that some practical aspects of this importance began to be recognised by numerous British institutions, following the Single European Act (of which more is said below). But the intended character of the Community, as a cooperative enterprise, was still not appreciated.

The European Coal and Steel Community, the Atomic Energy Community and finally the Economic Community, were founded in the 1950s to make another European war impossible, by integrating the economies of member countries. West European leaders hoped to attain political as well as economic union in the long run. Britain held aloof, refusing an invitation to the Messina conference in 1955 at which plans for the EEC were drawn up. The six original member states – France, Germany, Italy, Belgium, the Netherlands and Luxembourg – thus had the shaping of the Community and its legislation from 1957 to 1973, when Britain, Ireland and Denmark were admitted – Britain having regretted her original refusal, chiefly because it was now recognised that she could get a lot out of the EEC in material terms. This 'What's in it for us?' attitude to membership has, unfortunately, remained dominant in Britain, and not only at government level.

There was nothing in the Community Treaty about racism. Because EEC legislation has to be based on some element in the Treaty, there was no Community legislation concerning racism either. With this vacuum in EC law, anyone from a minority in Britain going to another EC country for work or on a visit had no protection against racial discrimination except under the national law of the country concerned. And nowhere but in Britain was there, in the 1970s, any comprehensive and effective race relations legislation. France had (and still has) a large body of law against racist utterances and discrimination, but this has been very little enforced. It is part of the criminal code, and so although an individual can make a complaint proceedings have to be taken by the public authorities, who have been very slow to prosecute. (Private prosecutions are legally possible but not a realistic option.) While most member countries had some constitutional provisions condemning racism, legal remedies were not in practice easily available. The situation changed somewhat as more countries joined – Greece, Spain and Portugal in the 1980s, Austria, Sweden and Finland in the 1990s – and as some countries began to change their national laws. The Netherlands rapidly developed its case-law on racism in the 1980s and has amended both its civil and criminal codes to deal more effectively with racial discrimination. Belgium passed an anti-discrimination law, of a rather limited kind, in the early 1980s, and in the 1990s has revised and strengthened it, setting up a body similar to the CRE, called the Centre for Equal Opportunities and the Struggle against Racism. Italy passed the Mancino Law in 1993, banning expressions of, and incitement to, racial hatred. At national level in these countries and others, some moves have been made since 1976, but implementation is everywhere a problem and the picture is patchy.

It is essential to distinguish between laws at national level and Community laws. Often British people confuse the two when talking about 'Europe'. Each nation has its own legal system and body of laws: each, except the United Kingdom, has its own written constitution. The Community is a supranational body which member states have voluntarily joined, and in joining they have committed themselves to observing the laws which their representatives make in the Community framework. The Community has not the powers to legislate in every area of life, but where it has powers conferred on it by the Treaty it can pass laws and its legislation must prevail over national legislation where the two conflict.

There is a complicated system of checks and balances, defined in the Treaty. The actual legislature is the Council of Ministers, with one Minister from each member state, but the Council cannot initiate a Bill as the Westminster cabinet can: it must rely on a proposal from the European Commission. Commissioners also are drawn from every member state, but their first loyalty is to the Community and not their home countries. They must consult the European parliament, which is democratically elected and which has amending powers. Many others are consulted, either formally or informally: the Economic and Social Committee, representing consumer groups, trade unions and other bodies in all member states; the Permanent Representatives in Brussels, who are national officials playing a part roughly comparable to ambassadors to the Community; voluntary associations of various kinds, and some individual experts and think-tanks. The process is in most ways an open one, with documents available to those who ask for them, and with anyone free to make suggestions. An Official Journal publishes proposals. Green Papers and White Papers are issued.

There are different types of legislation. The strongest is a Regulation, which becomes immediately binding on all member states. Slightly different is a Directive, which sets goals to be met and a time-limit for reaching them, and which requires each member state to pass its own national legislation so as to attain these goals. A Directive allows for some differences in the situations and legal systems of the member states. The Commission has a duty to watch over implementation, and the European Court of Justice, the Community's own Court (with judges from all member states) is the final court of appeal on interpretation.

By the early 1980s the Community's impetus towards closer union had slowed, bogged down by bureaucratic detail. Jacques Delors, then President of the Commission, and Britain's Lord Cockfield drew up a plan which resulted in the Single European Act 1986, a set of amendments to the Treaty which required that free movement of persons, goods, services and capital within EC territory should be attained by the end of 1992. This stimulated interest in Britain at last, and institutions began to consider how to prepare for 1992.

The Commission for Racial Equality had already produced some information on the Community and had been considering ways in which Community laws might affect the operation of the Race Relations Act in Britain. In 1989, the CRE set up a working group to study the likely effects of the Single European Act and to devise policy. The result was a three-point plan: to press for a Directive against racial discrimination, a Treaty amendment on racism and improved rights for third-country nationals.

'Third-country nationals', in Community jargon, are nationals of countries outside the Community. The name arises from the fact that a Community national has rights under Community law when in any second country within the EC. An Italian has the right to work in Britain on the same terms as British people; a British person has the same rights in Italy. But a Pole or a Jamaican, from outside the EC, may have been admitted to one of its member countries on a work-permit or with some other status permitting residence, but has no right to move elsewhere within the Community to work or reside. In Britain it was thus possible for two brothers, say, one born in Jamaica and one born in Britain, to have different sets of rights from each other: one could go and work in Denmark, the other could not; one needed no visa; the other did. A related matter of concern to the CRE was that qualifications gained in third countries were not among those recognised in Community legislation being passed to meet the Single European Act criteria: this was a matter of great concern to many doctors in Britain who had obtained their first degrees in India, for example.

The CRE's concerns arose out of its duties under the Race Relations Act to promote equality of opportunity and good relations between groups, and to work towards the elimination of discrimination. The uncertainty of protection at national level elsewhere, and the lack of protection under Community law impelled it to be part of a Europe-wide movement to tackle racism. Contacts had to be made, ideas and information exchanged with anti-racists in other European countries. Although the CRE was not new to such activities, there was now an added impetus.

It is impossible in a short space to give any clear idea of the character of 'race relations' throughout the European Community over the last twenty years. Recently, many studies have appeared which attempt at some length to do so.[7] Probably the two major difficulties are as follows. First, the terms of the discussion are set differently in different countries, and a British reader can easily misunderstand the whole structure of the debates elsewhere. Second, the kind of information a British person naturally seeks on the extent and character of discrimination is often not available. There is no equivalent elsewhere of the PEP and PSI reports which here have recorded extensive testing for discrimination in a comprehensive way.[8] Even the figures available for 'ethnic minorities' in other European countries are prepared on quite a different basis from ours, and are not comparable. Most countries simply record numbers of resident citizens and foreigners. These do not indicate ethnic origin or colour. In France it is illegal to classify a person as a member of an ethnic group. This general picture has begun to change, as more awareness of the problem develops, but there are still difficulties.

A Regulation of 2 June 1997 has opened new possibilities here. It provided that a Monitoring Centre on racism and xenophobia would be established by the Community, to collect information, attempt to find common terms and definitions, and provide data to public authorities and voluntary groups. The Centre is based in Vienna and will, like other Community institutions, be run by people from all member states. The European Commission has worked hard for several years to make this initiative possible. The Commission has also produced studies of anti-discrimination laws in member states and was the driving force behind the European Year against Racism, Xenophobia and Antisemitism in 1997.[9] Its White Paper of 1994 called for Community legislation against racial discrimination.[10]

To say this is not to depreciate the repeated attempts of the European parliament to get action on racism. These go back to the early 1980s. The electoral successes, mentioned above, of extreme-Right parties in several countries prompted the Parliament to set up a committee of enquiry on the growth of Fascism and racism. It produced the Evrigenis report, which set out alarming information and called for new policies recognising pluralism.[11] Most of its recommendations were ignored: they were repeated and added to in the Ford report of 1991, the work of another Parliamentary committee.[12] This time, the Commission set up, as recommended, a Migrants Forum to represent migrants in all member states and advise the Commission. The Parliament in 1991 also set up a new permanent committee on civil liberties (later renamed citizens' rights) and legal affairs: this produced further work on racism.

Nor should it be forgotten that the Economic and Social Committee had repeatedly called, in rather stronger terms than other European bodies were using, for action against racial discrimination.[13]

There were many political difficulties in the way. The British and Danish governments were opposed to any measures which, in their view, would damage national sovereignty by giving new powers to the Community. In some countries, right-wing politicians saw anti-racism as a left-wing stunt; others did not believe the problem of racism was very substantial. Others again would not define rights for non-citizens.

Meanwhile, throughout Community territory, there was massive inequality and daily discrimination. Minorities were facing violence and threats, petty harassments, insults, inferior housing, inferior job opportunities, in some cases insecurity of residence and fear of possible removal. The victims were various: in southern Europe Roma and Sinti were especially vulnerable. Jews continued to face prejudice and sometimes violence. Anti-Muslim feeling was growing, partly at high official level and partly at the base of society.

In 1991, a small group met informally to discuss how to achieve the goal of a Community Directive. The idea was to draft a model Directive in exactly the form draft legislation would take. Once a document had been agreed within the group, which included people from both official and unofficial anti-racist bodies, one of them the CRE, the draft could be used for lobbying. It would be much better to lobby for specific demands than for a vague, general one, and if the group itself (whose members came from six different EC countries) could agree, they might be able to anticipate and avoid the difficulties of producing a measure which had to deal with widely varying perceptions and situations.

The draft took over a year to complete, and was given a name, 'The Starting Line', to distinguish it from any other draft suggestions that might be made. Lobbying gained wide support in the member states. The whole initiative had been made possible, at the start, by the Churches' Committee (later renamed Commission) for Migrants in Europe.

The European parliament voted three times on a call for a Directive, specifically endorsing the Starting Line. But resistance was not only political: legal opinion was divided between those who thought that a Directive was possible under the Community's existing powers and those who held that the Treaty must first be amended to cover racism. The Starting Line group then turned to drafting a model Treaty amendment, calling it the Starting Point, and lobbied on that too.

In June 1994 the summit meeting of Community heads of government agreed to set up a committee to devise, as a matter of urgency, a strategy against racism and xenophobia and to report back within a year. The body then established, the Kahn Commission, reported in 1995 with several recommendations, one of which was to set up a European Observatory or Monitoring Centre (this was acted on in 1997: see above) and one was to amend the Treaty. The wording chosen by Kahn was almost identical with the Starting Point text.

The Community Treaty, amended in 1986 by the Single European Act, had been amended again at Maastricht in 1991, when it was agreed to set up a European Union of which the Community would form the first 'pillar'. The second pillar and the third rested on forms of intergovernmental cooperation outside the Community framework, the second dealing with foreign and defence policies, the third with cooperation in the fields of justice and home affairs. The third pillar included immigration and asylum issues. Another set of amendments was due in 1996, and conferences began in 1995 to prepare the agenda for changes to the whole structure. These conferences considered, among other matters, a 'race' amendment.

The Irish government took the initiative during its Presidency of the Union, in the second half of 1996, to press for an effective amendment along the lines of the Kahn proposal. But governments could not agree either on this or on the entire draft Treaty the Irish put forward. Discussions then proceeded under the Dutch Presidency. A very much watered-down race amendment was eventually agreed at the Amsterdam summit in June 1997.

The Amsterdam Treaty as a whole is a compromise document, reflecting the great difficulty of getting agreement from 15 states, ranging from Finland to Spain and Ireland to Greece, on institutional change. The priorities of the Community officials were to combat unemployment, to prepare for enlargement of the Community to the east as rapidly as possible, and to reform the Community's institutions, which had already become unwieldy with 15 members and would be in severe difficulties if unreformed once new members from eastern Europe were admitted. The Community did succeed in one aim: to get immigration and asylum matters shifted from the third pillar to the first. But the change was so hedged about with conditions and time-clauses that there could be little immediate effect. One valuable move, however, was to amend the third pillar provisions by placing the combating of racism and xenophobia first among the duties of police and judicial cooperation between member states. Race is thus mentioned twice in the new Treaty: in Article 13, formerly numbered 6A (the race amendment) and in Article 29 of Table VI, formerly Article K1.

The Treaty will not come into force until it has been separately ratified by every member state, a procedure which may take as long as two years. Limited though the racial provisions are, they represent an enormously important step forward. Religious as well as racial discrimination is covered, a vitally important point when hostility to Islam has become serious in many member states. Once legislation has been passed (though not until then) the European Court of Justice will have the opportunity to make judgments binding on all member states. The new Treaty outlaws other kinds of discrimination also, and gives very great weight to equality between men and women. It has a new section at the beginning, of which these measures are part, on fundamental rights as essential principles underlying the Union.

Article 13 says:

> Without prejudice to the other provisions of this Treaty and within the powers conferred by it upon the Community, the Council, acting unanimously on a proposal from the Commission and after consulting the European parliament, may take appropriate action to combat discrimination based on sex, racial or ethnic origin, religion and belief, disability, age or sexual orientation.

This text has 'may' where Kahn and the Starting Point had 'shall'. In other words, the Community is not required to legislate, but only permitted to do so. In other ways the text is much weaker than the Kahn and Starting Point texts. However, it opens the way to other measures besides legislation, and makes budgeting for anti-racism possible.

The above account has concentrated on developments in the European Community and Union – though even on these the information here is an inadequate summary of all that has passed – partly because these developments have not been well known in Britain and partly because they lead up to the climax of the Treaty amendment, which may produce great changes, provided the political will to make them is forthcoming. But if we look at the continent of Europe as a whole, there have been other happenings significant for race relations. The Council of Europe, a much larger and weaker organisation than the Community/Union, has had in succession two five-year projects, first on community relations and then on anti-racism, since 1984. The CRE has been represented in both series, and reports based on these activities have put forward numerous policy options.[14] There has been much discussion in the Council of Europe – so far without result – aimed at extending the provisions of Article 14 of the European Convention on Human Rights and Fundamental Freedoms. As it stands, Article 14 prohibits racial discrimination in the provision of any of the rights defined elsewhere in the Convention. But it does not touch upon discrimination in employment, housing, health care, education or the provision of goods and services. Thus the European Court of Human Rights at Strasbourg (to be distinguished from the Community's European Court of Justice – a distinction that British newspapers, even today, sometimes fail to make) has very limited powers to deal with discrimination.

It is rash to attempt a general overview, but perhaps timid to avoid it. Over the last twenty-one years, racism, xenophobia and anti-Semitism have been problems besetting every country in the continent in one form or another. In the Czech Republic thousands of Gypsies are denied citizenship. In France there has been desecration of Jewish cemeteries and violence against Muslims. In Germany, small neo-Nazi groups have attacked refugee hostels and committed arson attacks on Turkish homes: there have also been attacks on Italians and other foreigners of European origin. In Italy there have been attacks on Africans. Worst of all has been 'ethnic cleansing' in former Yugoslavia, a horrible conflict in which thousands died, but which somehow did not seem to count as having happened at all when politicians in the West proclaimed celebrations in 1995 for 'fifty years of peace in Europe'. Racist political parties have made gains in several countries, including France, Austria and Belgium. Yet also over the same period, there has been growing concern, increasing action, and a determination slowly spreading from voluntary groups into official thinking that racism must be stopped.

Unfortunately we are still a long way from full appreciation, at the level of governments, of what has brought about the present situation and what is needed to remedy it. Laws on racism will not do much by themselves. The manner in which they are administered is crucial. The next most pressing question is that of immigration and asylum policy: how can this be amended to avoid racist effects, not just on applicants but on the receiving societies? What can be done about structural unemployment, which affects minorities, particularly their younger members, disproportionately? How can the rights and opportunities of resident foreigners be improved, to bring them closer to those of citizens? How can minorities best be represented in decision-making that affects them?

Sadly, the contribution that British experience could make to answering some, though not all, of these questions is not being used. The Labour government elected in May 1997 has shown little sign of understanding its role in the European Community any better than its predecessors did. Community policies advance through negotiation between equals and depend on mutual understanding and a willingness to give as well as take. They need to be based on the fact that agreed policies will affect every member state, and must be considered for their effects on all the peoples living in EC territory, not just those who live in Britain. Of course every government tries to defend its own corner, and it must be said that Britain has one of the best records in Europe for applying laws once they have been agreed. But no other state has behaved in quite so obstructive and nationalistic a way, while claiming it is going to lead the others. A typical error was Britain's decision to support American policy towards Iraq early in 1998, at a time when Britain held the European Union presidency, without any consultation with other EC governments or even the pretence of seeking an agreed Community policy. This continuing British casualness towards its partners makes it very difficult for British proposals to find friendly hearers, especially if the proposals imply that Britain knows best.

Moreover, there is no indication that the present British government wants to make the tackling of racism a priority in Europe. Jobs, crime, the environment and a revised agricultural policy were the stated priorities at the beginning of the presidency, with no mention of minorities or their rights. The preceding government repeatedly objected to a strong 'race' amendment when the Amsterdam Treaty was under discussion, on the ground that this would remove some powers from Westminster to the Community institutions, and the present government appears equally determined to block some Community initiatives irrespective of their merits to maintain its own domestic powers. On immigration, for example, Britain opted out in June 1997 from a new agreement to transfer much of immigration policy towards the world outside the EC to the Community institutions within five years. Muddled and unsatisfactory though the details are of this section of the Treaty, and likely though it is that other governments too will be unwilling to yield their own controls when the time comes, it is significant that the Major government's determination to keep all Britain's controls, both inside and at the outer edge of the EC, exclusively in Westminster's hands is unchanged by our change of government. British contributions of a positive kind will have to come from sources outside the government itself – as indeed they have already done for some time. The British people who work in Community institutions and in Community-wide organisations such as UNICE (the association of European employers) and the ETUC (the European association of Trade Unions) together with the CRE, various non-governmental organisations, academic foundations, and numerous individuals have established contacts and exchanged information with other European countries for some years on racial equality issues. The work of one small but influential cross-border group, the Starting Line group, has already been mentioned above. Recently reconvened and enlarged with members from new member states, the group has redrafted its proposed text for a directive on racial discrimination, bringing its terms into line with the new Article 13 of the Treaty and adding provisions on religious discrimination. Proposed measures for greatly improved rights for third-country nationals are, at the time of writing, also being prepared by the group. This kind of initiative is in the spirit of the 'closer union between peoples' which the Community was founded to promote.

Ultimately, however, it is the Ministers in national governments who take the crucial decisions for the European Community. National governments have therefore to be lobbied on European as well as on domestic policies. And here we need to remember that policies are needed not only for the sake of minorities within Britain and of those among them who travel to other EC countries for work or study, but for all the millions of sufferers from racism on Community territory for whom we in Britain now share a responsibility.

In Europe at large, beyond the Community as well as within it, the great need is for a change of attitude to racism. A real determination to deal with it could accomplish much without the need for rhetoric or even for new anti-discrimination legislation. Policing everywhere needs to be transformed, and this could be done by much stricter discipline over racist behaviour and by incentives for improving racial equality. Governments could lead not just with empty declarations but with contract compliance policies and radical improvements to the administration of immigration controls and asylum cases. But such things cannot happen until the seriousness of the problem is understood. For Britain to make a contribution here it is necessary for the British government itself to understand that having a Race Relations Act is not enough, and that influence with other countries will be better gained by cooperation with a dash of humility than by asserting superiority.

NOTES

1. Numerous examples have been regularly reported over many years by *Searchlight* magazine.
2. Ray Hill with Andrew Bell, *The Other Face of Terror: Inside Europe's Neo-Nazi Network* (London: Grafton Books, 1988) pp. 28–29.
3. Geoffrey Harris, *The Dark Side of Europe: The Extreme Right Today* (Edinburgh: Edinburgh University Press, 1990).
4. Hill, *The Other Face of Terror*, p. 203.
5. Peter Evans, *Publish and be Damned* (Runnymede Trust: London, 1976).
6. S. Castles and G. Kosack, *Immigrant Workers and Class Structure in Western Europe* (London: Oxford University Press, 1973).
7. John Wrench and John Solomos (eds), *Racism and Migration in Western Europe* (Oxford: Berg Publishers, 1993); see also 'Antisemitism World Report' published annually by the Institute for Jewish Policy Research, London (dealing with minorities generally), and the European Commission's 'Communication to the Parliament and Council of Ministers' of 8 December 1995 on 'Racism, Xenophobia and Antisemitism', proposing 1997 as European Year against Racism. Also the Ford report (see note 12).
8. Political and Economic Planning, *Racial Discrimination* (London: PEP, 1967).
9. Most recently, *Legal Instruments to Combat Racism and Xenophobia*, Commission of the European Communities Directorate General for Employment, Industrial Relations and Social Affairs, Brussels, December 1992.
10. *European Social Policy*, White Paper COM (94)333 of 27 July 1994 (Luxembourg, 1994).
11. G. Evrigenis, *Report on the Findings of the Committee of Inquiry into Racism and Fascism in Europe* (Strasbourg: European Parliament, 1986).
12. Glyn Ford, *Report of the Committee of Inquiry into Racism and Xenophobia* (Luxembourg: European Parliament, 1991).

13.   For example, *Resolution of the Economic and Social Committee on Racism, Xenophobia and Religious Intolerance*, CES 1387/92 ht, 25 November 1992, (Brussels, 1992).

14.   Council of Europe, *Report of the Community Relations Project* (Strasbourg: Council of Europe, 1991).

7 Lessons from the US Civil Rights Experience
John Goering

OPENING QUESTIONS AND RESEARCH ISSUES

This chapter attempts to answer two straightforward questions: What have been the key features of the US legislative programme for racial justice, and what if any 'lessons' might be relevant for the United Kingdom or other European countries? Answering these questions sensibly, however, involves several basic difficulties which face outsiders attempting comparative assessments.

First, examining the multidimensional role of race and civil rights enforcement in the United States and the UK requires sensitivity to historical, cultural, social and political similarities and differences. As if this were not difficult enough, comparisons of such similarities and differences are constrained by the absence of heuristic social science understanding of the socio-political and economic dynamics affecting countries at relatively similar levels of economic and political development. The fact that the UK borrowed directly from the US when establishing its civil rights laws does not mean that the analyst can apply a 'cookie-cutter' methodology when comparing the impacts and effectiveness of these laws.

Some of these comparative difficulties are illustrated by understanding what minority status means in the two countries. For example, Michael Banton cautions that even between Britain and the United States the word 'race' has different associations. American visitors who interpret the British scene through the medium of a United States understanding of race easily come to oversimple conclusions.[1] Racial similarities may occur in populations with notably different experiences with slavery, racism and immigration and these require different social science understanding and programmatic solutions.[2]

Differences in the volume and recency of migration of minority groups, the social imprint of slavery, and different forms of minority political mobilisation between the two countries make it difficult to come to any simple conclusions about comparable patterns and processes. Thus, while it may appear that patterns of concentration of West Indians in British public housing are duplicating major parts of the US experience, they are occurring without a prior history of *de jure* and *de facto* discriminatory site selection and without a lengthy history of private market segregation to build upon. They are therefore only potentially comparable and it is the further terms of this comparability that we seek in this analysis.

The comparicist is constrained in his/her efforts by the absence of systematic, comparable data to determine the extent to which there are common or divergent social, economic and demographic patterns between 'racial' populations in the two countries. The current decentralised system in England for the reporting of information on the racial and ethnic composition of council-housing waiting lists and occupancy, for example, is even further limited by the voluntary nature of such reporting. This has been accompanied by apparent lack of interest among a number of councils in gathering such data. For example, in 1986, only 14 out of 32 London boroughs reportedly kept ethnic records, and of these only four did regular monitoring of the information.

Local authorities, at least in the recent past, have resisted minority data collection and equal opportunities policies on the grounds that 'we don't have a problem here', 'our allocation systems are already fair', or 'we prefer using a colour-blind approach'. Because of the greater primacy of race issues in the US, there are fewer egregious problems with US race data collection and most agencies collect some form of racial and ethnic information on a mandatory basis.

An area in which there has been comparably inadequate data gathering is racial violence. In the United States, such violence occurred frequently in the 1940s and 1950s when new housing projects were planned or built in previously white areas and such hostility continues to occur on an intermittent basis when African American or ethnic families buy homes in white areas. Less is known about predicting and explaining race-related rioting. In England, there is evidence of upwards of 200,000 racially motivated acts of racial violence annually, even though there is also evidence of under-reporting and no systematic scheme for gathering and reporting such information.[3] The inability to offer sensible social science and policy-relevant explanations for the occurrence of inter-racial hostility and race-based rioting, limits policy researchers' understanding of civil rights effectiveness since such acts suggest the limits of the legislative promise of equal opportunity and fair treatment.

Data limitations also include the absence of reliable time-series information describing the changing number, distribution and characteristics of minorities, including assessments of the impacts of policy changes intended to directly or indirectly influence their disparate situations. There is little systematic research on the effectiveness of civil rights in the US and UK in achieving more equitable or desegregated outcomes. The two countries are thus similar in the paucity of evaluations of the implementation and effectiveness of civil rights enforcement in changing discriminatory practices – thus making hazardous any confident cross-national comparisons. While some of these analyses have been done in the US by the US Civil Rights Commission (1994, 1995, 1996), much more effort is needed to assess impacts.[4]

Despite this string of cautions and caveats, it is both useful and, within limits, possible to address potential areas in which British and US race policies might converge. Because of the relatively small scale of the UK minority population, there is likely to be less sustained pressure to create broad-scale remedial programmes and affirmative relief but there is ample room for continued re-analysis of the need to strengthen civil rights entitlements and enforcement mechanisms.

In the following section, I briefly highlight the major US civil rights laws and their general system for enforcement. Following that I outline the best accumulated evidence of the effectiveness of these laws. An analysis of how the US and UK *might* be comparable follows.

MAJOR US CIVIL RIGHTS LAWS?

The following brief analysis condenses a large volume of research, legislative history and policy analysis on US civil rights laws and their effectiveness. US civil rights laws are administered through a variety of administrative procedures managed by federal, state and local civil rights agencies and through the system of federal courts. Administrative procedures typically include rights to conciliation or a hearing before an administrative law judge.

For cases filed in federal court, there are several interconnecting layers of civil rights protection available to an individual or protected class member including constitutional protections, most especially the 'new' constitutional protections provided in the 13th, 14th, and 15th amendments, the related 1866 civil rights act, and more recent Federal civil rights laws and executive orders. The latter have been promulgated within the last thirty to forty years and are at the heart of the provision of administrative and judicial anti-discrimination remedies for racial minorities.[5] In most instances the executive branch has worked with Congress to develop laws which are usually supported by the US Supreme Court, although there have been exceptions in which federal courts have led the way in enacting civil rights and desegregation remedies.

There are civil rights laws or orders addressing such issues as the military, schools, housing, and public accommodations. A sketch of these laws is provided below.

The Military

One of the earliest Executive Branch interventions to promote desegregation was the Executive Order (No. 9981) issued by President Harry Truman in July 1948, which instructed the armed forces to desegregate immediately.[6]

In the same year, the Supreme Court invalidated restrictive racial covenants in housing. In the 1950s, under President Eisenhower, a US Civil Rights Commission was established to help investigate and study discrimination in all aspects of American life. It was in 1954 that the Supreme Court ordered 'with all deliberate speed' the desegregation of education in the South.

Public Accommodations

In July 1964, Congress enacted major reforms in the Civil Rights Act of 1964. This statute prohibited discrimination in public accommodations, federally funded programmes, in employment and in schools.

Title II of the Civil Rights Act of 1964 prohibits discrimination or segregation in places of public accommodation. The law states that 'all persons shall be entitled to the full and equal enjoyment of the goods, services, facilities, privileges, advantages, and accommodations of any place of public accommodation without discrimination or segregation on the ground of race, colour, religion or national origin. There are very limited exemptions from this provision for private clubs or establishments. The law is enforced in large part by the Department of Justice.

Federally Assisted Programmes

Title VI of the Civil Rights Act of 1964 prohibits discrimination in all federally assisted programmes and activities based on race, colour or national origin. Title VI, unlike Titles VII and VIII, is administered by civil rights units located within approximately 25 separate federal agencies.[7]

School Desegregation

This is addressed through Titles IV and VI of the Civil Rights Act of 1964. The Department of Education's Office for Civil Rights (OCR) is responsible for enforcing prohibitions against discrimination based on race, sex, handicap and age in Title VI of the Civil Rights Act of 1964, the Age Discrimination Act of 1975, the Rehabilitation Act of 1973, and Title IX of the Education Amendments of 1972. OCR and the Department of Justice have primary responsibility for assuring equal educational opportunity in public schools on a non-discriminatory basis and for assuring that there is no discrimination against either faculty or administrators. Failure to effectively and promptly enforce these laws has subjected the agency to court orders for decades. Staff shortages have been given as the reason for failure to act.

Employment

Title VII of the Civil Rights Act of 1964 prohibits employment discrimination based on race, colour, religion, national origin or sex. Covered employers include those 'persons' with 15 or more employees as well as state and local governments. There are limited exemptions under this and other statutes for private clubs and Indian tribes.

The Equal Employment Opportunity Commission (EEOC) is an independent agency which enforces all aspects of Title VII, except litigation involving state and local governments which is handled by the Department of Justice. The EEOC handles all complaints of employment discrimination and funds many state and local government agencies to investigate and process such cases.

There has been a steady increase in employment discrimination cases filed in federal court from less than 350 in 1970 to roughly 80,000 in 1988. Unpublished data indicate that in 1991 there were a total of 8140 employment discrimination cases filed in federal court and another roughly 100,000 charges of employment discrimination filed with administrative agencies.

Voting Rights

The Voting Rights Act of 1965 was preceded by attempts in the Civil Rights Acts of 1957, 1960 and 1964 which 'depended primarily upon time consuming litigation for enforcement and consequently failed to achieve any significant minority voter registration or office holding'. The Voting Rights Act of 1965 guarantees the right to register and vote without discrimination or intimidation. Under the Voting Rights Act, the Department of Justice is responsible for preventing government officials and private parties from using voting practices to exclude minorities from full participation in the electoral process. Under Section 5 of the Act, certain jurisdictions with overt voting rights discrimination in the past must have any changes to their voting plans cleared by the Justice Department before implementation. Justice can file suit to enforce voting guarantees.

Fair Housing

Title VIII of the Civil Rights Act of 1968 prohibited discrimination based on race, colour, religion, sex or national origin in the sale, rental, advertising or financing of housing. The law was flawed in its grant of only conciliation powers and, in 1988, the Fair Housing Amendments Act provided the federal government with substantially improved enforcement powers, including temporary restraining powers, the right to file suit on behalf of aggrieved parties in federal court, and the right to impose substantial monetary damages on defendants.

Although further and more powerful enforcement provisions were granted to the US Department of Housing and Urban Redevelopment (HUD) in 1988, giving complainants access to free attorneys, the new law's benefits have not yet generated substantial interest in filing grievances against housing market actors (such as real estate agents). The number of cases is still substantially less than those in the employment arena. There were approximately 4500 complaints of housing discrimination a year up until the enactment of the new fair housing amendments which took effect in spring 1989. Of these almost 90 percent were from Afro-Americans. Under the new law, there have been roughly 8000 to 10,000 complaints in the last several years, of which roughly half were based on race.

Mortgage Market Discrimination

In addition to the Fair Housing Act, the Equal Credit Opportunity Act of 1974 (ECOA) prohibits discrimination in credit transactions based on race, colour, national origin, sex, martial status, age or derivation of parts or all of one's income from public assistance. The Act assigns administrative enforcement responsibility to twelve different federal agencies. The Department of Justice is responsible for litigation involving alleged violations of ECOA.

Disability

The Americans with Disability Act (ADA), signed into law in July 1990, covers persons with physical or mental impairments which limit a major life activity, and persons who have a record of such impairments. Under the Act, major life activities include walking, working, seeing, hearing, learning, breathing, performing manual tasks, and caring for oneself. There have been over 35,000 charges filed with the EEOC to date but a large proportion of these cases have been closed for administrative reasons or because no reasonable cause has been found.

CIVIL RIGHTS ENFORCEMENT

Political pressures as well as unstated or latent assumptions in the 'legal culture' of each country, and a myriad of other factors, have affected the formulation and implementation of anti-racist policies in the US. Some part of the implementation process has been affected by public opinion which typically is hesitant about the role of the federal government in enforcing civil rights laws and remedies.

Central to the enforcement paradigms, in both countries, is the decision that civil rights laws typically address the interests and complaints of *individuals* and only occasionally address broad *systemic* or institutional practices. Each country gives some support to effects-based enforcement in which the prejudice or intentions of the perpetrator are not involved.

In addition to the focus on individual acts of discrimination, several major civil rights laws in the US were initially framed to provide federal agencies with only the ability to talk or 'conciliate' with the offending party, despite the fact that blacks had been pressuring for the enactment of racial rights for decades and following several bouts of massive urban rioting. After their enactment, however, the employment and housing discrimination laws were amended to provide stronger enforcement and penalty powers. In 1988, for example, the US Congress amended the 1968 fair housing law by granting the federal government major new powers to bring suit directly in federal courts and offer major forms of relief to those mistreated.

The new law also permits HUD the authority to initiate its own investigations and complaints without any limits on the targets, methods or remedies sought. The latter systemic or pattern-and-practice authority is the closest to a *carte blanche* in law enforcement which, when coupled with other investigative and testing powers, creates the potential for substantial intervention in local housing and credit markets.

The principal civil rights enforcement agency in the United States is the Department of Justice, which has singular as well as overlapping enforcement authority regarding a number of different statutes. The Office of the Assistant Attorney General for Civil Rights at the Department of Justice, created in 1957, is primarily responsible for investigating and prosecuting violations of federal civil rights criminal and civil statutes.The Department of Justice is responsible for enforcing statutes guaranteeing the right to register and vote without discrimination or intimidation, which includes assigning federal personnel to conduct voter registrations and determine whether changes in voting provisions are discriminatory. They also litigate cases of employment discrimination by public sector employers.

The Department of Justice also has a unit which represents the federal government in school desegregation law suits based on Title IV, other statutory grounds, or on the Constitution. The Housing and Civil Enforcement Division at Justice is responsible for bringing suits involving patterns and practices of discrimination prohibited by the Fair Housing Amendments Act of 1988 and by fair lending statutes. As of 1996, there were an estimated 569 staff, some of whom were working part-time.[8]

The US system has not gone without major criticism. Halpern, among others, argues that by establishing a complex, fragmentary system for federal civil rights enforcement, Congress has limited prospects for integrated, targeted enforcement schemes.[9] The panoply of federal agencies, linked to state enforcement agencies, enforce dozens of civil rights statutes without any significant coordinating framework for educating the public, monitoring the effects of decisions, or deciding on targets for integrated investigations. Individuals are likely to be confused as to where their rights are best, or most logically, protected.[10] The system has also been criticised for being at the mercy of shifting political tolerance for aggressive, systemic enforcement.[11]

There have been intermittent efforts by the Department of Justice to establish coherent investigative strategies in certain areas and to promote communication among various federal agencies. Congress has also occasionally recognised the problem of coordination and designated one or another federal agency as the lead in linking the efforts of others. EEOC, for example has the responsibility for coordinating all federal agencies with equal employment opportunity responsibilities.

On the whole, however, the Department of Justice has effective control over the shape and timing of most major civil rights investigations, cases and policy debates. Their role as prosecutor of individual fair housing Act complaints is an exception to their role in tackling broad patterns and remedies. Their recent use of computer models and statistical analyses, as well as the initiation of their own testing unit, further strengthens their ability to target intent- and effects-based cases. Inevitable political (and resource) constraints, which occur as different political parties impose their broad-gauged policy choices upon civil rights enforcement, risk set-backs, delays and enforcement timidity but do not appear to permanently damage the ability of the government to promote racial equality. The vulnerability of civil rights to shifts in political paradigms or philosophy is not, of course, a comparative anomaly.

In Britain, the first race relations law in 1965 did not include coverage of either housing or employment but was superseded by the 1968 and 1976 Acts which provided for the examination of both 'direct' and 'indirect' forms of housing discrimination. The law also allows for the investigation of discrimination without having an individual complainant and empowers a quasi-governmental agency, the Commission for Racial Equality, to conduct investigations. The law, however, provides few if any sanctions and penalties for continued resistance and is weaker than laws enforced in the UK's Northern Ireland province. It is particularly troublesome that the CRE has initiated so few of their formal investigations in the last ten years.[12]

Given the heterogeneity of the American system for civil rights enforcement, and its relatively long history, is there evidence that it has major impacts? To answer this question, it is possible in the US to rely upon a number of social science and policy assessments of civil rights laws. In addition, there are a modest number of testing or auditing studies of the behaviour of real estate industry personnel and employers which help reveal if the level of measured discrimination in the behaviour of private sector agents has changed after the passage of these laws. It is these analyses to which we turn in an effort to see whether something can be gleaned from the US experience.

HAVE US CIVIL RIGHTS LAWS BEEN EFFECTIVE?

To answer sensibly the most general question of whether the era of civil rights laws has been associated with improvements in the quality and conditions of the lives of African Americans, it is important to appreciate how far African Americans have come in the last several decades. To understand how much change has occurred within the United States it is necessary to go back to the 1940s and into the 1950s when 'America was assumed to be a white country'.[13] A former Supreme Court Justice, for example, described conditions of African Americans living in the South in the early 1950s:

> They could not live where they desired; they could not work where white people worked except in menial positions. ... (They could not use the same restrooms, drinking fountains, or telephone booths. They could not eat in the same restaurants, sleep in the same hotels, be treated in the same hospitals). ... They could not attend the same public schools. ... They were not allowed to vote.[14]

It is, then, possible to describe a number of substantive and symbolic changes which have occurred since those times in order to illustrate improvements, some portion of which are attributable to civil rights reforms.[15] There is clear social science evidence that some of these changes would never have occurred without current civil rights laws. In other arenas there has been partial or limited success.

- A black middle class has arisen and it is no longer the segregated middle class of forty years ago – no longer only composed of Pullman porters, barbers, funeral parlour operators and insurance agents. In 1940, for example, black income was only 39 per cent of whites' while in 1989 in had risen to nearly 70 per cent.[16]
- In 1940, the average life expectancy of blacks was 54 years, it rose to 70 years by 1985, and was at 69.6 years in 1994.
- In 1940 only one in 29 of voting age blacks were registered to vote in the South. Now blacks are very much a part of the nation's political life, occupying thousands of local and appointed offices across the country.
- Desegregation of the military has resulted in 30 per cent of all non-commissioned officers, 11 per cent of all army officers, and 7 per cent of generals being African American (as of 1996).
- More importantly, blacks are 'no longer in the basement of moral discourse in American life'. They have both greater

dignity and greater voice in public affairs – along with an accompanying 'outrage of liberation'.[17]

These broad-scale changes in the American social structure have, of course, occurred for a variety of economic, social and juridical reasons and might well have occurred without the enactment of specific federal statutes. It is then necessary to make use of more carefully targeted evaluations and research data to understand, as far as possible, the causal role of civil rights initiatives in creating positive, or negative, change.

To the question, have US civil rights programmes succeeded or failed, the most sensible answer is that they have done both; some civil rights initiatives have been generally effective while others have had partial achievements, and there are cases where they appear to have failed.[18] The following sections review what is known about these more direct impacts.

EMPLOYMENT DESEGREGATION: LARGELY SUCCESSFUL

Many of the early civil rights statutes enacted were explicitly targeted at patterns of *de jure* segregation and formally approved segregation in the Southern region of the US. In the area of employment discrimination, specific sectors of the economy in the South were targeted for enforcement actions and there is evidence that this targeted enforcement had clear, measurable effects.

The most rigorous research aimed at assessing the power of any civil rights statutes has been the work of Professor James Heckman and his colleagues on employment discrimination. Their research makes use of evidence of changes in the levels of employment and relative wages paid to Afro-Americans and whites over the last seventy years, with particular attention to changes in wages following the enactment of the equal employment statute in 1964.

The research indicates sharp increases in employment and wages in the Southern sections of the US immediately after 1965 and up until the mid-1970s. 'Black relative progress was dramatic in the decade following 1965, particularly in the

South, but virtually non-existent thereafter.' Heckman and Payner carefully examined the effect of Title VII on the textile industry in South Carolina and report that:

> Regression analyses of black employment reveal a structural shift in employment equations that cannot be accounted for by conventional measures of output or the growth in alternative opportunities. There is some evidence of greater black employment in counties that sold more goods to the U.S. government. Both the timing evidence and the regression evidence suggest that government activity played an important role in integrating textiles.[19]

Leonard also provides evidence that, even with weak enforcement, 'affirmative action has been effective in increasing the black male share of employment'.[20]

It is, however, impossible to distinguish the distinctive contributions of equal employment civil rights enforcement provisions as they were administered by the EEOC or the Department of Justice from all the 'noise' of surrounding influences. Heckman and Payner, and Donohue and Heckman, for example, cannot dismiss the possibility that some of the effects on Afro-American labour were also due to the overall tightness of the labour market. Also, changes in aggregate economic statistics do not prove causality since the underlying reasons which helped create the climate for civil rights laws could also have been simultaneously the cause in the rise of Afro-American wages. The substantial migration of Afro-Americans from the south to the north, for example, had clear positive effects on aggregate black incomes.

Following the period of the mid-1970s, an increasing proportion of Title VII cases which were filed in federal courts alleged discrimination in firing rather than hiring and appear to have had negligible effect on aggregate wage or employment patterns. In 1993, for example, one study by Ronald Mincy reported 'significant hiring discrimination against young African American and Hispanic men in three metropolitan areas where indicators of poverty and social distress are high'. Another recent report, by Mark Bendick from the Fair Employment Council of Greater Washington, summarising the use of testers looking for employment discrimination, estimates that nearly 20 (19.4) per cent of African American and 33 per cent of Hispanic job applicants are discriminated against. Jobs that were not formally advertised experienced higher levels – between 33 and 67 per cent. Discrimination was found in jobs ranging from entry level to managerial.[21]

Thus while there has been some aggregate, earlier success, there is continuing evidence of employment discrimination. Recent changes in affirmative action hiring rules have not been enacted for sufficient time to evaluate their impacts on federally funded or private sector employment.

SCHOOL DESEGREGATION: PARTIAL SUCCESS

Some of the most effective solutions to the problems of school segregation and discrimination in the US have been those imposed by federal courts. Federal courts made major efforts to redress the *de jure* segregation of schools in the South and appear to have been effective in reducing the racial isolation of Afro-American students up though 1976. The South and the border states witnessed a gradual reduction in racial segregation; racial isolation has increased in the North-East and is accelerating.

The effect of court-ordered school desegregation extends beyond the simple measurement of racial composition of student enrolments. School desegregation also appears to have modest effects on school performance of Afro-American pupils. It is also clear that many factors and governmental policies have operated to affect the educational performance of Afro-Americans and whites and that it is quite problematic to isolate the distinctive impact of school desegregation within the larger context of policy innovation, budget changes, and other federal interventions aimed at assisting poor and minority students.

African Americans are, with greater frequency, questioning the goal of school or housing integration. Some have argued that:

racial subordination experienced in integrated schools may be more damaging than that experienced in segregated schools. For example, institutionalised white racism may cause disproportionately high discipline and suspension rates for black students.[22]

There has, however, been so little monitoring of – or research on – case settlements established by US courts that it is hard to determine whether and to what extent defendants have fully complied with all aspects of the remedial orders and whether all of the intended benefits from integration have been achieved. A major summary of evidence in this field concluded:

> over the relatively short period from 1970 to 1980, the gap between average academic performance of white and black school children narrowed appreciably. The data suggests that the largest impact was in rural areas. It is not possible to conclude from the evidence that achievement gains of black students are due simply to school desegregation or to programs initiated in the 1960s that were designed to increase educational opportunities for minority students.[23]

CONTINUING HOUSING SEGREGATION: LARGELY A FAILURE?

While housing segregation has declined slightly since the 1980 census, the rate of change has been slow and the causal link to fair housing laws quite uncertain. The index of dissimilarity declined from 69 in 1980 to 65 ten years later, with segregation declining in nearly 200 metropolitan areas over the last decade.[24] There is, however, considerable uncertainty as to the causes of this decline, given that some portion of the decline is due to economic changes, some due to shifts in whites' and African Americans' preferences for integration, and some part due to persisting housing discrimination.

In 1990, George Galster published research evidence on the forms of housing discrimination up through the later 1980s. Using audit data for 1981–88 provided by private fair housing organisations, Galster found, for example, that the average of discrimination in rental cases was 41 per cent. In the sales market, he found an unweighted mean of discrimination of 21 per cent. The audit findings, although variable across cities, revealed that discrimination was most likely to be practised by offering blacks fewer apartments, establishing different application procedures, and providing less courteous treatment. In the sales market, there were differences in the number of homes shown, information provided and qualifying requirements cited.

Galster also reported on those few audits which attempted to measure the level of discrimination over time. While he reports some instances in which the pattern was 'clearly downward', his overall judgement is 'that little substantial change in the nature or incidence of discrimination nation-wide has occurred since 1977.'

CHANGES IN HOUSING DISCRIMINATION SINCE THE FAIR HOUSING AMENDMENTS ACT OF 1988

The above audit data suggest that the 1968 Fair Housing Act did not cause a major change in, or have a measurable impact on, the manner in which rental and sales agents treated African American homeseekers up through the late 1980s. While few blacks were denied outright, there were abundant instances and clear patterns in which blacks were treated differently.

Did, however, the enactment of the 1988 amendments to the Fair Housing Act, with its stronger set of fines and punishments, result in measurable change in the behaviour of rental and sales agents? There is limited information about the post-1988 laws' implementation,[25] although there are a number of audit studies done by private fair housing groups since 1990 which shed some light on the issue of the change or persistence in levels of housing discrimination.

In these audit studies whites are, typically, told about more apartments and it is easier for them to get longer term leases. In some cases whites are offered reductions of half off their rent, while such offers are not extended to African Americans. No racially derogatory remarks were made, making it unlikely that the black person would be aware that they had been treated differently. The use of such testing data are essential, therefore, because 'subtle' forms of mistreatment are not easily seen or felt. Indeed, survey research indicates that only 21 per cent of Afro-Americans and 13 per cent of Hispanics report or believe that discrimination in housing, for example, is a major problem compared with income- and credit-related issues.

Table 7.1   *Incidence of racial discrimination in the Washington, DC, Metropolitan Statistical Area rental market, 1986–97*

Year	No. of Audits	Incidence*
1986	280	49.3
1987	111	46.8
1988	295	28.1
1989	215	54.4
1990	200	54.0
1991	100	48.0
1992	129	40.0
1993	107	39.0
1997	163	35.0

*Incidence refers to the net difference in percentage of audits in which white auditors are favoured over black auditors. Some of these per cents differ from those contained in issued reports because a different method for calculating differences in treatment was used with special tabulations provided by the Fair Housing Council of Greater Washington.

While no nationally representative audit study exists to compare 1989 with 1997 discrimination levels, one agency (in the Washington, DC, metropolitan area) conducted comparably designed audits over the period from 1989 to the present which provide an indication of whether the level of discrimination has changed.[26] Table 7.1 presents data regarding the incidence of racial rental market discrimination for most years between 1986 and 1997.

The data reveal a modest overall decline in the level of measured housing discrimination over the period 1986–97. For the years after full implementation of the Fair Housing Amendments Act, discrimination declined from 54 per cent in 1989 and 1990 to roughly 35 per cent in 1997. It is important to note that the level of discrimination for 1989 was the highest level reported for any of the nine audit studies. If, instead, the benchmark year for comparison was 1988 then the level of discrimination increased from 28 to 35 per cent. There is no information available as to why the measured levels of discrimination fluctuated so markedly between 1988 and 1990.

There is, then, some suggestion, although not careful causal analysis, that both housing discrimination and segregation have declined slightly in the period after the enactment of the 1988 amendments to the fair housing Act. Research currently under-way will, it is hoped, begin the process of documenting how the law has achieved these effects, for whom, and with what long-lasting effects.

It is important to note that although testing studies document still high levels of housing discrimination against blacks, and also Hispanics, relatively few members of these protected classes ever file a formal complaint. Through the 1990s roughly 9000 complaints a year have been received by federal, state and local agencies. There appears to be a wide discrepancy between the incidence of discrimination and complaints.

WHAT EXPLAINS THE SUCCESSES AND FAILURES?

Civil rights programmes appear to achieve their clearest effects when the policy is lodged within a robust, centralised institution such as the armed forces or the Justice department. When mandates are issued to tightly controlled, hierarchical organisations rather than to those which are loosely organised or regulated there appear to be faster and more comprehensive impacts. For example, it has been easier to deal with military units than the diffuse system of locally controlled school boards. It has also been easier to get the well-organised National Association of Realtors to discipline members regarding unequal treatment than the diffuse and poorly managed apartment house owners.

When civil rights helps to 'free' the market from distortions or clear inefficiencies it also appears to have an impact. This includes when markets are freed of their own or their customers' discriminatory preferences so that it is possible and profitable for businesses, such as hotels and restaurants, to take everyone's money without distinction.

It is also clear that civil rights policies succeed when key administrative officials are politically motivated. The American experience suggests that political leadership matters in the formulation and implementation of civil rights.

Civil rights programmes have been less successful when limited or few benefits are achieved at the expense of many. School and housing desegregation are examples of such limited achievements. When costs are not concentrated and when benefits are distributed widely it appears possible to succeed, as in the desegregation of employment opportunities in the South.

Another key to the success of civil rights has been the targeted use of enforcement resources. In the thirty years since the enactment of the major civil rights laws, most analysts agree that the processing of *individual* complaints has yielded little measurable change, large expenditures, and often increasing case backlogs (US Commission 1995), while systemic or pattern-and-practice cases have been influential in setting legal precedent and in altering the behaviour of economic actors for whom large penalties are an obvious cost. Martin MacEwen elaborates:

> The reason legislation in the USA is more effective, particularly with regard to employment, is that there is a hierarchy of controls with the state and federal courts encouraging constructive adaptation, the courts are generally less hidebound by a narrow common law construction of the legislation and are prepared to ditch unhelpful and marginal precedence, and the concept of indirect discrimination has developed more bite through the power of class actions and the heavier resultant penalties. In the United States, therefore, it has become easier and cheaper to obey the law than be threatened with the real costs of remedying an illegal practice as it affects an entire class of litigants rather than merely having to meet the marginal costs borne by an individual litigant.[27]

It is also understood that: 'Laws alone are ineffective when the behaviour they forbid is not confined to a small part of the population, when the behaviour goes on behind closed doors, when the violations are difficult and expensive to prove, and when the penalties are not easy to apply.'[28]

HAVE US AND UK RACE RELATIONS ANYTHING IN COMMON?

Having described US civil rights laws and what is known of their effects, it is necessary to ask whether there are sufficient commonalities between the US and the UK to warrant drawing comparative conclusions or recommendations. Over a decade ago Michael Banton has cautioned in this regard that:

> the United States has pioneered many programmes relevant to policy-making about ethnic equality in Britain; but before attempting to transplant any of them it is necessary to identify the nature of the differences between the two societies so that like may be paired with like.[29]

Some British social scientists conclude that Gunnar Myrdal's 'Americans' dilemma is indeed, and has been for some time, a British dilemma.[30] Other analysts point to notable incomparables, especially the small scale and relative recency of racial immigration and the absence of any constitutional framework comparable to that in the US, upon which to pivot a more aggressive programme of rights and remedies.[31]

In this section, I sketch out those similarities which appear to warrant more careful cross-national policy sensitivity and research so that any cross-breeding of ideas and policies is not unwarranted. The key similarities that may be noted are listed below.

(1) Racial Disadvantages Affect African Americans in Both Countries

For the US, Ian Haney Lopez provides a fairly typical description:

> The race-conscious market screens and selects us for manual jobs and professional careers, red-lines financing for real estate, green-lines our access to insurance, and even raises the price of that car we need to buy. Race permeates our politics. It alters electoral boundaries, shapes the disbursement of local, state, and federal funds, fuels the creation and collapse of political alliances, and twists the conduct of law enforcement. In short, race mediates every aspect of our lives.[32]

While the situation may appear less dramatic for most minorities in the UK, there is clear evidence of a number of striking disadvantages. Small provides one recent overview:

> Discrimination is institutionalised in immigration legislation, and is widespread in every other area of life from

employment to education. ... Blacks were more likely to be unemployed, and if they worked, earn less than non-blacks ... Despite the comparatively favourable pattern of housing integration in England, discrimination has often been at its most rampant, some of the most violent confrontations have occurred, and deep-seated animosities become embedded, as a result of conflict over housing, especially council housing.[33]

Muhammad Anwar, in this collection, also takes note of racial disadvantages, including comparably high levels of employment discrimination, notable levels of housing discrimination based upon the use of testers in 1990, and significant under-representation in government.

(2) The Divergent Attitudes of African Americans and whites in Both Societies

While racial attitudes in the two countries have necessarily had different historical trajectories, there are none the less important similarities in whites understating the degree of active discrimination and blacks feeling more of it.

In the US, whites and African Americans have come to view racial disadvantages in divergent, often diametrically opposed ways. This divergence of views constitutes a potentially fatal flaw in the civic culture (of each society) that endangers sustained public policy commitments for racial justice. For the US, Jennifer Hochschild summarises this issue:

> African Americans increasingly believe that racial discrimination is worsening and that it inhibits their race's ability to participate in the American dream; whites increasingly believe that discrimination is lessening and that blacks have the same chance to participate in the dream as whites.[34]

The legal analyst Richard Delgado elaborates:

> One structural feature of human experience separates people of colour from our white friends, accounting in large part for our differing perceptions in matters of race. This structural feature, which dwarfs almost everything else, is simply stated: white people rarely see acts of blatant or subtle racism, while minority people experience them all the time.[35]

This divergence represents a not insubstantial policy dilemma. For example, recently released research reveals that while 87 per cent of blacks believe that banks and lenders will not loan money to blacks, only 51 per cent of whites feel this way.[36] Should federal policy act to address blacks' perceptions of credit constraint or accept whites' views of ample mortgage funds?

Indeed, a variety of recent research suggests the emergence of new forms of 'symbolic' racism which are less sympathetic to policies of racial integration and affirmative action. A number of social scientists have argued over the last decade that new forms of racism have emerged in the United States, driven by both structural factors and changing sets of attitudes. McConahay, for example, argues that a new form of 'modern racism' has emerged which includes the belief that 'discrimination is a thing of the past because blacks now have the freedom to compete in the marketplace and to enjoy those things they can afford ...'.[37] Gaertner and Dovidio report that 'aversive racism' has replaced old-fashioned red-neck racism and has 'evolved in a new type that is, at least temporarily, resistant to traditional attitude-change remedies that emphasise the evils of prejudice as a means of eliminating racism'.[38] Whites now express a new form of 'racial resentment' which strongly affects their support of civil rights policies and programmes.

Larry Bobo, in a series of papers, provides a careful analytic exposition of the demise of 'Jim Crow racism' and the emergence of what he terms '*laissez-faire*' racism based upon his analysis of recent surveys of racial attitudes. This new form of racism includes a denial by whites that discrimination is a serious societal problem and the belief that blacks' disadvantages are (largely) their own fault. His argument does not, however, imply that the experience of discrimination is likely to improve, and indeed it may worsen:

Laissez Faire Racism involves persistent negative stereotyping of African Americans, a tendency to blame blacks themselves for the black–white gap in socio-economic standing, and resistance to meaningful policy efforts to ameliorate America's racist social conditions and institutions. ... Rather than relying on state enforced inequality as during the Jim Crow era, however, modern racial inequality relies upon the market and informal racial bias to recreate, and *in some instances to sharply worsen, structured racial inequality.*[39] (emphases added)

This latest wave of research highlights the divergence of views held by whites and blacks and suggests limited prospects for civil rights progress until, and if, this ossification of racial choices is redressed. This research is a deeply troubling portrait of how racial divisions can calcify and freeze options for change and improvement.

In Britain racial attitudes appear be mimicking those of the US with the difference that racially identifiable perceptions were at first relatively neutral towards black immigrants. These views changed in the period of the mid-1950s as black immigrants became competitors for scarce resources and were increasingly seen as lower class. By 1967, Elizabeth Burney was concerned enough to warn her fellow countrymen that:

> the habit of prejudice, or the equally insidious habit of expecting others to act prejudicially and taking evasive action accordingly, may be all that is necessary to maintain and reinforce the relationship between coloured minorities and socially underprivileged people. There is not much time to put things right, for a new generation is already entering the vicious cycle.[40]

Social surveys reveal that as of that time, roughly 1964, half (51 per cent) of English respondents said that they would not accept 'coloured' people as neighbours and often felt that it would be better for 'different races to live in separate districts'. The percentage had increased somewhat to 59 per cent by 1981. The fact that roughly 45 per cent of those in England believe that race prejudice is increasing suggests good reason to assume a growing comparability of attitudinal structures, and all they potentially bring with them.

More recently, Small finds that in the UK most whites support the principle of colour-blind meritocracy 'much less in practice than they do on paper', just as their US counterparts. Civil rights policies too are met with 'both legal and administrative resistance'.[41]

In both the US and the UK there appears to be a relatively constant, resistant one-third of the population for whom blacks are the subject of persistent negative stereotyping. The *1986 British Attitudes Report*, for example, indicated that just over one-third of the white population admitted to being prejudiced. This group can form the basis for considerable organised race-based resistance which, in its most militant forms in the US, has the potential for strategic destabilisation of communities.

Despite apparent differences in the level of racial intolerance, the social basis of these prejudiced or racist beliefs appears similar in the two countries. McKay, for example, describes the origins of British racial fears, which include a set of beliefs quite common to those in the US:

> to whites, and certainly to mostly white property interests, all blacks are perceived as a threat to the economic integrity of property and neighbourhoods. They are believed to lower property values and to lack the future-oriented financial prudence of middle-class whites. As a result, middle class blacks are excluded from the large, varied and highly advantaged middle-class housing markets.[42]

Analogous fears have been a part of minority encounters in the United States for roughly a century. Acts of racial violence appear, in both societies, to stem from a mixture of collective status and racial fears coupled with the security that whites are seldom punished for such collective rancour. The opposition, anger and violence associated with substantial levels of immigration has been addressed in different ways in each country, with enough attitudinal similarity to add concern about growing comparabilities.

There exist, therefore, varying levels of racial prejudice and sporadic inter-racial violence in both countries, including scattered instances of brutal racial violence by mainly working class whites against blacks in inner city neighbourhoods – episodes which were conspicuous occurrences in the United States twenty to thirty years ago that now appear 'reproduced' in Britain. The irrational and violent character to such colour-coded judgements, linked to political demagoguery and opportunism, makes them powerful tools in redirecting resources and policies in both countries. If there is a single, striking point of comparability between the two countries it is, then, in the tendency to hate solely because of race.

(3)   Race and Poverty

The third similarity is the linkage between race and concentrated poverty. The landscape of race relations in the US has become inextricably linked to systemic economic disparities whose persistence has created serious obstacles to a race-only solution.[43] The white–black gap in male unemployment, for example, has remained constant for several decades, with blacks experiencing roughly twice the rate of whites. It appears impossible, then, to address the US 'race' problem solely with the machinery of anti-discrimination laws since the problem has its harshest and most intractable forms in concentrated poverty and underclass social behaviour.[44]

The probable evolution of race relations in Britain, with British patterns 'solidifying' into an American style of race prejudice, discrimination, segregation appears a not-unlikely outcome to a number of social researchers. Evidence of decades-long racial isolation and impoverishment of West Indians in a number of major British cities appears to simulate US-style underclass concentrations even at lower levels of density. Banton is among those scholars in England who note that rising black crime and 'transmitted deprivation' could constitute a new political agenda for England.

The reconfiguration of race, poverty, social unrest and anti-social practices, labelled as 'underclass' behaviour, may constitute, although at relatively different scales, the basis for blacks and whites in each country to pull further apart and to render that much more irreconcilable the fissioning of support for further improvement in civil rights enforcement.

(4)   Good Will

A fourth commonality is that blacks in both countries necessarily have to rely on the 'commitment and good will of whites to dissolve prejudice, eliminate discrimination, guarantee legal and civil rights and abolish poverty' since there are no local initiatives which have the ability to serve as an effective alternative.[45]

At the same time, blacks in both societies have a necessary, complementary role.

It is blacks who must take the initiative, suffer the greater pain, define and offer the more creative solutions, persevere in the face of obstacles and paradoxical outcomes, insist that improvements are possible and maintain a climate of optimism concerning the eventual outcome.[46]

(5) Vulnerability of Laws to Reform

A final similarity is the vulnerability of civil rights laws to unintended reform once such laws are proposed for improvement. The US has had a series of increasing innovations and legal improvements to address discrimination but many of them have had to be argued through the judicial system, with all that uncertainty. For many years it was politically hazardous to undertake a reopening of major laws because of the prospect of unintended, 'negative' change. It appears that the UK has been similarly affected in its approach to reform of the Race Relations Act 1976. The political timing of such changes might appear more promising now that a new government has begun the formulation of an agenda for change.

CONCLUSIONS

There are unquestionably many far more qualified than I to answer the question of whether the US and UK have anything substantive in common in the area of race and civil rights enforcement and what, in consequence, the most sensible policy recommendations might be. Small, for example, reports a virtual army of such comparative policy makers:

policies introduced by national and local government to achieve radicalised equality have drawn extensively upon the United States. Substantial parts of the legislative and institutional framework of 'race relations' in England have been begged, borrowed or stolen from the United States, and England has not hesitated to send cohorts of theoreticians and policymakers across, or to invite their counterparts to England. ... In the 1990s we are seeing increasing efforts to learn from the American experience of a multi-cultural workforce. All of this is because many in England – Black and white, policymaker and public – see the policies and practices of the United States as the way forward for achieving 'good race relations'.[47]

My own personal views are centred on the concern that the United Kingdom has not enacted tough civil rights enforcement procedures comparable to those in the US, and is suffering from the unwillingness of prior governments to initiate strengthened civil rights legislation, despite continued requests for its improvement by established civil rights representatives. These recommendations for modest improvements have been made in the face of substantial, growing racial inequalities and persistent prejudice.

Nor have prior governments, or the CRE, evaluated how well the law has worked to achieve its goals. It appears initially sensible to promptly review and decide on recommendations made to the Home Office in the 'Second Review of the Race Relations Act of 1976' by the CRE. The analysis should also include assessing the benefits of retaining the quasi-governmental character of civil rights enforcement, which permits the CRE to be neither fish nor fowl. Is it indeed still appropriate, twenty years after the enactment of the current law, to retain a civil rights policy implemented by an agency operating without the full force, credibility and effectiveness of the government?

It seems reasonable to initiate a major inquiry to ascertain the form and likelihood of a reproduction of racist institutions and patterns occurring in Britain, including a careful empirical examination of the forces associated with crystallising and solidifying British patterns of racial subjugation in comparison with the US. This analysis needs to be accompanied by an independent evaluation of the effectiveness of current civil rights enforcement practices in redressing these problems.

There is another set of issues which need to be sketched in order to appreciate the strengths and weaknesses of anti-discrimination law in the US. The first characteristic is the paradox that civil rights laws are both heavily institutionalised, after thirty years, but also systematically ignored by many of their intended beneficiaries. The US and UK both receive relatively few complaints, with Anwar, in this collection, estimating that there are only roughly 100 complaints a year in the UK. This sign of the disinclination of minorities in both countries to rely upon governmental civil rights agencies is an issue much in need of careful examination and improvement.

The American experience, in my opinion, therefore speaks to four simple principles: (1) the importance of concentrating the power of direct enforcement directly in a central government agency, like the Justice Department, and not marginalising it; (2) the need to gather the most indisputable evidence of discrimination to counter arguments that existing reforms have been adequate; (3) the need to gather and analyse racial and ethnic data about the conditions of protected classes in arenas of social and economic life which are most central to the progress of minorities; and (4) open the Pandora's box of legislative 'reform' judiciously when there is an appropriate level of public support for a fresh start for new, stronger approaches to remedying clear inequities. Otherwise one should fear that the opening may be used to impose unwanted legislative restraints.

(1)   Evaluate the Merits of Concentrating Strengthened Enforcement Powers in a Single Governmental Agency

It can be argued that a strong system of governmentally administered legal enforcement is a necessary, if insufficient, basis for ensuring race equity. Unless the laws are enforceable through the system of courts, and there are meaningful civil and punitive damages, then civil rights appears as window dressing and the sham serves no remedial function when times of stress and riot occur. The converse of this argument is that ineffective methods of enforcement, such as the conciliation powers initially provided to enforce the fair housing Act, do more harm then good in that they discourage belief by victims that the law is reliable and effective.

It would be useful to consider establishing a commission of independent analysts and policy makers to evaluate the benefits to be gained from rooting civil rights enforcement powers within a central government agency with a solid institutional basis which can command a fair share of necessarily limited resources. The power of such an agency to conduct well-regarded pattern-and-practice cases appears essential for efficient success in changing white institutional patterns of racial subordination.

Such strong, centralised enforcement capability provides the teeth in a system which also relies upon voluntary compliance and cooperation in creating effective remedial orders. Voluntarism without the threat of credible punishment has been shown to be clearly ineffective in the US. Speaking of the Race Relations Act, MacEwen comments:

> perhaps, its most significant weakness remains its failure to impose sanctions which are strong enough to force major employers and service providers to review their practices in order to secure compliance.[48]

(2)   Continually Measure the Forms and Level of Discrimination

Testing job, housing, and credit markets appears an indispensable basis for demonstrating the level – virulence – of racist practices and for estimating the costs of discrimination to the average citizen – white or black – of either country. Such evidence has been used by numerous analysts to great policy advantage.[49] In the US, the Justice Department's own testing programme is growing and there are plans to fund the design for an ongoing panel of tests in multiple markets, over many issues, so that there is a permanent monitoring tool for national and local civil rights policies.

The atrophying of the use of testing in the UK by governmental agencies in recent years suggests the benefits from examining both the US Justice Department's testing programme as well as proposals to institute ongoing testing of multiple issues as a method of rigorous monitoring. Policy makers in the UK cannot, at this point, rely upon current limited evidence to prove whether, to what degree, and for whom active forms of discrimination are most prevalent. Testing data from years past suggest the presence of a virulent disease but without more current information there appears no sensible means of prescribing improved remedies.

(3)   Racial and Ethnic Monitoring Data Should Be Required of Public and Private Sector Agencies

The UK has succeeded in having ethnic monitoring done by the police and there appears clear momentum to make stiffer requirements for the private sector.

In addition, employers, bankers and others should make this information available to all parties upon request. I understand that the compulsory requirement of such data gathering will appear intrusive and costly. However, until the government has complete and accurate information on the actual distribution of racial opportunities in major sectors of British life, no one can be sure what remedies and what policies are most needed, including those corporations inclined to develop racially and ethnically sensitive outreach to new markets. The US experience suggests that employers find that it is in their clear interest to understand both the racial and ethnic composition of their workforce but also more about the race of the markets they serve; market share analyses using race are becoming quite standard for banks.

Such monitoring should also be tied to continuing independent evaluations of the performance of government civil rights enforcement efforts. In the US, there has been evaluation or assessments of the Reagan, Bush and Clinton administrations' records on civil rights by a Citizen's Commission on Civil Rights, as well as major evaluations of fair housing and Title VI by the independent US Commission on Civil Rights.[50]

(4)   Beware Opening the Pandora's Box of Legislative 'Reform' for Fear that the Opening May Be Used to Impose Unwanted Legislative Restraints

Opposition forces will readily attempt to extract their own pound of flesh once they see the opportunity to press home an anti-race quota or anti-big government message.

Collaterally, there is a need for continuing dialogue about the place of race, class and subordination in each of our societies – because law enforcement mechanisms will always fall short in creating effective civil discourse and full citizenship. It is only through such civilising debate and reasoned discourse that it will be possible to reduce what one observer calls the 'acid rain of white racism' in contemporary America – and Britain.[51]

In brief, there is a need for an understanding of the structural basis for racism in each society that will permit a clearer view of how much of the problem is a matter of perceptions and beliefs and how much is more deeply rooted. The recent decision by the US President to establish a commission on racial reconciliation is one necessary step in building support for such fundamental change.

ACKNOWLEDGEMENTS

The author would like to thank many colleagues in Great Britain for their courtesy and cooperation in providing comments, suggestions and research reports addressing many different aspects of the racial housing issue. Without their cooperation this paper would not have been possible. In particular, I would like to express my appreciation to Michael Banton, Ceri Peach, Valerie Karn, Peter Ratcliff and Colin Hann. In the US, I would like to thank Douglas Massey, Joe Feagin, George Galster, John Yinger, David Berenbaum and Reynolds Farley. All of the mistakes, omissions and failures of insight contained herein are exclusively my own doing.

NOTES

1. This discussion does not extend to include an analysis of the political, legislative and historical background of these laws which would highlight the fundamental provisions and compromises inherent in each.
2. Stephen Small, *Racialized Barriers: The Black Experience in the United States and England in the 1980s* (New York: Routledge, 1994).
3. Muhammed Anwar, 'What Impact has Race Relations Legislation Made on British Race Relations?', paper presented at the Conference 'From Legislation to Integration?' held at the University of Warwick, Coventry in September 1996.
4. US Commission on Civil Rights (1994), the Fair Housing Amendments Act of 1988: the Enforcement Report (September) (Washington, DC: GPO, 1995); Funding Federal Civil Rights Enforcement (June) (Washington, DC: US Commission on Civil Rights, 1996); Federal Title VI Enforcement to Ensure Nondiscrimination in Federally Assisted Programs (June) (Washington, DC: US Commission on Civil Rights).
5. See note 1 above.
6. 'It is hereby declared to the policy of the President that there shall be equality of treatment and opportunity of all persons in the armed services without regard to race, color, religion or national origin. This policy shall be put into effect as rapidly as possible, having due regard to

the time required to effectuate any necessary changes without impairing efficiency or morale' (*Federal Register*, 28 July 1948, p. 4313).

7. In 1987, Congress passed the Civil Rights Restoration Act which declared that Title VI covers the entire operation of the federally funded recipient and not solely the particular programme receiving federal funds. This was enacted to offset a Supreme Court decision in the *Grove City College* v. *Bell* case. There are several other federal statutes which also prohibit discrimination in any programme receiving federal financial assistance, including Section 109 covering HUD's community development programs.

8. Congress, for example, provides funding to both the EEOC and HUD to fund identical state and local fair employment and fair housing agencies. No principles are established for the coordinated training of investigators, or provisions to identify weaknesses in one enforcement scheme that may effect the other. Some state agencies argued that because they got higher levels of funding for complaint processing from the EEOC that HUD's fair housing cases were necessarily secondary. After HUD increased its level of funding for housing cases the reverse criticism has been made. There are also no requirements in place that address the linkages between housing and school desegregation actions.

9. Stephen Halpern, 'Title VI Enforcement', pp. 137–56, in Tinsley Yarbrough (ed.), *The Reagan Administration and Human Rights* (New York: Praeger, 1985).

10. See note 8 above.

11. Corrine Yu and William Taylor, *New Challenges: The Civil Rights Record of the Clinton Administration Mid-Term* (Washington, DC: Citizen's Commission on Civil Rights, 1995).

12. Anwar, 'What Impact has Race Relations Legislation Made on British Race Relations?'; Martin MacEwen, *Tackling Racism in Europe: An Examination of Anti-Discrimination Law in Practice* (Oxford: Berg Publishers, 1995).

13. Orlando Patterson, 'The Paradox of Integration', *The New Republic*, 213 (6 November 1995), pp. 24–7.

14. Gerald Jaynes and Robin Williams (eds), *A Common Destiny: Blacks and American Society* (Washington, DC: National Academy Press, 1989), pp. 40–2.

15. The exact causal role of other concurrent forces cannot be accurately measured. Jaynes and Williams list five factors involved in the transformation but state that civil rights 'perhaps more than any single event' caused the new institutional changes.

16. Jaynes and Williams, *A Common Destiny*.

17. Patterson 'The Paradox of Integration'.

18. The absence of good evaluations and thorough social science research makes this a hazardous undertaking. I am indebted to conversations with Professor Jennifer Hochschild, of Princeton University, as well as her 1996 conference paper for helping me understand the best means to categorise civil rights achievements. I have borrowed from her work and acknowledge my great debt. See Jennifer Hochschild, ' "You win some, you lose some ..." ': Explaining the Patterns of Success and Failure in the

Second Reconstruction', paper presented at the annual meeting of the American Sociological Association, 19 August 1996 New York.

19. J. Heckman and B. Payner, 'Determining the Impact of Anti-Discrimination Policy on the Economic Status of Blacks: A Study of South Carolina', *The American Economic Review*, 79 (1989) pp. 138–77.

20. Jonathan Leonard, 'The Impact of Affirmative Action Regulation and Equal Employment Law on Black Employment', *Journal of Economic Perspectives*, 4 (Fall 1990) pp. 47–63.

21. Ronald Mincy, 'The Urban Institute Audit Studies: Their Research and Policy Context', in Michael Fix and Raymond Struyk (eds), *Clear and Convincing Evidence: Measurement of Discrimination in America* (Washington, DC: The Urban Institute Press, 1993). Mark Bendick, *Discrimination Against Racial/Ethnic Minorities in Access to Employment in the United States: Empirical Findings from Situation Testing*, International Migration Paper 12, Employment Department (Geneva: International Labour Office, 1996).

22. Lisa Stewart, 'Another in Skirmish in the Equal Education Battle', in *Harvard Civil Rights – Civil Liberties Law Review*, 28 (1993), pp. 217–36.

23. Jaynes and Willliams, *A Common Destiny*.

24. Reynolds Farley and William H. Frey, 'Changes in the Segregation of Whites from Blacks during the 1980s: Small Steps toward a More Integrated Society', *American Sociological Review*, 59 (February 1994) pp. 23–45.

25. US Commission (1994; 1995). See note 4, above.

26. One private fair housing organisation operating in New Jersey reported that the results of over 1500 investigative tests (those driven by specific complaints) reveal evidence of discrimination in 75 per cent of the cases in the years 1990–91. That level declined only slightly to 70 per cent in 1995–6.

27. MacEwen, *Tackling Racism in Europe*.

28. Barbara Bergmann, *In Defense of Affirmative Action* (New York: Basic Books, 1996), p. 169.

29. Michael Banton, 'Transatlantic Perspectives on Public Policies Concerning Racial Disadvantage', *New Community*, II (Spring 1984) pp. 280–87.

30. See Jaynes and Williams, *A Common Destiny*, p. 4; MacEwen, *Tackling Racism in Europe*, pp. 157–9; Small, *Racialized Barriers*, p. 12.

31. David McKay, *Housing and Race in Industrial Society: Civil Rights and Urban Policy in Britain and the United States* (London: Croom Helm, 1977).

32. Ian Haney Lopez, 'The Social Construction of Race: Some Observations on Illusion, Fabrication, and Choice', *Harvard Civil Rights – Civil Liberties Law Review*, 29 (1994) pp. 3–63.

33. Small, *Racialized Barriers*, pp. 162–3.

34. Jennifer Hochschild, *Facing up to the American Dream: Race, Class and the Soul of the Nation* (Princeton, NJ: Princeton University Press, 1955), p. 55.

35. Richard Delgado, 'Rodrigos Eighth Chronicle: Black Crime, White Fears – On the Social Construction of Threat', *Virginia Law Review*, 80 (March 1994) pp. 503–48.

36. Reynolds Farley, 'Racial Differences in the Search for Housing: Do Whites and Blacks use the Same Techniques to Find Housing?', *Housing Policy Debate*, 7 (1996) pp. 367–86.

37. John McConahay, 'Modern Racism, Ambivalence and the Modern Racism Scale', in John Dovidio and Samuel Gaertner (eds), *Prejudice, Discrimination, and Racism* (New York: Academic Press, 1986), pp. 91–125.

38. Dovidio and Gaertner, *Prejudice, Discrimination and Racism*, pp. 85–6.

39. Larry Bobo, James Kruegel and Ryan Smith, 'Laissez Faire Racism: The Crystallization of a "Kinder, Gentler" Anti-Black Ideology', Russell Sage Working Paper No. 98 (New York: Russell Sage Foundation).

40. Elizabeth Burney, *Housing on Trial* (London: Oxford University Press, 1967).

41. Small, *Racialised Barriers*, p. 163.

42. McKay, *Housing and Race in Industrialial Society*, p. 175.

43. See, for example, William J. Wilson, *The Truly Disadvantaged* (Chicago: University of Chicago, 1987).

44. See, for example, Wilson, *The Truly Disadvantaged*, and Hochschild, *You Win Some, You Lose Some*.

45. Michael Banton, 'Transatlantic Perspectives on Public Policies Concerning Racial Disadvantage'.

46. Patterson, 'The Paradox of Integration'.

47. Small, *Racialized Barriers*.

48. MacEwen, *Tackling Racism in Europe*, p. 171.

49. For example, Bergmann, *In Defence of Affirmative Action* pp. 50–2; John Yinger, *Closed Doors, Opportunities Lost: The Continuing Costs of Housing Discrimination* (New York: Russell Sage Foundation, 1995); John Goering and Ron Wienk, *Mortgage Lending, Racial Discrimination, and Federal Policy* (Washington, DC: The Urban Institute Press, 1996) pp. 589–617.

50. Yu and Taylor, *New Challenges: The Civil Rights Record of the Clinton Administration Mid-Term*.

51. Joe Feagin and Melvin Sikes, *Living with Racism: The Black Middle Class Experience* (Boston, Mass: Beacon Press, 1994).

8 Strategic Vision in Combating Racial Discrimination
Michael Banton

In 1919 the United Kingdom opposed the Japanese proposal to include in the Covenant of the League of Nations a statement of the principle of racial equality. In 1944 it resisted a similar proposal from China concerning the Charter of the United Nations.[1] It is therefore noteworthy that in 1969 it was so quick to accede to the International Convention on the Elimination of All Forms of Racial Discrimination. Only one West European state deposited an instrument of ratification of this convention earlier than the UK. The new stance may have been associated with the ending of empire. So long as the UK was a colonial power it probably saw any question of accepting such a principle as a matter of foreign (or commonwealth) policy. By the late 1960s that had changed. The UK experienced substantial labour immigration from Third World countries earlier than other European countries. The new settlers entered as British citizens with the expectation that their equal citizenship would be acknowledged; this distinguished their situation from that of immigrants to countries where they were counted as aliens. The UK had benefited from bipartisan political leadership on the issues and an accumulation of social research which, though it may not have borne directly upon the 1969 decision, was educating the public in the nature of racial discrimination as a domestic and everyday problem.

Within a democratic country, progress in combating racial discrimination depends significantly upon strategic vision, and the ability of a political élite to utilise whatever opportunities arise in the course of events in order to translate that vision into policy. In the foreseeable future those opportunities are as likely to arise in connection with the United Nations or with European developments as with domestic events, so this essay discusses the former first. Other advances can stem from the strategic enforcement of the available law, such as when the Commission for Racial Equality conducts formal investigations under section 49(1) of the 1976 Act or, discharging its duties under section 66 (1 & 2), selects some cases rather than others for assistance in bringing proceedings.[2] Any selection must depend upon an appreciation of the potentialities within the existing law, so the essay then turns to a criticism of the House of Lords judgment in the leading case of *Mandla* v. *Dowell Lee* in order to contend that the scope of the 1976 Act for protecting Muslims has not been exhausted and that advances are possible without the introduction of any new legislation.

THE INTERNATIONAL VISION

The International Convention on the Elimination of All Forms of Racial Discrimination (ICERD), adopted by the UN General Assembly in December 1965, aims 'to build an international community free from all forms of racial segregation and racial discrimination'. Its preambular paragraphs recognise two causes of racial discrimination: 'colonialism and all practices of segregation and discrimination associated therewith' and the dissemination of doctrines of superiority based on racial differentiation. These paragraphs represent racial discrimination as a political pathology and refer three times to the desirability and possibility of 'speedily' eliminating it. Yet the first substantive paragraph, which has the legal consequences, defines racial discrimination quite differently. Borrowing from an International Labour Organisation convention designed for regulating interpersonal relations in the workplace, it runs as follows:

> the term 'racial discrimination' shall mean any distinction, exclusion, restriction or preference based on race, colour, descent, or national or ethnic origin which has the purpose or effect of nullifying or impairing the recognition, enjoyment or exercise, on an equal footing, of human rights and fundamental freedoms in the political, economic, social, cultural or any other field of public life.

Thus it represents racial discrimination as resembling a crime rather than a sickness. Note also that it restricts its prohibition to fields of *public* life.

The definition covers actions with a discriminatory 'purpose or effect' (that is, what is now called direct and indirect discrimination); and makes it possible to decide whether an individual's human rights have been impaired. It recognises two important exceptions. One is to exclude the power of governments to differentiate between the rights of citizens and non-citizens; the other is to allow them to introduce the kinds of measure that have been called 'positive action', described in the Convention as special measures for the advancement of groups to ensure their equal enjoyment of rights, with the qualification that these may not be continued after their objectives have been achieved.

The text of the Convention reflects some of the assumptions that were current in the UN at the time, like the way colonialism was charged with responsibility for racial discrimination, but these assumptions also made the Convention possible. Its adoption was providential, for if discrimination had been seen, like crime, as a normal social phenomenon, then no governments would have wanted to draft a convention against it. What matters now is that 153 states have undertaken extensive legislative and administrative obligations as parties to the Convention. Twenty-five of them have accorded the right of individual petition, and the UK is currently considering whether it should do likewise. In that event anyone who believes that the government has failed to protect his or her rights under the Convention will be able to refer the case for review in Geneva. The Convention is an important part of the UN's framework for guaranteeing the right of everyone to enjoy human rights and fundamental freedoms.

The central component of that framework is the International Bill of Human Rights, which includes the Universal Declaration of Human Rights and the two covenants. Within the International Covenant on Civil and Political Rights, Article 27 stipulates that:

> In those States in which ethnic, religious or linguistic minorities exist, persons belonging to such minorities shall not be denied the right, in community with other members of their group, to enjoy their own culture, to profess and practice their own religion, or to use their own language.

The rights recognised in this article are not very extensive. Even so, they are sometimes circumscribed by individual states.

The French government, which accorded resident foreigners the right of association only in 1981, has declared that no such minorities exist in France. Under German law only a group of citizens of the same origin and living in the same area is considered a minority. So while the persons of Danish origin near the frontier with Denmark constitute a minority, Jews do not, and most persons of Turkish origin are accounted aliens rather than as members of a minority.[3]

Limited though they may be, these agreements constitute the best available framework for policy in an increasingly interdependent world. That interdependence poses ever-new problems. A recent newspaper article described how a company had moved production of plastic bags from Telford, in Britain, to Xin Hui, in China, for a saving in cost of between one-third and one-quarter of a penny per bag.[4] When a factory makes 21 million bags per week, such a saving can be important. There are now very few people in Hong Kong working in manufacturing industry, but 150 million in south-eastern China. Singapore farms work out to Bangladesh and India. Globalisation means that production moves to wherever labour is cheapest. While the money saved by making plastic bags in Xin Hui could be used to ease restructuring in Telford, any such development is improbable because people make short-term choices with insufficient information about who will bear the costs and what will be the likely long-term consequences. Globalisation destroys old solidarities; it weakens the sense of belonging in local communities, and it transforms people's conceptions of identity. If present trends continue there are likely to be major increases in social inequality as the fortunate members of society pursue their individual interests. In the United States the effects of continuing globalisation will not eliminate the differentiation of African-Americans as a hyphenated group within US society because that has such deep historical roots, but those effects will militate against any increase in black solidarity in Britain.

If any vision of a future with less racial discrimination is to be a strategic vision, one capable of realisation, it will have to reinforce current procedures for state reporting under the Convention, extend the right of individual petition, and balance the sovereignty of states against the constraints that globalisation imposes.

THE EUROPEAN VISION

European countries led the movement for human rights, yet the spectre of Nazism hangs over them as a crushing historical reproach. They failed to protect the rights of people in Yugoslavia and they have the greatest difficulty agreeing a common approach whenever there is any conflict between their shared ideals and their national interests. The Council of Europe and the Organisation for Security and Cooperation in Europe have required states which seek to join these organisations to observe certain human rights standards, but they have not been able to exert much pressure upon states that are already members.

Since 1984 concern has been expressed within the European Parliament about the revival of fascism and the increase in xenophobia. There is a desire to progress towards a 'Europe with a moral dimension' which will require a Directive to enable the Commission and the Court of Justice to act against racial discrimination in a manner paralleling their action against sex discrimination. Member states have agreed that they will act, separately and in cooperation, to punish incitement to racial hatred and participation in the activities of groups which promote such hatred.[5] At the 1997 Amsterdam meeting of the intergovernmental Council it was agreed that the Treaty of European Unity be amended to empower the Council to act against racial discrimination, but any proposal for action will require the support of all 15 governments.

As can be seen from the European Year Against Racism, the vision is still a negative one of removing a political pathology rather than a positive one of promoting equal opportunities and equal participation in social life. Nor has there yet been any effective action against everyday discrimination. The denial that there are minorities in France, and the restricted conception in Germany, are reminders that the European conception of the integration of immigrants from overseas is still narrow and individualistic. Sweden and the Netherlands have been unusual in their readiness to recognise Third World immigrants as forming communities, and to help them maintain distinctive cultures if they wish, but both these countries have recently revised their policies to put more stress on individual freedom of choice and to move closer to an emergent European outlook.

The UK's experience in this field has much to offer the development of European policy.

THE BRITISH VISION

The British vision was implicit in the 1950s bills which never reached the statute book, in Roy Hattersley's speeches of 1964, the subsequent White Paper, the often-quoted 1966 address by Roy Jenkins, and the Acts of 1965, 1968 and 1976. Based upon a shared citizenship, it tried to ensure that everyone would be protected from racial discrimination – black, brown, white and yellow.[6] The Community Relations Commission, and the Commission for Racial Equality, were to be for everyone, not just for ethnic minorities.

The UK's Thirteenth periodic report under ICERD, dated April 1995, declared that

> It is a fundamental objective of the United Kingdom Government to enable members of ethnic minorities to participate freely and fully in the economic, social and public life of the nation, with all the benefits and responsibilities which that entails, while still being able to maintain their own culture, traditions, language and values. Government action is directed towards addressing problems of discrimination and disadvantage which prevent members of ethnic minorities from fulfilling their potential as full members of British society.[7]

The Runnymede Trust observed approvingly that 'this statement valuably stresses two main goals – cultural pluralism and full participation in society – and succinctly summarises what may be called a "multi-ethnic good society".'[8] The reader should pause and reflect upon these words because the expression 'cultural pluralism' is of uncertain meaning. What the Government's statement emphasises is, firstly, participation with its attendant rights and responsibilities, and then, secondly, approval for groups to maintain distinctive practices provided they do not conflict with others' rights or derogate from their members' responsibilities. The Jews, the Irish and the Gypsies are presumably precedents. The Government's statement does not authorise the expression 'multi-ethnic society'. By its very silence about any name suggesting that it aims for a kind of society different from that before the settlement of New Commonwealth immigrants, the statement illustrates the difficulty of formulating a strategic vision that might guide the efforts of those who want to move on from the negative goal of preventing discrimination.

Most countries have written constitutions, and these often provide guidance on the rights and responsibilities of citizens and non-citizen residents. The British constitution is not written, which has both advantages and disadvantages, but this makes it the more instructive to examine in detail a policy statement like the one just quoted. Participation in the 'social and public life of the nation', followed by the reference to the freedom of groups to maintain characteristic practices, suggests a differentiation of a public realm and a private one. Yet such a division is bridged by the Church of England which, as the established church, exercises important public functions while organising and expressing the private faith of its members. Any strategic vision for the future will have to address the difficult question of whether a line is to be drawn between the public and private spheres, and, if so, whether other religions should also be seen as bridging the division.

NEW TIMES, NEW PROBLEMS

Roy Jenkins in 1966 was reacting to the issues posed by the settlement of immigrants from the Caribbean rather than from Pakistan, and he was influenced by his knowledge of developments in the United States where African-Americans posed a special challenge. Put simply, he did not perceive the distinctive implications of the growth of a Muslim minority. Later, alarmed by the threats to Salman Rushdie, he wrote that 'In retrospect we might have been more cautious about allowing the creation in the 1950s of substantial Muslim communities here ...' He went on to echo recent writing about citizenship as requiring the consent of both the state and the citizen, observing 'Not the least advantage of having a written constitution is that under it such an obligation [to accept British tolerance] would be explicit ... we can at least proclaim that an acceptance of British law and of British liberties is expected by all who wish to live in this country.'[9]

In its comments on the UK's Thirteenth Report, the
Runnymede Trust referred to a growth in anti-Muslim sentiment. Hostility towards Muslims may have appeared in some
localities, and there may be some incidents which can properly
be described as Islamophobia, but there are genuine political
conflicts which cannot be equated with street-corner prejudices.
Two implications of the growth of a Muslim minority deserve
particular mention. Firstly, with the collapse in Marxism, Islam
has become the richest source of inspiration for movements
critical of prevailing regimes. In the Middle East and in Asia
electoral support for Islamic political parties has increased
because of popular dissatisfaction with governmental corrup-
tion and inattention to popular needs. In Europe, Islam inspires
the strongest criticisms of family breakdown, sexual immoral-
ity, the neglect of the elderly, and the materialism associated
with consumer capitalism. Any society needs criticism, and one
rooted in religion can be more thorough-going than one based
on social science.

Secondly, and very importantly, a Muslim cannot accept the
separation of the public and private spheres and the
confinement of religion within the latter. In Islam there is no
distinction between the secular and the spiritual, the sacred
and the profane.[10] 'Render unto Caesar the things which are
Caesar's' maybe, but only if the rendering is sanctioned by religious law.

France and the USA have, in their constitutions, attempted
to separate church and state. France declares itself a secular
republic which respects all faiths. The Bill of Rights in the USA
stipulates that 'Congress shall make no law respecting an
establishment of religion ...'. Yet these provisions have not kept
religion out of politics. The French delimitation is challenged
even by so trivial an incident as a girl coming to school wearing
a Muslim head-scarf. The controversy over the legality of abor-
tion can affect the outcome of a US presidential election.

An underlying issue, in both Christianity and Islam, is the
interpretation of sacred texts. There are theologians who ask,
'If God spoke in these words to the people of that time, what
should they mean to us in our time?' Are the texts to be read
literally or in a historical context? Jesus and Muhammad
addressed some of the problems of the societies of their own
day; how should their teaching be applied to the problems of a

later age? It sometimes seems today as if proportionately more Muslims than Christians favour a literal reading of their scriptures, but this may reflect only recent political and doctrinal shifts. One of the most significant *hadiths* (or traditions) says that 'Every verse of the Qur'an has seven levels of meaning'. Every faith which relies on sacred texts must have problems in interpreting them. A simple example of the room for interpretation in Islam concerns the method for calculating the hours of fasting in Ramadan. Most Muslims maintain that the fast should end with the appearance of the moon in the believer's country of residence, but a minority within Islam believes that it may end at the time when the moon appears in Mecca.

How the sacred texts are to be interpreted is particularly important if a faith is to help guide young people facing pressures and choices which may be new even to their parents. When a religious group imports its teachers from seminaries overseas which interpret its scriptures literally and do not understand the local conditions, the new generations may continue to identify themselves with that religion because of the social oppositions in their environment, but they will not draw upon the full resources of their faith.[11]

Roy Jenkins' argument for a written constitution was repeated from a Muslim standpoint by Modood when he wrote:

> the greatest psychological and political need for clarity about a common framework and national symbols comes from the minorities. For clarity about what makes us willingly bound into a single country relieves the pressure upon minorities, especially new minorities whose presence within the country is not fully accepted, to have to conform in all areas of social life, or in arbitrarily chosen areas, in order to rebut the charge of disloyalty. It is the absence of comprehensively respected national symbols in Britain, comparable to the constitution and the flag in America, that allows politicians unsympathetic to minorities to demand that they demonstrate loyalty by doing x or y or z, like supporting the national cricket team in Norman Tebbit's famous example.[12]

One criticism of the Race Relations Act 1976 is that while it provides remedies to Sikhs and Jews who are victims of indirect discrimination on grounds of race, it does not give equal protection to Muslims. Some infer that new legislation is therefore necessary, but it may be too early to draw any such conclusion. The protection of Sikhs derives from case-law, from the courts' interpretation of the statute, not from any mention of Sikhs in the Act. The courts might yet be brought to interpret the Act in a manner which gives equal protection to Muslims. The reasoning on this point has to be complex because some of the law on racial discrimination is shared with the law on sex discrimination. The issues in respect of the English law of blasphemy are very different, but the reasoning which permits the Sikhs to be differentiated as an ethnic rather than a religious group has a bearing upon this issue also.

INDIRECT DISCRIMINATION

A perhaps audacious contention underlying the first point in the argument is that the case of *Mandla* v. *Dowell Lee* was wrongly decided by a unanimous House of Lords.[13] It turns on the phrase 'group of persons' in the definition of 'racial group' in section 3 of the Act; but it also raises a question about the extent to which the criteria for determining indirect discrimination may be independent of those for direct discrimination.

The second point also arises in the law on sex discrimination. In *James* v. *Eastleigh Borough Council* the House of Lords reaffirmed that 'whether a person was afforded less favourable treatment than another because of his sex was a matter to be determined objectively' (and not by reference to any subjective intention or motive).[14] In cases of sex discrimination, indirect discrimination can be separated from direct discrimination in this way because gender grouping is unidimensional. A set of individuals who suffer sex discrimination share the common attribute of gender, but they do not necessarily share any other attribute. By contrast, an ethnic group is multidimensional. For a set of individuals to constitute an ethnic group they must, according to the House of Lords decision in the *Mandla* case, share some common attributes of historical memory and cultural tradition plus, possibly, language, literature, religion, and so on. When questioned about his refusal of a place to Mandla junior, the headmaster wrote that 'the boy was not rejected because he was a Sikh since we do not make racial distinctions and we have several Sikhs in the school. It was the turban that was rejected, and I believe your Acts cover people, not clothes.' In the House of Lords Lord Fraser observed that

> When the present proceedings began in the county court, direct discrimination was alleged, but the judge held that there had been no direct discrimination, and his judgement on that point was not challenged in the Court of Appeal or before your Lordships' House. The appellants' case in this House was based entirely on indirect discrimination ...

The headmaster's motives were therefore regarded as irrelevant, but it was still his action that should have been the Court's focus of attention, and not the character of the ethnic minority.

The main question in the *Mandla* appeal to the Lords was whether Sikhs were a 'racial group'. The Act specifies five classes of persons who can constitute such a group; four of them could be set aside, so the appeal concentrated upon the definition of 'a group of persons defined by reference to ... ethnic ... origins'. The House of Lords concluded that the 'ethnic origins' of the Sikhs brought them within the definition of a 'racial group', but they found little relevance in the religious differences between the Sikh group and the ethnic majority. The headmaster would not permit an exception to the school rules about uniform on the grounds of religion; he had admitted other Sikh boys who did not wear turbans. (Incidentally, Mr Mandla senior would not have pursued his application to the school had he known that, if admitted, his son would have been expected to attend classes in the Christian faith.)[15]

Speaking for the whole court, Lord Fraser concurred with the remarks of a judge in the New Zealand Court of Appeal who had said that 'The real test is whether the individuals or the group regard themselves and are regarded by others in the community as having a particular historical identity in terms of their colour or their racial, national or ethnic origins.' Those words are close to the British Act's definition of a racial group as *a group of persons*, but Lord Fraser departed from them when he dropped the reference to *persons* and stated that 'For a group to constitute an ethnic group in the sense of the 1976 Act, it must, in my opinion, regard itself, and be regarded by others, as a distinct community by virtue of certain characteristics.' The necessary attributes were '(1) a long-shared history, of which the group is conscious as distinguishing it from other groups, and the memory of which it keeps alive; (2) a cultural tradition of its own, including family and social customs and manners, often but not necessarily associated with religious observance.' Five more 'relevant' but not essential attributes were then listed.

The expression 'a group of persons' allows for the multi-dimensionality of ethnic grouping and the way that individuals may belong to the same group for some purposes and to different groups for other purposes. The expression 'a distinct community' has no statutory justification; it changes the emphasis and implies that if a person is a member of the community for one purpose he is a member of it for very many other purposes. Its adoption in the *Mandla* judgment led to an incorrect interpretation of the statute.

The court had to decide whether the headmaster had applied to Mandla junior a condition 'which he applies or would apply equally to persons not of the same racial group' as the Mandlas. In deciding that Sikhs were a racial group, the House of Lords treated section 1(1)(b) of the Act as if it were separate from the earlier part of the section. In defining the class of persons entitled to a remedy against indirect discrimination, the judges concentrated on defining the criteria for a group of persons to constitute an ethnic group without attending sufficiently to the purpose for which a definition was required and the multi-dimensionality of ethnic grouping. They treated Sikhs as if they were a homogeneous or a unidimensional group. None of the ethnic minorities in Britain is completely 'distinct'; they are all blurred at their edges, while the tendency for them to become more diverse as one generation succeeds another gives additional force to the objection urged here.

The Sikh grouping is characterised by commonalities of ethnic origin, faith, and other attributes, but there are some converts to the faith who are not of Sikh descent and there are some Sikh atheists (the same could be said of Jews, Copts, and possibly of some other groups, like Armenians). Thus a distinction can be drawn between ethnic Sikhs and religious Sikhs, even if most Sikhs are both. This was recognised in the Court of Appeal where Oliver LJ noted that 'a substantial proportion do not assume the turban',[16] and, with reference to the school, 'there was at the material time a number of Sikhs in the school whose parents did not insist, as the first plaintiff did, on their sons wearing their distinctive religious headgear'.[17] Lord Fraser said of the Sikhs, 'the community is no longer purely religious in character'.[18] But earlier he spoke of a group being capable of 'excluding apostates' as if such persons were no longer members of an ethnic group for the purposes of the Act.[19] In deciding the appeal the House of Lords should have paid particular attention to those who did not insist on the turban. To class non-religious Sikhs as 'apostates' would be to adopt the viewpoint of their critics without investigating the facts. On Lord Fraser's own terms, 'Provided a person who joins the group feels himself to be a member of it, and is accepted by other members, then he is, for the purposes of the 1976 Act, a member.'[20] Did the parents who did not insist on the turban regard themselves as Sikhs? Did other Sikhs regard them as Sikhs? These questions were overlooked.

In the terms of the statute, the headmaster applied a condition ('no distinctive religious dress or headgear') which he applied equally to all persons whether ethnic Sikhs or ethnic English people. The further questions of whether the condition was of disparate effect, unjustifiable and detrimental, therefore did not arise.

ETHNIC MUSLIMS

Such a conclusion has a wider relevance, as is suggested by the observations, already quoted, of the Runnymede Trust on the UK's Thirteenth Report. It expressed concern about anti-Muslim sentiment and the lack of protection for Muslims, submitting that

> In the case of Muslim communities in Britain, the general perception at present – both in the communities themselves and in mainstream society – is that the markers of difference are exclusively religious. In consequence, Muslim communities and individuals are unrecognised and unprotected by race discrimination legislation, and by legislation on incitement to racial hatred. At the same time, however, other communities whose defining features are primarily (though not

exclusively) religious do have protection; this is the case for Jews and Sikhs in Great Britain, and Catholics and Protestants in Northern Ireland (para 38).

The Trust continued:

> In certain other countries, for example most obviously in the former republic of Yugoslavia, the concept of a secular or cultural Muslim is recognised: the term 'Muslim' refers to membership of an ethno-religious community, not necessarily to religious belief and observance. It may be that this concept will develop eventually in the United Kingdom also. If indeed it does, 'Muslims' will presumably be defined as an ethnic or ethno-religious group, like Sikhs, and will be recognised by case law as protected under the Race Relations Act (para 40).

At the present time any representative of Muslims in Britain would criticise the concept of an 'ethnic Muslim' as a contradiction in terms, but the views of the religiously orthodox do not decide the legal issue. Legal reasoning often has to follow a different course from that used in everyday debate. Following the *Mandla* decision a court has to consider both how persons regard themselves and how they are regarded by others. The parallel with Jews is instructive. Commenting on the findings of a recent survey which revealed high rates of out-marriage, the director of the Institute of Jewish Affairs said that 'British Jews are coming together more like an ethnic community than a religious one.'[21] By way of contrast, in 1993 the Court of Appeal held that Rastafarians were not a racial group for the purposes of the Act because their shared history did not go back far enough. The court could, instead, have considered the position of 'locksmen' who wear dreadlocks and adopt a Rasta style without being true believers. It could have asked whether such persons regarded themselves, and were regarded by others, as Rastafarians.[22] If the answer was in the affirmative, that would show the existence of a group larger than the religious group, though it would not necessarily be an ethnic group. If the answer was in the negative, that would be evidence that the Rastafarians were not an ethnic group.

The less favourable treatment of Muslims might be brought within the legal definition of racial group if they could be likened to Jews rather than to Rastafarians, and distinguished from the definition of an ethnic group in *Mandla*. A further possibility was opened up in a decision of the Industrial Tribunal in Sheffield.[23] An employer had faxed a job centre in Rotherham requesting them to advertise job vacancies. When telephoned, he said he wished the job centre to exercise discretion when sending applicants to his company; he was not ready to employ either males or Muslims. Before the Tribunal, the employer explained that he would not wish to employ 'extremists', citing 'the activities of the Muslim community in Bradford' (where there were currently demonstrations against Salman Rushdie's *Satanic Verses*) and the IRA. He denied having issued any instructions to discriminate racially. The Tribunal accepted that when the telephone conversation started the employer had no intention of giving any instructions to restrict applicants to non-Muslims but concluded that, however indirectly and unnecessarily he arrived at the point, he had attempted to procure the job centre to implement a discriminatory condition. The Tribunal had next to consider whether that condition had a disparate impact upon a racial group, as in *Mandla*'s case. It found that the group in question was a class of persons defined by reference to colour, the great majority of whom were of the Muslim faith. This decision was not tested by appeal so its authority is uncertain. Nevertheless, some other Industrial Tribunal decisions appear to have been influenced by it.[24]

Thus in *Yassin* v. *Northwest Homecare Ltd* at Liverpool, the tribunal held that expecting the applicant to give up any attendance at the mosque on Friday afternoons 'was a requirement that a greater proportion of black than white people could [not] comply with, because most adherents of Islam are black.'[25] In *Azam and others* v. *J. H. Walker Ltd*, a tribunal found that there had been indirect discrimination against 17 Asian Muslims who had persisted in their intention to absent themselves for the Eid festival, and then been disciplined for doing so. The tribunal heard evidence that the workforce consisted of two main racial groups, one originating from the Indian subcontinent and the other European. It found that the applicants were 'knowingly and intentionally treated unfavourably on racial grounds' and were awarded damages. The respondent company appealed against the award of damages but not against the finding of discrimination, presumably having been advised by leading counsel that it would have little chance of success on this point.[26] Were the House of Lords to attempt to refine the *Mandla* definition it might begin by modifying the opening words of Lord Fraser's definition to read 'For a group to constitute an ethnic group in the sense of the 1976 Act, it must be a group of persons who regard themselves, and are regarded by others, as distinguished by certain attributes some of which are essential and others not essential but relevant if they help to distinguish the group from the surrounding community.' It could then repeat the characteristics listed by Lord Fraser, but would need to qualify that list with a limitation like: 'An action will not be discrimination under section 1(1)(b) of the Act unless the requirement or condition is applied in respect of one of the essential attributes.' Some such condition is needed to ensure that the definition of a racial group for the purposes of prohibiting indirect discrimination is not severed from the concept of racial grounds, even if that concept is not as central for these purposes as it is for the prohibition of direct discrimination.

In cases of direct discrimination on the ground of sex (but not indirect discrimination, *per* Lord Goff in *James* p. 619 at *a*) the courts have accepted the 'but for?' question as a test for sex discrimination.[27] Since gender grouping is unidimensional, as explained above, the question may be a good test for the purposes of the Sex Discrimination Act, but it should not be used as a test for racial discrimination unless allowance is made for the multidimensionality of ethnic grouping.

OTHER BRANCHES OF LAW

Earlier the Union of Muslim Organisations of UK and Ireland drew up proposals for the introduction of a system of Muslim family law to be applicable to all British Muslims. Jews and members of the Society of Friends have been exempted from many legal requirements regarding the solemnisation of marriage, but other religions have not. The Islamic marriage contract has no basis in English law. The Islamic prohibition on marriages between Muslim women and non-Muslim men is disregarded and polygamous marriages may not be contracted. Divorce and its legal consequences cannot be regulated by

Islamic law. Nor can the division of a deceased person's estate. Muslims may see this situation as placing them at a disadvantage, but there are no strong arguments for maintaining that in this respect Britain discriminates unlawfully against Muslims.[28] Whether the Secretary of State for Education has exercised his (or her) powers to grant voluntary status to private schools equitably as between applications from Muslim and non-Muslim schools is more arguable.

On the other hand, there is little room for doubt that the way in which English law protects the faith of the Church of England from blasphemy but not the faiths of other Christian churches or other religions, embodies a discriminatory restriction contrary to Article 10.2 of the European Convention on Human Rights and Article 18.3 of the International Covenant on Civil and Political Rights. There is a compelling case for either repealing or replacing the English law. As a perspicacious essay by Tariq Modood explains, Muslims do not want the state to evade what they see as one of its obligations; they seek equal protection. The case for replacing the present law has been made by those who signed the minority report of the Law Commission, endorsed by the Bishop of London's working group, for a new statute protecting all religions.[29] A new law could have a declaratory value even if it inspired few prosecutions.

Poulter contends that English law should be flexible enough to accommodate the cultural needs of the ethnic minority communities.[30] In this there is a certain parallelism between his approach and Bhikhu Parekh's plea for Britain to see itself as an ethnically plural society.[31] Yet the case for religious pluralism as sketched by Modood is stronger than the case for ethnic pluralism advanced by Poulter and Parekh. It might be better were English law flexible enough to accommodate the needs of those who profess different faiths.

In the *Mandla* case the Court of Appeal held that

> communities or movements whose members or adherents merely shared a common religion ... and whose members could freely move into or out of the community or movement could not be described as a group defined by its "ethnic origins"... Sikhs were merely a distinct religious and cultural community to which anyone might belong.[32]

This view of the issue kept religion and ethnicity separate, but the distinction was smothered by the judgement of the House of Lords. Underlying the argument for restoring that distinction is the question of consent. Adherents of different faiths, and those of no faith, can surely agree upon this. Muslims will always be ready to recall the Qur'anic verse 'There is no compulsion in religion'.[33] The idea of consent has its problems because humans can give or withhold it only in social settings. They will be influenced by the views of their kin and their peers, and by their personal plans. One characteristic of racial classification was that it was supposed to be objective; an expert did the classifying and individuals could exercise no choice about how they were classified. Ethnic classification often allows for a degree of voluntary self-identification, but when there is tension between groups an individual may in practice have little alternative but to identify with kin and neighbours. Many persons of immigrant origin feel excluded from significant sectors of British society, so that ethnic identification is unlikely to become simply a matter of consent within the foreseeable future. Religious faith, however, is supposed to express a purer form of consent, to stem from personal commitment and not to reflect social pressures. It is supposed to relate to things outside and above human society. It changes less rapidly than ethnic identification; it has greater legitimacy and it is easier for governments to accept institutions as representing religions than any which claim to represent ethnic communities.

CONCLUSION

After a slow start, the UK has acted to combat racial discrimination more effectively than most states. The next steps may need to be taken in conjunction with others as part of international or European programmes, but the opportunities will be missed if those in positions of influence have no strategic vision of how the objective of enabling members of ethnic minorities 'to participate freely and fully in the economic, social and public life of the nation' can be realised. A group is more likely to remain ethnically distinctive if its members practise a distinctive religion.

While Muslims may constitute a religious group, preliminary indications suggest that for legal purposes they may also be counted as a racial group, or, more precisely, as a group based on ethnic origins. This implies that there can be ethnic Muslims as well as religious Muslims, just as there are ethnic Jews and ethnic Sikhs. This conclusion will be incomprehensible to many devout Muslims and highly contentious in the views of others. Yet by calling attention to an important distinction between the nature of a religious group and an ethnic group, it strengthens the arguments for enhancing the position accorded to faiths outside the established church in the life of the nation, starting, perhaps, with the reform of the law against blasphemy. Such a vision could well inform the CRE's strategy for exploiting the potentialities of the 1976 Act.

NOTES

1. Paul Gordon Lauren, *Power and Prejudice: The Politics and Diplomacy of Racial Discrimination*, 2nd edn (Boulder, Colorado: Westview, 1996).
2. Mary Coussey, 'The Effectiveness of Strategic Enforcement of the Race Relations Act 1976', in Bob Hepple and Erika M. Szyszczak (eds), *Discrimination: The Limits of Law* (London: Mansell, 1992) pp. 35–49.
3. Michael Banton, *International Action Against Racial Discrimination* (Oxford: Clarendon Press, 1996), pp. 35–7.
4. *Guardian*, 28 September 1996.
5. *Official Journal of the European Communities*, L185 24 July 1996.
6. E. J. B. Rose *et al.*, *Colour and Citizenship: A Report on British Race Relations* (London: Oxford University Press, 1969).
7. The reception of this report by the UN Committee on the Elimination of Racial Discrimination is described in Michael Banton, *Ethnic and Racial Consciousness* (London: Addison Wesley Longman, 1997) pp. 149–52.
8. In its memorandum of March 1996 published as a supplement to *The Runnymede Bulletin*.
9. *Independent Magazine*, 4 March 1989.
10. Mashuq Ibn Ally, 'Second Introductory Paper,' in *Law, Blasphemy and the Multi-Faith Society* (London: Commission for Racial Equality, 1990) pp. 21–9.
11. Philip Lewis, *Islamic Britain* (London: I. B. Taurus, 1999).
12. Tariq Modood, 'Establishment, Multiculturalism and British Citizenship', *Political Quarterly*, 66 (1994) pp. 53–73.
13. *Mandla* v. *Dowell Lee* [1983 All ER 1062].

14. *James* v. *Eastleigh Borough Council* [1990 2 All ER 606].
15. See 3 All ER 1982 1118 at *c*.
16. 116 at *g*
17. 1118 at *d*.
18. 1069 at *b*.
19. 1067 at *c*.
20. 1067 at *d*.
21. *Independent*, 15 February 1996.
22. Michael Banton, 'Are Rastafarians an Ethnic Group?', *New Community*, 16 (1989), pp. 153–7.
23. *CRE* v. *Precision Manufacturing Services Ltd*, case 4106/91.
24. Having, in paragraph 7 of their decision, identified the victims of the discrimination as 'a group of persons defined by reference to colour', the Tribunal went on to throw doubt upon their own line of reasoning. In paragraph 23 they accepted that there were Jewish atheists, and continued 'There cannot be by definition any such thing as an atheist Muslim and it is that factor it seems to us which separates in the Jewish case faith from membership of a race within the meaning of the Act.' (But they did not ask whether there were in Rotherham persons who did not attend the mosque or keep the fast but nevertheless regarded themselves as Muslims, and were so regarded by others.) In paragraph 27 the Tribunal added 'the true nature of Islam is not within the Race Relations Act 1976, although for practical purposes the person that discriminates against Muslims probably discriminates indirectly on grounds of race.' If Muslims are a group defined by religion they are not protected under the Act. 'Racial grounds' are a necessary condition for an action to be held direct discrimination; as the law presently stands, they are irrelevant to indirect discrimination, so the last four words quoted from paragraph 27 would have been better omitted.
25. *Yassin* v. *Northwest Homecare Ltd*, case 19088/92.
26. *Azam and others* v. *J H Walker Ltd*, 1996 IRLR 11 EAT.
27. *James* v. *Eastleigh Borough Council*,. p. 619 at *a*.
28. Sebastian Poulter, 'Cultural Pluralism and its Limits: A Legal Perspective', in *Britain: A Plural Society* (London: Commission for Racial Equality, 1990) pp. 3–28.
29. Modood, 'Establishment, Multiculturalism...'. See also Simon Lee, 'First Introductory Paper', *Law, Blasphemy and the Multi-Faith Society* (London: Commission for Racial Equality, 1990) pp. 4–20.
30. Poulter, 'Cultural Pluralism and its Limits'.
31. Bhikhu Parekh, 'Britain and the Social Logic of Pluralism', *Britain: A Plural Society* (London: Commission for Racial Equality, 1990) pp. 58–76
32. 3 All ER 1982 1109 at *d*
33. *The Qur'an* (2:256).

9 Race Relations in New Britain

Yasmin Alibhai-Brown

'The law,' said Martin Luther King, 'does not change the heart – but it does restrain the heartless.' But on both sides of the Atlantic, those who pushed through anti-discrimination legislation, including King, had far greater ambitions than this minimalist view would suggest. The 1975 Home Office White Paper *Race Discrimination* states: 'Legislation is the essential precondition for an effective policy to combat the problems experienced by the coloured minority groups and to promote equality of opportunity and treatment. It is a necessary pre-condition to deal with explicit discriminatory actions or accumulated disadvantages.' Elsewhere the paper also declares: 'It is the Government's duty to prevent ... morally unàcceptable and socially divisive inequalities from hardening into entrenched patterns. It is inconceivable that Britain in the last quarter of the 20th century should confess herself unable to secure for a small minority of ... coloured citizens their full and equal rights as individual men and women.'[1]

And yet as we approach the millennium, these laudable aims remain largely unfulfilled. It is becoming increasingly clear to those concerned that legislative measures to combat race inequality have failed to shift in a significant way the beliefs and values underpinning the actions of people who discriminate and of society in general. Back in 1989 John Solomos wrote: 'It is difficult to be optimistic about the prospects for radical change within the constraints of the existing legislation. It is now over a decade since the 1976 Race Relations Act came into force and there is little ground to argue that it has achieved in practice the kind of radical changes which it promised.'[2]

Disenchantment is even greater in 1997, perhaps because expectations are higher, and in spite of some indisputable signs of progress on several fronts. The results of the election are a reminder of how such contradictory realities can and do exist as

they do even more starkly in the United States. The resounding
victory achieved by Labour and the unprecedented number of
women MP's has been welcomed by most black and Asian
Britons. But the fact that black and Asian women (with the
exception of Dianne Abbot and Oona King who is half African
American and half Jewish) have been left out in terms of representation is striking. The number of male ethnic minority MPs
has risen by only three. Unsurprisingly, therefore, the response
of black and Asian Britons to the new political age is at best
ambiguous, at worst, cynical. Remarkably, neither of the major
parties seem concerned about this. None of the key senior ministerial posts in the Blair Government have gone to experienced
black or Asian MPs, a full ten years after they were elected. Nor
do there appear any ethnic minorities in the large and dynamic
group of advisors to the new Government.

In order to go forward there needs to be a deeper understanding of how white people and black people actually think
and feel about exclusion, racism and the mechanisms to combat
these continuing problems. Greater awareness is also required
of the changing nature of discrimination and prejudice as well
as the political, economic and social landscapes which have
been so utterly transformed in the past fifteen years and which
will continue to change over the next decade, perhaps at an
even greater pace than before. The last Policy Studies Institute
survey into ethnic minorities shows that some ethnic groups
have started to outstrip other groups and in some cases even
white Britons. But the study also points out that the 'glass
ceiling' shuts off the top 10 per cent of jobs and also that discrimination and disadvantage continue to blight the lives of
black men, Bangladeshis and some Pakistani communities.[3] It
would, therefore, be a mistake to read this study as portending
the end of racism, as some in the media are already attempting
to do.[4] Discrimination is still excluding those with high
qualifications and there is no indication that, apart from a few
ever-present individuals, there has been any shift in the entry of
black and Asian people into political and other influential
areas. Basic discrimination continues to blight the lives of
young black and Bangladeshi men and, increasingly, Muslims.

Those who had faith that the law in itself – being an unequivocal declaration of public policy – would in time achieve
a change in perceptions and morality were reflecting the

misplaced optimism of the 1960s. And in any case, they could not possibly have imagined the massive ideological, economic and social changes that swept through Britain in the 1980s, nor the obstinacy of human nature.

This was recognised by Bernard Levin when he wrote this a few years ago: 'Societies like ours which live by the law are appallingly likely to believe that if legislation is enacted and generally obeyed the problem to which the legislation was addressed in the first place, must have been solved.' Levin also warned: 'Like bees trapped behind a window, human beings strive however fitfully towards the light but the progress in that striving cannot be rapid and those who yell and threaten that it must be increased, are inevitably and tragically ensuring that it will slow down.'[5]

He was contemplating growing racial tensions in America, but the complex and paradoxical position he is describing would echo powerfully with some influential white Britons today. Many of them accept that racism remains a concern but also argue (curiously) that demanding more effective action would be counterproductive especially in the precarious, uncertain 1990s. There are other shades of opinion which have emerged over the past decade too. Sophisticated theories were developed by the New Right which argued that 'too many' minority groups constitute a threat to the unity and nationhood of Britain itself. This more acceptable face of racism reverberated with many white Britons. Margaret Thatcher represented this view with conviction not only when she made her famous 'swamping' speech on a *World In Action* programme in 1978, but much later in Bruges when she described her exclusive and white view of Europe: 'From our perspective today, surely what strikes us most is our common experience. For instance, the story of how Europeans explored and colonised and yes, without apology – civilised much of the world is an extraordinary tale of talent, skill and courage.'[6] The view of Britain as exclusively white with an ancient shared history was promoted not only by the Conservatives, but by the British National Party and Labour during their television party election broadcasts in the 1997 election. Labour used the symbol of the bulldog during one of these and played Land Of Hope and Glory in another – symbols which were not likely to draw in the hopes and sympathies of ethnic minority voters. Bernie Grant, Darcus Howe and many others publicly condemned these images and tactics.[7]

Nor is it only during elections that such images and threats are raised. In June 1996, MP Nicholas Budgen continued to use these very arguments to justify his vociferous anti-immigration views on a programme for BBC Radio Five Live. Whilst accepting that immigrants have brought certain economic advantages and that the Powellite nightmares of 'rivers of blood' have not materialised, Budgen nevertheless claimed that:

> there have been quite a few thunderstorms and a lot of raining down of social and racial tensions which would have been avoided ... there have been very considerable social disadvantages from the scale of immigration that we have received since the war; different customs, different religions, different attitudes towards all that is important in a nation's subconscious and of course different loyalties.[8]

Then there is a view increasingly gaining credence which proclaims that racism is far from widespread in British society. People who argue this include those on the right like Ray Honeyford, the Bradford headteacher who was forced to resign in the 1980s because of his published views on ethnic minority pupils and his opposition to multicultural education. For years he has propagated the idea that racism is a minor problem in this country. In this letter published in *The Independent* in 1990 these views are clearly expressed: 'Our ethnic minorities are not "victims of the system" ... Prejudice undoubtedly exists – though it is by no means confined to the majority population. But the determining factor in a group's fortunes is not prejudice but the group's own cultural values.'[9] But increasingly these views are also to be found on the centre left. Here, for example, is what the intellectually formidable Bryan Appleyard wrote in *The Independent* in 1993 when he was attacking the anti-racist material in social work training courses:

> racist attitudes exist and there are many nasty incidents with a racial component that can be proved; it is meaningless and utterly unjustified to inflate this into the conviction that all British society is riddled with it. ... In fact, Britain in world terms is a society relatively free of racist tension and historically it was the British rather than the equally implicated Arabs and Africans who abolished the slave trade. [The truth

is that racism] is simply a stupid and occasionally evil distortion of the human impulse to treat the alien with caution and some unease.[9]

There are also those – again well represented across the political spectrum – who go further than this. They would blame multiculturalism and anti-racism for the sense and even experience of injustice that is felt by non-whites and, more seriously, for creating a divided society. The law and the policies of the seventies and eighties, they say, have created a self-serving 'race relations industry' with a vested interest in keeping alive the myth of racism in Britain. Worse still, they might be failing the very people they are attempting to help. Melanie Phillips best exemplifies this position when she writes:

> In the public sector, the drive to eradicate racism for example, has created pockets of oppressiveness which are not only unjust but also increase racism and disadvantage Black and other vulnerable people. ... Anti-racism which started out with the worthy intention of righting a wrong, has developed into a zealotry which creates instead fresh victims.'[11]

Such arguments have prevailed, making white people uneasy about any moves to strengthen the law and leading some to suggest that they could be abolished because they are a destructive distraction. The elected president of the Law Society in 1996, Martin Mears, publicly denounced anti-discrimination measures as 'corrupt and debased.'[12] For him, the law has worked rather too well so that the new disenfranchised people are now white middle-class men who need more sympathetic attention than those traditional victims of society – women and ethnic minorities.

Perhaps this is why so many liberals who once espoused with enthusiasm the ideals of multiculturalism are now withdrawing from the enterprise. There might also be more self-serving reasons. Once, if you were middle class, it was easy to support multiculturalism because it did not really affect your job, lifestyle and children. It was largely a problem for working class or poor white people living in deprivation themselves who were called upon to treat black people as equal citizens. Now not only is there increasing job insecurity among the professional classes, they are finding themselves in competition with up-

and-coming blacks and Asians. Interviewed for a BBC Radio 4 programme, the *Guardian* journalist Gary Younge (black himself), put it like this:

> What is happening with white middle class people is that they are catching up with what the white working class have been dealing with for quite a long time. They didn't have to really worry about what their opinion would be if a black family moved in next door because it was never going to happen. That's not the case now. There are black people who could be moving in next door, there are black people who could be threatening them for their jobs.'[13]

Another reason for this withdrawal might be that the ideal once seemed less complicated than it really was. When the Rushdie affair erupted, for many white liberals it was a moment of truth. The principles they deemed sacrosanct – secularism, freedom of expression, artistic integrity – were not only being scrutinised by British people who did not wish to buy into those values, but were rejected and even derided by many of them. And it was this provocation that revealed not just the limits of liberal tolerance, but a disturbing presumptuousness and intolerance that underpinned their world view.

Bhikhu Parekh described this reaction accurately in his essay 'The Rushdie Affair and the British Press':

> All the newspapers, including the liberal, debated whether British society had an obligation to tolerate the intolerant and whether multiculturalism was not a dangerous doctrine. ... A *Guardian* editorial asked Muslims to recognise that they were living in a secular society and that they must change their ways of thought and life. Several newspapers wondered if they had made a 'mistake' in 'letting in' too many Muslims. Even Roy Jenkins, father of the Race Relations Act, lamented that 'we might have been more cautious about allowing the creation in the fifties [sic] of a substantial Muslim community here'.[14]

Tariq Modood believes this watershed event has had a deep effect on those who once thought they could embrace multiculturalism with little cost and effort: 'Many people underestimated what pluralism meant. Some people signed up for a cause they weren't ready for, and many want to burn their tickets.'[15]

And nowhere can we see this more clearly than in the area of
education. Where in the late 1970s and mid 1980s, the recommendations of the Rampton and Swann reports were getting
through into the curriculum and the practical operations within
schools, especially in urban areas, now the national curriculum,
league tables and back-to-basics campaigns have banished the
emerging principles and practices of multicultural education
either to the margins or out altogether. From left to right, intel-
ligent people will now argue that this kind of education left
their children illiterate or innumerate or worse. One white
middle-class parent whose child was in a mixed inner-city
school wrote in *The Observer* in 1994:

> Our experience during Matthew's first half term is that
> many of the people we know, some impeccably liberal, others
> decidedly not, do not expect teachers to be Asian and, when
> they find one that is, question his or her competence. Let
> slip, 'he's the only white boy in his class,' and the image of
> the urban jungle is complete; an isolated child, dumped by
> his parents when only five into an alien jungle, all mosques,
> chappatis and chutney, unable to receive notions of
> 'Englishness' that are his birthright. ... They fear corruption
> of culture, they fear mingling of race, they fear the Babel of
> language.[16]

There is another reason why white people in Britain are less
enthusiastic about remedial laws and other policies to promote
race equality and it is the visible evidence of advancement. In
the United States, where many people of colour have reached
positions of unimaginable power, people are turning against
affirmative action even though racism remains a fact of life for
the rest. Here too it is obvious that in some areas ethnic minority people are getting to the top – television for example – and
yet the exclusion of most of the rest continues. Both countries
find it hard to accept that the forces of progress and regression
can coexist. The 1990s have also been a time when victimhood
became unfashionable, when everyone was obliged to think positively and to take responsibility for their lives. Rabindranath
Tagore once wrote: 'Power takes as ingratitude the writhings of
its victims.'

Looking at the broad picture, therefore, at present there
seem to be very few individuals in the white community who

accept both that racism continues to exclude and to blight the lives of non-whites and that something more energetic needs to be done about this, or that multiculturalism has been an unmixed blessing for this country. A survey carried out by the Institute for Public Policy Research into attitudes towards existing laws and racial minorities in general, shows that although there is support for the race relations law, twenty years on among most white people there are also growing anxieties about the state of their country as the millennium approaches. The two studies, one qualitative and one quantitative, revealed that 94 per cent of white Britons accept that white racial prejudice is a problem in this country. Inter-ethnic prejudice is also manifesting itself in all kinds of ways and there is little sense of a joint purpose among the various ethnic and religious groups which make up this nation. The fear that the English identity is in danger of disappearing both because of internal 'alien' forces and pressures to become more European as the EU matures also manifested itself in this study.[17]

It is never very difficult to find examples of this paranoia. The highly paid and highly regarded journalist Linda Lee Potter spoke for many when she wrote of her dislike of multicultural activities in schools: 'Traditional customs in schools are going to disappear to be replaced by strange and foreign ones which would be both sad and wrong.'[18] Charles Moore, editor of the *Daily Telegraph,* expressed the first of these fears in an article in *The Spectator* in 1993: 'We want foreigners as long as their foreignness is not overwhelming. ... Britain is basically English speaking and Christian and if one starts to think it might become Urdu speaking and Muslim and Brown, one gets angry and frightened.'[19]

The anti-European jingoism and xenophobia which is regularly generated by events like the beef crisis indicates how vulnerable white Britons are indeed feeling. There are accumulating examples of how people look for such events in order to vent this nationalistic panic, and it is a combination of both of these fears that need to be understood. As Philip Dodd pointed out in his Demos pamphlet:

even if Mrs Thatcher is no longer in power, the signs of the continuing Battle over Britain and its national identity are everywhere, not least in the political parties. They are most

visible in the Tory Party which seems intent on tearing itself
apart over what kind of Britain it wants – in the one corner
there's Mr Major, trying to hang on to his Baldwinite love of
country and cricket and Constitution ... while on the other,
Michael Portillo defends a kind of Britishness ... which actually has deep historical roots within a culture which has long
defined itself in terms of its superiority to its 'untrustworthy
neighbours'.

Dodd sees the battle within as well, especially on the streets
'in the escalating number of racial attacks on the black British
fuelled by a conviction that those who complicate the simple
equation British = white deserve all the hatred they get.'[20]
Stuart Hall believes that these anxieties arise out of history
but have acquired a potency because the present (and future)
seem so problematic:

> The official ideology in the sixties was a liberal patronising
> assimilationism. Now it is a defensive strategy which derives
> from a deep sense of national trauma. The desperate bid to
> recreate a notion of 'Englishness' has come out of a realisa-
> tion that we are in a post-colonial decline which not even
> Thatcher could reverse. So the nightmare of multi-ethnic
> identities within and without Europe is producing a huge
> wishful thinking into the past where so many of the fondest
> memories of this country are lodged.[21]

There are other changes, too, to confront. The free market
philosophy which is obsessively non-interventionist is having a
negative impact on how some people feel about the Race
Relations Act. If there is so little protection available to
workers, if the minimum wage and other rights have been
eroded, if we all have to live with the terrors of the contract
culture, why should there be 'special' protection for black
people? The loss of the political consensus which gave us the
Act in the first place, and the drive of the main political parties
to make themselves attractive to voters anxious about multiculturalism and also law and order has created an atmosphere
where any kind of anti-racism is viewed with suspicion.
The Conservatives have continued to do what they have
always done: maintain minimal support for the race laws, and
yet proudly claim that Britain has the most comprehensive

anti-discrimination legislation among our European partners; or, more dishonourably, pass racist immigration legislation, whip up hostility among white Britons towards immigrants and refugees and still maintain that fairness and tolerance lie at the heart of Conservative politics. The 1995 Asylum Bill has been used by ministers to stereotype most asylum seekers as 'bogus' and as cheats who have come here, in the words of the Home Secretary, Michael Howard: 'to live off our taxpayers'.[22] The CRE first recommended changes to the Act in 1985. They remained ignored by the Thatcher government. Michael Howard more or less continued that tradition while at the same time invoking the legislation as an example to defend himself against the accusation that the Conservatives were using the race card in the increasingly draconian immigration and asylum policies. To add insult to injury, ethnic minorities are told that it is in order not to destroy 'good race relations' that they ought to support, or at least accept, immigration policies and regulations which in effect deny so many basic human rights, like those of family unification and political asylum. With New Labour now in power, it remains to be seen how much of this practice and rhetoric will be changed. The primary purpose rule is set to be abolished and Labour has promised a fairer and more efficient asylum policy.

However, the pre-election behaviour of New Labour when it came to the issue of racial equality caused so much concern that many black and Asian Britons opted out of the democratic process, preferring not to vote at all rather than give their votes to a party which expects them to do so as a continuing act of faith without giving anything back or publicly declaring their importance to the party. In order to counteract this disengagement from the political process, Charter 88 and the National Black Caucus launched a campaign to mobilise the black vote in the elections. Conflicts over the selection of prospective parliamentary candidates, especially in inner city areas, also caused rifts between New Labour and ethnic minorities. Although all the real facts have been incredibly difficult to ascertain, what is clear is that perceptions have grown that the Labour Party is not committed to getting more black and Asian MPs and that the concern shown by the party leaders over the need to have better representation of women is not extended to the representation of minorities. Professor Zig Layton-Henry is convinced that this is a strategy the Labour Party consciously adopted in the lead-up to the 1996/7 election.[23] By spring 1996, Labour had put up three Asian candidates and the Tories nine. It was also evident that there were no black or Asian advisors in the inner circle where so many key decisions are made. There also appeared to be an embargo on talking about such thorny issues within New Labour. Says Roy Hattersley: 'There has been no time when Labour has been so silent on immigration and race. I think Labour is being extremely cautious at the moment. In this country there is a potent well of prejudice to be tapped. Some parties are prepared to tap such base instincts and Labour is afraid of it being tapped.'[24] Even when it comes to the ideas that are central to the thinking of New Labour, there are serious implications for the racial minorities that do not seem to have been addressed. If your aim is to create social cohesion and a sense of community, white people and black people could feel they can only build this with people like themselves. Advocating curfews for young adults may be a popular – and maybe a wise – policy as long as there are real safeguards to ensure that black youngsters are not unfairly picked on by the police.

Meanwhile black and Asian people do feel hopelessness and impatience at the lack of progress. Many are alarmed at these more recent definitions of Britishness which still exclude them, and the backlash against equality measures. Others feel that the lame law simply piles up promises and expectations, that it is failing to deliver and – worse – that it gives Government a convenient exit when it is called upon to show that it is committed to the eradication of racism in Britain.

Such cynicism is understandable because so much less has been achieved than might have been had there been greater political will, like there has been with women's rights. This is probably why we are seeing a mirror image of what is happening in the white community, with ethnic minority individuals increasingly uncomfortable with the 'race industry', feeling that it somehow demeans blacks and Asians through endless special pleading and that it encourages them to wait for others to deliver instead of taking control of their lives themselves. The black British journalist Donu Kogbara put forward this view in a public debate held in London in May 1995. Similar arguments have emerged in the United States with right-wing academics like Dinesh Desouza, whose book *The End of Racism* puts forward the controversial view that anti-racists cause more damage than racists by making excuses for inept, violent and anti-social blacks.[25] The more radical voices have long felt that anti-discrimination initiatives have merely served to give the illusion of progress, draining black communities of the rage they might have had to push for real change in their status.[26] People also appear divided about where to go from here. There are those that argue that strengthening the Act, for example, will only increase white antipathy and anxieties and those who feel that not extending the scope of the Act is likely to persuade even more people that the legislation is there simply to pacify and nothing else.

This is the backdrop of multiracial Britain twenty years after the creation of the Commission for Racial Equality. Little wonder then that research commissioned by the BBC in 1996 shows that a third more people – white, black and Asian – think racism is a more serious problem today than five years ago. The recession of the early 1990s has affected non-whites disproportionately. Figures of 1995 show that unemployment among black and Asian people is double that for white people. There is one ethnic minority civil servant over Grade 5, one national newspaper columnist, no editors, critics, hardly any professors, hospital consultants, or business board members. They are under-represented in quangos and commissions. The army is riddled with racism, and it also infects our police force where payouts for alleged brutality have been rising. Several black men have died in police custody; others have received huge payoffs after alleged maltreatment by officers. In 1996, one young black motorist received £320,000 for one such incident – one of the biggest awards ever. Since the failure of the criminal justice system to punish the killers of Stephen Lawrence, it is hard to find anyone in the black community who feels that the law protects them. According to the British Crime Survey, there are 130,000 racially motivated crimes in Britain each year.

But this is only a part of a complex picture. Other evidence shows that in spite of the growth of negative feelings and perceptions, major positive and real developments have taken place. Even the most avowed racist has been shamed enough over the decades to need to disclaim his racism. That sense of shame is significant progress for a country which less than three decades ago had white people putting out notices that said 'No Blacks, No Dogs'. Support for the Commission has grown over the years especially among large organisations, across the private, public and voluntary sectors. Sponsorship deals from companies like those that the CRE was able to facilitate for the campaign to kick racism out of football might have been unthinkable a few years back. The incorporation of equal opportunity into corporate thinking has also been gradually happening. For example, this statement by Robert Ayling, Chief Executive of British Airways, says: 'As a country we have thrived, improved and become more wealthy by taking the best of the immigrant community and utilising their skills. If we can't break down racial barriers between people, we won't work successfully as an organisation.'[27]

The rise in the number of successful black and Asian individuals across the board is obvious for all to see. Key areas of influence now have powerful ethnic minority individuals and companies are now becoming increasingly aware of both the purchasing power and the skills and talents of ethnic minority individuals.

The way forward must therefore include arguing for an extension and strengthening of the current legislation; that much is obvious and no doubt argued by others in this book. But this is unlikely to happen if we don't influence the broader issues which have taken hold – public attitudes, perceptions, anxieties and fears. There are a few major areas which need to be addressed before real progress can be achieved.

Unlike Germany, Canada and other countries, we have no research base which can indicate what the costs and benefits of immigration have been to this country. In Germany, for example, work done by an economic audit of immigration to West Germany has recently produced some interesting findings which bear serious consideration, according to Dr Allan Findlay, Director of the Applied Population Research Unit, University of Glasgow:

A study produced by the Rheinish-Westfalische Institute (RWI) in 1991 provided a range of evidence to support the view that the immigrant community contributed substantially to the state's affluence. The 3.5 million immigrants who entered West Germany between 1988 and 1991 would not be described as skilled transients. ... Instead they were made up of refugees, economic migrants and family members seeking re-unification ... the new labour supply enabled German firms to extend their productive capacity and far from taking up jobs which otherwise would have been taken up by West Germans the wealth generated as a result of the immigrants created a net increase in employment (i.e., in addition creating extra jobs to match the jobs taken by the immigrants) of 20,000 jobs. The RWI also calculated an increase in economic growth of between 0.5 and 1 per cent per annum which was attributed to the increase in foreign labour.'[28]

In Britain we know that labour shortages in key areas in the 1950s and 1960s prompted recruitment drives in the West Indies and that much of London Transport and the National Health Service depended on black labour, but we have as yet little substantial research which would provide us with an economic audit of the sort available in Germany. Also lacking is detailed research on immigration flows which could be used to counteract the panic that is easily generated by politicians and others claiming that millions of people are entering this country every year. MP Winston Churchill regularly claims that 150,000 illegal immigrants are getting into this country every year, a figure found by the National Audit Office to be without foundation. When ex-Immigration Minister Charles Wardle resigned saying he feared that 15 million new immigrants would be entitled to settle here if passport checks were abolished, he was including EU, EFTA and other European nationals and also black and Asian British citizens. Fertile confusion and fear can be generated by these people because reliable official figures are not available.

The European Commission has recently accepted that public hostility in Europe towards minority groups is 'often based on feeling rather than facts' and argued that governments should engineer 'an evolution of public and political perceptions of immigration and asylum issues.'[29] The Council of Europe has consistently argued that for anti-discrimination policies to work, public attitudes need to be changed and governments and the media need to take a lead on this.[30] In the UK, an All-Party Parliamentary Group on Race and Community concluded: 'The law alone cannot solve the problem [of racial violence]. What we need to do is create a culture of civility conducive to harmonious coexistence between citizens of different colours and races.'[31] The way this might be done is being explored by the Institute for Public Policy Research and the recommendations will be available in autumn 1997. They will include a detailed comparison with what governments in countries like Canada are doing.

The chairman of the Commission for Racial Equality said in the annual report for 1995: 'real progress depends particularly on those in our society with power, resources and influence to act in a socially responsible way without racial bias, and to give positive leadership in rejecting racial hatred and eliminating discrimination'. That call is relevant to all political parties but most particularly to the two main parties. Negative actions or statements and the absence of positive leadership is an irresponsible and inefficient way to govern a country which is now a mature and irreversibly multiracial democracy. There are public order implications as well as arguments for social cohesiveness which should impel all politicians into taking their responsibilities seriously.

There needs to be a re-instatement of the moral reasons why racism is an evil which all right-minded people should wish to fight. You cannot eradicate racism through complacency or by comparing Britain with worse examples. There is enough to build on. If so many people say that they are not racist, even when they are, then they are saying that to be racist is undesirable. But if white Britons are constantly told that they are indeed fair and tolerant and that those who say otherwise are making problems, fifty years from now we will not have made any progress. When most asylum seekers lost their right to claim benefits, the Court of Appeal ruled that the Social Services Secretary had exceeded his powers. In his statement, Lord Justice Simon Brown partly made a strong moral case for this judgment, saying that such 'draconian' measures could not be tolerated in any 'civilised society'. Without such moral foundations anti-racism is bound to fail. Merely providing economic reasons for change will prove to be inadequate.

Our immigration policies need now to be dislocated from race policies. We need rational immigration policies based on the needs and resources of this country, not on the containment of xenophobia. The tethering of immigration and race policies has been deeply damaging. Roy Hattersley, the architect of the equation, interviewed on the BBC, now accepts this absolutely.[32] In our education system and through the way we interpret ourselves and the world we will have to create new definitions of Britishness which include not only the ethnic communities but proud Englishmen and women who are proud, at least partly, because they have been able to accept multiculturalism, finally shedding the trappings of a colonial history. To achieve this ideal white English people will need to feel that their heritage and identity matters too. With devolution and greater ties with Europe gathering momentum, this is a priority area. In order to re-engage the commitment of white liberals, a lot more thinking will have to go into new kinds of multicultural education which include the white identity. There also needs to be a rethink on how long a nation can be held collectively culpable for historical sins.

Recent research reports indicate serious levels of exclusions of black boys from schools which are disproportionately high. There is also evidence that among ethnic minority youngsters there is increasing splitting-off into ethnic and religious groups and also tensions between white and minority teenagers as well as within the different Asian communities.[33] No political party at the moment seems interested in tackling these fissures, but to have the kind of future everyone is seeking this is surely a priority social policy area.

Since the Rushdie affair, Muslims in this country are increasingly regarded as the alien wedge within. High-minded thinkers and writers, who would not dream of denigrating blacks and Jews, regularly portray all Muslims as barbaric and ill-suited to fit into a secular modern nation. When Connor Cruise O'Brien says that Muslims are regarded as 'repulsive' because they *are* 'repulsive';[34] when Bernard Levin pronounces that the Oklahoma bombs must have been the work of Muslims determined to turn it into 'Khartoum on the Mississippi',[35] you know that prejudices against this community have dug deep into the entire culture of British society. Extending our discrimination laws will be part of the answer, but the education which is needed in order to arrest the growth of this is not being discussed at any level. The fact that militancy and separatism is beginning to manifest itself within young Muslim groups is also something that needs to be urgently tackled by politicians and educators. Those who think in traditional ways about racial inequality as applying to those of a different skin colour have not registered the other inequalities that have emerged in recent years. This has been pointed out repeatedly and eloquently by people like Tariq Modood, who believes

> surely one of the most prominent forms of racism in Britain ... may be characterised as cultural racism. Groups are opposed, feared, despised in terms of *both* their colour and their culture. This combination makes their oppression more acute even though some individuals can escape on one or the other front. It follows that remedies must address both dimensions of this duality: just attacking colour prejudice will not remove the hostility that has built up against some non-white groups.[36]

The issues facing multiracial, multi-ethnic Britain are complex and will require a holistic approach where the responsibilities for change rest not simply with legislators, but with other people in positions of power and influence who can see the need to transform the way we live our lives, who we are and what, as a society, we want to be in the next century.

NOTES

1. Home Office, *Racial Discrimination*, White Paper Cmnd 6234 (London: HMSO, 1975).
2. John Solomos, *Race and Racism in Contemporary Britain* (London: Macmillan, 1989).
3. T. Modood, and R. Berthoud *et al.*, *Ethnic Minorities in Britain: Diversity and Disadvantage* (London: PSI, 1997).
4. Quoted in *The Guardian*, 23 January 1990, 'Community Whitewash' by Yasmin Alibhai-Brown.
5. Bernard Levin, in *No Entry*, Radio Five Live, 8th June 1996.
6. Margaret Thatcher, *Independent*, 18 October 1990.
7. *Independent*, 4 August 1993.
8. 'Illiberal Liberalism', in Sarah Dunnant (ed.), *The War of the Words* (London: Virago press 1994).
9. Ray Honeyford, *Independent*, 18 October 1990.

10. Bryan Appleyard, *Independent*, 4 August 1993.
11. Melanie Phillips, 'Illiberal Liberalism', in Sarah Dunant (ed.), *The War of the Words*.
12. Martin Mears, *Independent*, 31 May 1996.
13. Gary Yange, in *Race Matters*, BBC Radio 4, 28 September 1995.
14. Bhikhu Parekh, in *Free Speech*, report of a seminar organised by the Commission for Racial Equality and the Policy Studies Institute, September 1989, Discussion Papers 2 (London: CRE, 1990).
15. Tariq Modood, in *Race Matters* (see note 13 above).
16. Peter Aylmer, 'The Hidden Delights of Babel', *Observer*, 30 June 1994.
17. IPPR research surveys into attitudes towards racial minorities and inter-ethnic attitudes carried out by NOP and Opinion Leader Research, 4 February 1997.
18. Yasmin Alibhai-Brown, in *The New Europeans and the Olde Worlde Order*, Bradford and Ilkley Community College Research and Policy Papers no. 4 (1992).
19. Charles Moore, *Spectator*, October 1991.
20. Philip Dodd, *The Battle over Britain*, Demos Paper no. 13 (1995).
21. Quoted in Yasmin Alibhai-Brown, 'Race and the Single Nation', *Guardian*, 29 January 1992.
22. Michael Howard, *The Today Programme*, BBC Radio 4, 5 January 1997.
23. Quoted in Yasmin Alibhai-Brown, 'You have been Silent about Racism for Too Long', *Independent*, 5 June 1996.
24. Roy Hattlersley, in *No Entry* (see note 5 above).
25. Dinesh Desouza, *The End of Racism* (New York: The Free Press, 1995).
26. See, for example, the various essays of A. Sivanandan of the Institute of Race Relations, particularly since 1984.
27. Robert Ayling, *Independent*; see also Yasmin Alibhai-Brown, 'You have been Silent ...' (see note 23 above).
28. Sarah Spencer (ed.), 'An Economic Audit of Contemporary Immigration', in *Strangers and Citizens* (IPPR: Rivers Oram Press, 1994).
29. Communication from the Commission of the European Communities to the Council and the European Parliament on Immigration and Asylum Policies, Office for Official Publications of the European Communities (1994), COM (94)23 Final.
30. Council of Europe, 1206 (1993), 1222 (1993).
31. *Racial Violence: A Separate Offence?* All Parliamentary Group on Race and Community Relations, May 1994.
32. Roy Hattersley, in *No Entry*.
33. See the report of tensions between Muslim and Sikh youth in Southall in Rifat Malik, 'West Side Story', *Evening Standard*, 22 May 1997.
34. Conor Cruise O'Brien, *The Times*, 11 May 1989.
35. Bernard Levin, *The Times*, 21 April 1995.
36. T. Modood, *Not Easy Being British: Colour, Culture and Citizenship* (London: Runnymede Trust/Trentham Books, 1992).

10 National Identity in a Multicultural Society
Bhikhu Parekh

Every society tends to, and even perhaps needs to, form some conception of itself in order to unite its members, encourage them to behave and relate to each other in a desired manner, mobilise their collective energies, and to give them a reasonably clear idea of who they are and how they differ from others. If the society happens to be multicultural, the tendency and the need to develop a shared national identity is even greater. It is therefore hardly surprising that the question of national identity has dominated the public agenda of almost all contemporary multicultural societies for the past three decades. In this paper I intend to discuss the meaning and logic of national identity and how it should be defined in a multicultural society. I shall end by relating the discussion to the current British debate on the subject.

I

The term 'identity' is of relatively recent origin. Its cognate 'national identity' is even more recent, and seems to go back no further than the 1950s when it replaced such earlier terms as national character, national culture, national soul and national peculiarities, that had dominated European thought since the rise of the modern nation state. The term 'identity' primarily refers to individuals and is analogically extended to human collectivities including nation states. It would, therefore, be useful to begin with a brief discussion of individual or personal identity.

To ask what is our identity as individuals is to ask what defines us or makes us the kind of persons we are and distinguishes us from others. As individuals we possess countless attributes and qualities and stand in a host of relationships

196

with others. Some of these attributes and relations are contingent and transient whereas others are central and tenacious and shape us profoundly. The fact that we are golfers or members of a particular social club is a contingent fact of our lives and we would not become altogether different persons if we ceased being either. By contrast our humanity, gender and age and, at a different level, our culture, religion, values, moral commitments, dominant passions, psychological and moral dispositions and so forth are constitutive of us in the sense that we either cannot abandon them at all or cannot do so without becoming very different kind of persons. Since they constitute us they are an integral part of us, making it almost impossible to define ourselves independently of them. This is not to say that some or many of these characteristics and relationships cannot change over time, for as reflective and self-determining agents we can redefine and change ourselves, but rather that when they change, we ourselves change however imperceptibly and recognise ourselves as no longer what we were before.

Identity refers to those features and relationships that are constitutive of us and define and distinguish us as a certain kind of person. We are necessarily the products of countless influences. Some of these influences go back to our childhood and largely remain inaccessible to us, and some others operate so surreptitiously and unconsciously that we can only become partially aware of them, and that too after a most rigorous self-reflection. Our identity therefore contains large areas of opacity and we can never fashion ourselves into wholly coherent and harmonious wholes. In the course of trying to make some sense of ourselves and introduce a measure of order in our lives, we form some conception of ourselves, define ourselves in a particular manner, and act and organise our lives on that basis. Since our self-knowledge is never wholly accurate and complete, there is always a gap between who we think we are and who we really are. Our identity therefore has two dimensions, ontological and epistemological, the former refers to who are, the latter to who we think we are or self-understanding. The two necessarily shape each other and our identity is a constant and dialectical interplay between them. Our self-understanding is based on and can be checked against who we really are; conversely the latter can be altered, sometimes decisively, by the way we define ourselves. Our identity is neither fixed and unalterable nor wholly fluid and subject to unlimited reconstruction. We can alter it but only within the constraints imposed by our inherited constitution and our inherently inadequate self-knowledge. Since it evolves over time and is often marked by several retrospectively identifiable turning-points, it has an inescapable historical dimension and is best told in the form of a story or a narrative of how we came to be who and what we are. The narrative is never wholly accurate both because it is constructed from a particular standpoint with all its attendant biases and exaggerations, and because our memory of our past is inevitably hazy and coloured by the present. The narrative, further, is never formal and external in the sense of being a chronicle of successive events but is a story of the substantive transformation of its bearer, narrating how he or she developed certain attachments, aspirations, passions, temperament, etc., and became a certain kind of person.

Although identity is closely related to difference the two are not the same, and much confusion is created when they are equated. Obviously to know who I am is also to know who I am not and how I differ from others. And since the need to define my identity arises partly because I wish or need to distinguish myself from others, every statement of identity is also a statement of difference. However, it is wrong to suggest that my identity consists in my difference from others. I differ from others because I am already constituted in a certain way, not the other way round. If others became like me, my differences from them would diminish, but it would be absurd to say that my identity has changed, for while they have changed I have not. This means that in order to cultivate or maintain my identity, I don't need to concentrate on or stress my differences from others, let alone frenetically endeavour to retain them. The fallacious equation of identity with difference leads to misguided views about the nature of the self and its relation to the other, and lies at the basis of many a romantic theory of individuality including that of J. S. Mill.

Our identity is not always a source of pride. As we discover who we are, we might not like some or even most of what we find. We might find that we harbour deep sexist, racist and other prejudices, or that we are mean, jealous, greedy and unable to respond to others' achievements in a spirit of generosity. We might then feel ashamed of ourselves and even of our culture which encouraged these prejudices and moral traits in us, and might explore ways of reconstituting and reforming ourselves. We might decide to convert to another religion, embrace another culture, change our occupation, or abandon a way of life in which we cannot flourish without trampling on others. It is difficult to think of an identity of which one is wholly proud or totally ashamed; the former breeds narcissism, the other self-hatred, and both alike are recipes for psychological and moral disintegration. For the most part we are both content with and critical of our identity in different degrees. Identity necessarily involves self-evaluation and has a normative dimension. It is ultimately about who we wish to be as determined in the light of who we are. To say that 'this is my identity' does not imply that this is how I wish to – or should – remain for ever, for I need to ask if I am happy with it and approve of what it entails. Just as I can evaluate my identity, so can others. While my identity deserves their respect, the respect cannot be uncritical, for they might legitimately object to those aspects of it that they find unacceptable and even repugnant.

Just as personal identity is the identity of a distinct self, national identity is the identity of a political community. It refers to the kind of community it is – its central values and commitments, its characteristic ways of talking about and conducting its collective affairs, its organising principles, the way in which it constitutes the public realm, its self-understanding, its deepest collective passions, fears and aspirations, and so forth. Like personal identity, national identity is too complex and elusive to be summed up in a set of specific features or neat propositions. Every definition of it highlights some features and ignores or marginalises others, and is necessarily partial. Its constitutive features can be identified, and the story of their development told, in several different ways, some albeit more accurate than others. The most truthful view of it can only be developed in the course of a critical and open-minded dialogue between its different accounts.

Much of what we said earlier about personal identity is also true of national identity. National identity is neither unalterable nor a matter of unfettered choice. It is alterable within limits and in a manner that harmonises with its overall character and organising principles. It is not wholly transparent either, and parts of it sometimes surprise even its keenest students as Britain discovered on the occasion of the death of Diana, Princess of Wales. No one had expected an allegedly reserved people to be capable of publicly expressing their

deepest emotions in a relatively uninhibited manner. And as if
this were not surprising enough, there was a further surprise
when it was discovered that nearly 40 per cent of Britons did
not watch her funeral on the television, partly out of lack of
interest and partly as a reaction against the excessive media
coverage. National identity, again, is not always a matter of
pride. In the aftermath of the Nazi era, many Germans
intensely disliked what they discovered about themselves.
Deeply afraid to trust themselves, they decided to restructure
and regulate their identity by tying themselves closely to a
federal Europe. In Britain, too, not all its citizens feel comfortable with its imperial history. While some are very, and some
moderately, proud of it, others feel deeply ashamed at the way
their country burst into and took over other societies.

National identity then is both given and constantly reconsti-
tuted. We might not like parts of it. And even when we do, we
might feel that they need to be changed to suit new circumstances. Such changes as we make in it must be consistent with
the rest of its constituents, for otherwise they cannot graft and
take roots. All such redefinitions and changes require both a
deep historical knowledge of the country and a feel for its past,
as well as a rigorous and realistic assessment of its present circumstances and future aspirations. While remaining firmly
located in the present, we need to make a critical appraisal of
our history and use its resources to develop a new sense of
national identity that is both loyal to the past and that res-
onates with the experiences and aspirations of the present. This
means that national identity can neither be preserved like an
antique piece of furniture nor discarded like an old pair of
clothes. To talk of preserving or maintaining national identity is
to use misleading metaphors, for a country's identity is necessarily tied up with its circumstances and self-understanding and
changes with the changes in the latter. And since national identity shapes and constitutes us in certain ways and limits our
choices, we cannot reject or arbitrarily reconstruct it either.

II

We live today in a world in which our traditional ideas of
national identity need radical revision. One of the important

reasons for this has to do with the fact that, unlike their predecessors, almost all societies today are multicultural and include communities and individuals who take different views about the meaning of life, live by different values, and assign different meanings and significance to different activities. Although multicultural societies existed in premodern times as well, contemporary multiculturality is wider, deeper, more defiant, democratically legitimised, and closely bound up with the process of globalisation.

A multicultural society needs to strike a balance between the equally legitimate demands of both unity and diversity. If it privileged unity, it would provoke resistance and violate the important cultural rights of minorities. If it did the opposite, it would degenerate into a collection of mutely coexisting cultural ghettos obsessed with their differences and unable to work together to pursue common goals and create a wider and richer identity. Strange as it may seem, the greater and deeper the diversity in a society, the greater the unity and cohesion it requires to hold itself together and nurture its diversity. A weakly held society feels nervous in the presence of differences, sees them as potential threats to its unity and survival, and lacks the confidence to welcome and live with them. Prima facie this seems odd, for a strong sense of unity is widely regarded as inhospitable to diversity. We are thus confronted with a paradox. A multicultural society requires a strong sense of unity, yet the latter can also reduce and even undermine its ability to accommodate diversity!

The paradox is only apparent and arises because unity is defined in two different ways in the two halves of the paradox. When we say that a multicultural society requires a strong sense of unity, we mean that its members should have a strong sense of mutual commitment and common belonging, that they should trust each other enough to know that despite all their differences, they wish to continue to live together and would do nothing to break up their society. When we say that strong unity can undermine diversity, we mean that if a multicultural society insisted on a uniform and comprehensive national culture as the basis of its unity, it would leave little space for diversity. If we can show, as indeed we can, that a multicultural society can foster a strong sense of unity (in the sense of a strong sense of mutual commitment and belonging) without requiring a shared comprehensive national culture, the paradox disappears. There is nothing surprising about this for it is a common experience in many areas of life. Members of a family not only tolerate but delight in their deep differences of temperament and interest because they feel sufficiently committed to each other not to feel threatened by their differences. This is also true of friends, political parties and even large organisations. A multicultural society, then, needs to find ways of developing a strong sense of mutual commitment and common belonging without insisting upon a shared and comprehensive national culture and the concomitant uniformity of values, ideals and ways of organising significant social relations. In this respect a multiculturally constituted state radically differs from the long familiar nation state. The latter rested the unity of the state on the uniformity of culture. This alternative is closed to a multicultural society, which needs to derive its unity not from cultural uniformity but from cultural diversity and to turn it into a source of strength. Its unity can be as deep and strong as that of the nation state, but it has a very different nature, texture and source.

While accommodating cultural differences and creating a climate in which different communities can flourish and make their contributions to the creation of a plural collective culture, multicultural societies need to ensure that members of these communities identify with each other and develop a spirit of mutual loyalty and solidarity. This is made possible by, among other things, a shared national identity, a shared sense of belonging to a single community and a broad agreement on what that entails. A shared identity both holds them together and gives them the confidence to live with and even delight in their differences.

If national identity in a multicultural society is to serve this purpose, it should satisfy the following conditions. First, it should be so defined that it does not exclude or delegitimise any of the constituent communities. Disputes about national identity are ultimately about who belongs to the community and who does not, who is a legitimate and valued part of it and who is not. When Malaysians discuss whether their country is Malay Malaysia as the bulk of the majority insists, or Malaysian Malaysia, as the rest and especially the minorities do, they are debating the importance to be given to the Malay community.

'Malay Malaysia' makes Malays the sole legitimate owners of the country and treats the Chinese, the Indians and others as relative outsiders who are, no doubt, entitled to full legal protection but not to participate as equals in the determination of the country's identity. Disputes between the advocates of Arab Sudan versus African Sudan, Arab Lebanon versus Muslim Lebanon, Algerian Algeria versus Arabic-Muslim Algeria, white and Christian Britain versus multi-ethnic Britain, and Hindu India versus Indian India have a similar thrust. In each case one party offers an exclusive and the other an inclusive definition of national identity. The exclusive definition, which is generally favoured by the dominant group, alienates minorities and even some sections of the majority and prevents the emergence of a common sense of belonging. Minorities cannot feel part of a society if its self-definition denies them political and moral legitimacy.

Recognising cultural and religious minorities as an equally legitimate and valued part of the community requires a number of things. They should not be discriminated against in significant areas of life and should enjoy equal rights and opportunity. They should be accorded equal respect, not be made objects of patronising remarks, silly jokes and demeaning stereotypes, and their membership should not be a subject of dispute or contingent on good behaviour. They should also be free to cherish and retain their differences without inviting charges of disloyalty. And they should be able and, when necessary, encouraged and helped to participate as equals in the public life of the community. Without equality in these and other areas of life, minorities remain unintegrated outsiders, surviving on the precarious goodwill of the wider society, and only an inclusive definition of national identity can create a climate conducive to such equality.

Secondly, the national identity of a society is embodied in and nurtured by not only its self-understanding but also by such emotional symbols of collective self-expression as the national anthem, the flag, national ceremonies, political rituals, and monuments to the dead heroes. The symbols mobilise political emotions, draw people together in common acts of self-identification, and generate and affirm the consciousness of a collective 'we'. Habermas's 'constitutional patriotism' is too cerebral to move and inspire people and needs to be embedded in and nurtured by a healthy emotional patriotism. It is therefore essential that symbols of national identity should, whenever appropriate, affirm the multicultural character of the society and grant suitable public recognition to its diverse communities. Prince Charles expressed this well when he said that he would, as a monarch, like to be the 'Defender of Faith' rather than of 'the faith' as is currently the case. The same multicultural spirit was at work when the public ceremony at the Commonwealth Remembrance Day in Britain was revised to include multifaith worship, when the newly independent state of India included the green colour of Islam in its national flag, and when the Canadian flag included the maple leaf as both a culturally neutral and nationally representative symbol of the country's identity. At a recent banquet to mark the golden jubilee of Indian independence, Cherie Blair, the Prime Minister's wife, wore a red sari with great elegance and ease. Although some conservative newspapers thought it un-British and trendy, it was a striking and sensitive way of respecting the dignity of the occasion, identifying with British Indians, and celebrating their presence and contribution. Although largely symbolic, such gestures reassure the minorities, help their emotional integration, and play an important part in affirming and sustaining the society's multicultural ethos.

Thirdly, as I argued earlier, the national identity of a community is articulated in its collective values and shared historical self-understanding. In a multicultural society it is critically important that both these should recognise and reflect the imperatives of cultural diversity. The common values should be such that the various communities do or can be persuaded to share them, and the understanding of the country's history should appreciate minority contributions and see them as its valued part. This is not always easy, as the Rushdie affair in Britain showed. When a small minority of Muslims endorsed Ayatollah Khomenei's *fatwa*, British society rightly refused to compromise on the inviolability of Rushdie's right to life. When Muslims in turn criticised the British anti-blasphemy law which only protected Christianity, many Britons agreed that not only the law but the very institution of the established church, a long-standing part of British national identity, should be reconsidered in the light of Britain's multicultural character. In every multicultural society common values and the accepted view of national identity are subject to a heated debate and even contestation. However, such a debate need not prove insoluble, get out of control or lead to violence if the minorities accept the constraints of the inherited historical identity of the wider society and the majority recognises the need for such changes as that identity might need.

Fourthly, a multicultural society requires that the prevailing view of national identity should allow its members to entertain dual and even multiple identities without arousing fears of divided loyalties. It should be accepted as a matter of fact that we belong to different ethnic, religious, cultural and other groups, that these identities matter deeply to us, and that they do not necessarily stand in the way of a shared national identity. One can be both Scottish and British, both Quebecois and Canadian, both Basque as well as Spanish, and also both Hindu or Muslim and British. Citizens have different cultural biographies and enter the mainstream of national life in their own different ways. National identity must therefore be capacious enough to accommodate these and other identities and draw strength from them. National identity is like a language that can be spoken in different accents and with different degrees of facility and felicity. Within the framework of a shared body of values and collective self-understanding, to the definition of which minorities should have an equal opportunity to contribute, one can be British in several different and equally legitimate ways. Even as they all speak English in their own different ways and accents, Indians, Pakistanis, Scots, the English and the rest can all be British in their own unique ways.

Finally, in a multicultural society there is always a danger, or at least a suspicion, that minorities might either be discriminated against, as is usually the case, or pampered and privileged. And while it is vital that the courts and the agencies of government should be sensitive to cultural differences in enforcing laws and implementing policies, there should be some check on them to ensure that this does not result in discrimination or privilege. For these and related reasons, the shared values of a multicultural society should be translated and embodied in a constitutionally guaranteed statement of fundamental rights. Such a statement provides the minimal basis of national unity, prescribes the limits of the permissible range of diversity, and leaves no room for suspicion of partiality, whether in the form of discrimination or privilege. It is striking that, historically speaking, every successful multicultural society has a constitutionally guaranteed system of rights, and that every society that becomes multicultural increasingly finds itself moving in that direction.

III

In the light of our discussion it would be useful to examine briefly how Britain has attempted to define its national identity to take account of its increasingly diverse character. Its current cultural diversity emerged from two different sources and appeared on the public agenda in two related but different forms in the late 1960s. The first related to the arrival of a large number of Afro-Caribbean and South Asian immigrants from the erstwhile colonies and their concentration in the major cities, and the second to the pressure from influential quarters to join the European Community and the consequent fear that this would deepen its diversity and put at risk not only its cultural and political identity but also its capacity to safeguard it. The two sources of diversity were closely related in the minds of many British citizens. By and large those who opposed or welcomed internal pluralisation brought about by ex-colonial immigrants were also respectively hostile or hospitable to external pluralisation likely to be precipitated by Britain's entry into Europe.

The cultural diversification of Britain provoked anxieties about the country's national identity and threw up two different definitions of it, namely the New Right and the liberal. Very briefly, the New Right attacked both forms of cultural diversity, bitterly complained about the increasing 'dilution' or 'erosion' of British identity, and canvassed a particular view of it. Led by Enoch Powell, Margaret Thatcher, Roger Scruton and others, it defined British identity in narrowly nationalist and ethnic terms. Britain was an island, singular, unattached, and unique both in its geography and history. For all its history it had, in Powell's words, 'stood with her face to the oceans, her back to Europe'. And even when it crossed the oceans to rule the world, it never struck roots anywhere and 'remained true to itself'. Its greatness was derived from its internal homogeneity and strong sense of identity and was now threatened by the interrelated forces of immigration and Europe. For the New Right Britain must reaffirm its traditional identity by staying out of Europe or entering it only to transform it into a loosely structured common market, and by repatriating or vigorously assimilating the ethnic minorities into the British way of life. The British people were of a 'single ethnic stock', bound together by strong ties of common culture, kinship and solidarity, and felt 'instinctively' antipathetic to outsiders. Since multiculturalism threatened to destroy its sense of nationhood and unity, it must at all cost be rejected in favour of a vigorous reassertion of the monocultural identity that was supposed to have served the country so well in the past.

Basically, the New Right and its supreme spokesperson Margaret Thatcher took a highly moralistic, puritanical, ethnic, nationalistic and largely petty bourgeois view of British identity, stressing only those elements that supported the kind of Britain she intended to create. She was determined to rationalise British society and launch the long-delayed capitalist revolution under the petty bourgeois leadership, and to challenge the cultural and political establishment in the interest of an upwardly mobile, economically ambitious, socially resentful, morally arrogant, and culturally philistine social class. Not surprisingly, her view of British national identity assigned no role to British aristocracy, trade unions, the intellectuals, the educationists, artists, and the ethnic minorities. It had no room either for British scepticism, humility, love of diversity, self-doubt, sense of irony, deep suspicion of the messiah, playfulness, love of eccentricity, traditionalism, and spirit of compromise. The virtues she stressed were narrowly based, largely economic, and centred around self-interest.

Although Thatcher's view of British identity captured some of its important elements, it was deeply imbalanced and led to results opposite to what she intended. She wanted to 'set the individual free' but ended up creating a highly centralised state. She could not set the individual free without equipping him with the required qualities of temperament and character and guarding against the consequences their unregulated actions. She had no choice but to turn to the state for both these tasks, especially as she had little patience with the intermediate social and civic institutions. She talked of parliamentary democracy but could not trust it to sustain her vision of Britain, and tended to personalise power. Her view of Britain required a strong sense of public spirit and national solidarity, both of which were undermined by her brand of economic individualism that denied the very existence of society. The kind of national self-definition she offered was internally contradictory and did the country some good but much harm.

The New Right view of British national identity was challenged by the liberals, who welcomed both the internal and external pluralisation and redefined British identity to make space for the growing cultural diversity. This was eloquently expressed by Roy Jenkins who rejected the 'flattening' process of assimilation which deprived the ethnic minorities of their 'national characteristics and culture' and turned them into 'a series of carbon copies of someone's misplaced vision of the stereotyped Englishman'. He pleaded instead for 'equal opportunity accompanied by cultural diversity in an atmosphere of mutual tolerance'. For liberals multiculturalism was not inimical to or even incompatible with British national identity but an integral part of it. They also offered a more nuanced view of the country's history, including its imperial phase, its cultural ties with Europe, its rationalist heritage, sense of social justice, spirit of toleration and fairness, and so forth.

Although there is much to be said for the liberal definition of British identity, it suffered from an important limitation. It divided national life into the public and private realms, and confined cultural diversity to the latter. So far as the public realm was concerned, it was to be governed by a uniform set of traditional and non-negotiable liberal values. While the minorities were free to retain their cultural identities in the private realm, they were expected to endorse and assimilate into the monocultural public realm. Like the New Right, liberals too demanded assimilation, with the twofold difference that it was now limited to the public realm and involved assimilation not into the British stock but British cultural values. It was therefore hardly surprising that when British Muslims demanded reassessment of some of these values in the aftermath of the Rushdie affair, especially the nature and limits of free speech, most liberals felt frightened by the 'barbarians' in their midst and refused even to debate the issue. Even Roy Jenkins lamentably remarked that if he had known all this earlier, he would have opposed Muslim immigration into Britain, and that he had now decided against admitting Turkey into Europe! The liberal definition of British national identity had a dark underside and its own characteristic biases and blind spots. It does not meet some of the basic preconditions of national identity in a multicultural society and needs to be deepened and broadened. During the past few years several new definitions of British national identity have been canvassed. I shall mention two that have deservedly attracted much attention. In an influential and well-argued monograph published by *Demos*, an independent think-tank brilliantly guided until recently by Geoff Mulgan, Mark Leonard marshals much valuable evidence to support an engaging view of British national identity. He stresses Britain's global connections, European roots, multi-ethnic composition, multicultural character, creativity, sense of fair play, socially and technologically innovative spirit, and commercial dynamism. While much of this eclectic list in terms of which British national identity is redefined makes good sense, Leonard's view has several troubling features.

He wants Britain to have a clear identity *in order* that the latter can generate economic benefits and help British business and industry. Not surprisingly, like Margaret Thatcher he sees Britain in the image of a business corporation, and its identity as a kind of commodity that can be manufactured, attractively packaged, and sold abroad. By and large he thinks of national identity in terms of how we want foreigners to see us rather than how we wish to see ourselves. As a result he takes an instrumental view of national identity, seeing it as an easily mobilisable commercial asset rather than as a basis of national unity and a vital political and moral resource. Like Margaret Thatcher, Leonard also sets up an untenable contrast between tradition and modernity, and his view of British identity has a deeply anti-traditional thrust. It also has a strong positivist ethos, for it is largely celebratory, stressing Britain's strengths and only cursorily analysing its weaknesses. Since it lacks a critical and reflective dimension, its reconstitution of British identity remains somewhat superficial. Leonard's proposal that Britain should mobilise all its institutions to project his view of its identity both at home and abroad is no less troubling. It homogenises British identity, leaves no space for dissent, and is likely to prove morally suffocating.

The Prime Minister, Tony Blair, has offered yet another and in my view more mature view of British identity. He has rightly stressed Britain's cultural and technological creativity, youthful spirit, multicultural character, European roots, global connections, tolerance, compassion and so forth, and obviously any convincing view of British identity would have to include all this. However, so far Blair's vision remains somewhat sketchy and inadequate. At times he too tends to see national identity as a kind of commodity, a way to sell Britain abroad. And he also tends to concentrate on the narrow economic gains of national identity rather than its domestic moral and political value. I am not sure that calling Britain young when a quarter of its population is over 60 offers a sufficiently inclusive vision of it; and that we should strive to become a beacon to the world or its moral leader. If others find something worth learning from the way we solve our moral and social problems, we should obviously be pleased, but to think that we have some special talents in this area and that the rest of the world should look up to us for guidance is to invite disappointment and the charge of hubris.

Although the Prime Minister has passionately complained about inadequate minority representation in the upper echelons of our major political, economic and other institutions, his vision of Britain is not fully sensitive to cultural plurality. It is intended to open up spaces for minorities *within* the dominant culture rather than to broaden that culture, to create greater opportunities for members of minority communities to rise within the dominant culture rather than to enable them to help pluralise it in the light of their distinct cultural sensibilities. This may perhaps explain why his vision has not resonated with the ethnic minorities, as also why he has not so far been able to do for them what he has most commendably done for women. Women meet the requirements of his cultural vision; ethnic minorities do not so easily fit into it and require a greater imaginative effort. In spite of these and other limitations, Blair's vision of British national identity is basically correct. It is generous in its sprit, is both realistic and inspiring, and is capable of uniting and inspiring our culturally diverse society. I hope I have said enough to indicate how it can be deepened and broadened.

The past three decades have changed Britain beyond recognition, and the coming ones will do so even more. Britain cannot coherently navigate its way through the rapidly changing world and define its place in it without a clear sense of what it stands for and the kind of country it wishes to be, and that requires both a deep and unbiased understanding of its past and a realistic assessment of its present and future. This is not the first time in its history that it has faced the task of self-definition. It did so successfully in the seventeenth century and, again, in the early years of the nineteenth century. There is every reason to believe that it can do so today.

Index

housing
in Britain: of immigrants, 46–7;
legislation on, 28, 41, 133; racial
discrimination in, 5, 19, 62, 87,
144; statutory codes of practice,
13, 58
in the United States: civil rights laws
and policies, 129–30, 131, 132,
133, 139–41; continuing
segregation, 138–9; and racial
violence, 125
Howard, Michael, 85, 187
Howe, Darcus, 86, 180
Howe, Sir Geoffrey, 28
Human Rights Commission,
establishment of a UK, 21, 102
Hurd, Douglas, 78

Imbert, Sir Peter, 65
immigration
anti-immigration propaganda, 109
and the European Community, 97, 120
and right-wing racist organizations,
107–8
to Britain, 1–3, 24–5, 104, 108:
attitudes to black immigrants,
146; controls and legislation on, 2,
3, 4, 25–7, 187, 192–3;
discriminatory procedures, 63; and
equal citizenship, 158; lack of
reliable figures, 191
to European countries, 108–9, 119,
162
Immigration Act (1971), 26
incomes, African-American, 136
India
immigration from, 1
and national identity, 204
indirect discrimination
and employment, 15, 58
in housing, 133
interpretation of by the courts, 52
PSI surveys on, 59–60
and the Race Relations Act (1976), 10,
33–4, 42–3, 70, 71
and sex discrimination, 167, 173
and Sikhs in Britain, 167–70
individual identity, 196–9
individuals
and civil rights laws in the United
States, 131
complainants, and employment
discrimination, 72–3
and the CRE, 56
power to bring proceedings, 41–2, 54

industrial machinery, and the Race
Relations Board, 41
industrial tribunals, 42, 56, 58, 102
and Amari Plastics, 48
and the concept of ethnic Muslims,
172–3
weaknesses of, 89
Institute for Public Policy Research, 185,
192
institutional discrimination, and the 1976
Act, 42, 53, 56
institutional racism, and the CRE, 88, 98,
102
integration, and the limits of tolerance,
91–3
inter-ethnic prejudice in Britain, 185
International Bill of Human Rights, 20,
160–1
International Convention on the
Elimination of All Forms of Racial
Discrimination, 20, 36, 158, 159–60
International Covenant on Civil and
Political Rights, 36, 160–1, 174
International Covenant on Economic,
Social and Cultural Rights, 36
international human rights law, 34,
159–63
Islam *see* Muslims
Italy
Movimento Sociale Italiano, 108
racial discrimination laws, 112
racist attacks, 119

Jasper, Lee, 86
Jenkins, Roy, 4, 5, 8, 9, 17, 26, 27, 28,
163
and the CRE, 34
on multiculturalism, 208
and Muslims in Britain, 92, 164, 166,
183, 208–9
and the Race Relations Act (1976), 33,
83
on racial discrimination and
integration, 30–2
and the Sex Discrimination Act (1975),
33
Jewish immigrants, 24
Jews, 94, 97
and anti-Semitism, 24, 104, 115–16,
119
in Britain, 166, 171, 173
in European Community territory,
115–16
and right-wing racist organizations,
107, 108

Kant, I., 31
King, Martin Luther, 27, 178
King, Oona, 179
Kogbara, Donu, 188
Kosack, Godula, 110

Labour Party/governments
 and asylum policy, 187
 and the CRE, 12, 82, 85, 87
 election victory (1997), 178–9, 180
 and the establishment of a Human
  Rights Commission, 21
 and ethnic minority MPs, 187–8
 and the European Community, 120
 and immigration control, 25
 and legislation on racial
  discrimination, 3–4, 25–8, 32–5
laissez-faire racism, 145–6
Lane, Sir David, 80, 85
Lawrence, Stephen, 104, 189
Layton-Henry, Professor Zig, 187–8
Le Pen, Jean-Marie, 78
legislation (race relations)
 aims of, 178
 European Community countries,
  111–13
 impact of, 58–75
 racial discrimination, 3–4, 25–7, 28, 29;
  in Britain, 3–4, 25–7, 28, 29, 32–5,
  113–14
 United States civil rights laws, 126–31
 see also Race Relations Acts
Leonard, Jonathan, 136
Leonard, Mark, 209
Lester, Anthony (Lord Lester of Herne
  Hill), 4, 24–37, 81
Levin, Bernard, 180, 193
liberalism, and British national identity,
  208–9
life expectancy, of African-Americans,
  134
Liverpool City Council, CRE formal
  investigation into housing policies,
  62, 87
local authorities
 and contract compliance, 17–18, 74
 and equal opportunities policies, 85
 ethnic minority councillors, 64
 and ethnic monitoring, 14
 and the improvement of race relations,
  75
 and the Notting Hill Carnival, 86
 and race data collection, 125
 and the Race Relations Act (1976), 16,
  58–9

and social and racial inequalities, 87
Local Government Act (1988), 17–18
Lopez, Ian Haney, 143
Lyttle, John, 28

Maastricht Treaty (1991), 116–17
McConahay, John, 145
MacEwen, Martin, 142, 152
McKay, 147
Major, John, 103, 121, 186
Malaysia, 202–3
marriage law in Britain, and Muslims,
  173–4
Mears, Martin, 182
media
 and the European Union, 97
 and the improvement of race relations,
  75
 and Muslims in Britain, 92–3
 and racial discrimination, 16
 and the Rushdie affair, 183
middle class
 blacks, 134, 147
 whites, and multiculturalism, 182–3,
  184
Migrants Forum, 96
Mill, J. S., 198
Mincy, Ronald, 136
Ministry of Defence, 90
Modood, Tariq, 166, 174, 183, 194
Mosley, Sir Oswald, 107
Mulgan, Geoff, 209
multiculturalism
 in Britain, 22, 94, 103, 193, 208; attacks
  on, 181–3; in schools, 184, 185
 and national identity, 201–6, 208
Muslims
 in Britain, 21, 74, 91–4, 103, 164–7,
  170–5, 193–4; and the 1976 Act,
  159; and the concept of ethnic
  Muslims, 170–3, 176; and the law,
  173–5; and national identity,
  208–9; and the Rushdie affair, 74,
  92, 93, 94, 164, 172, 183, 193, 204
 in European Community countries,
  116, 117–18
 in France, 95
 and the interpretation of sacred texts,
  165–6
 secular or cultural, 171
mutual tolerance, 31
Myrdal, Gunnar, 143

named-person investigations, and the
  CRE, 45–6, 48–9, 54